Sidgwick & Jackson Ltd
in association with Thames Television

The Day Before Yesterday

An illustrated history of Britain from Attlee to Macmillan

by Alan Thompson
Historical consultant: John Barnes

Designed by Paul Watkins

Acknowledgments

This book is based on the Thames Television series *The Day Before Yesterday*, first broadcast in the autumn of 1970. The six programmes dealt with the political history of Britain from Attlee to Macmillan. The series was inspired by Phillip Whitehead, who produced it.

There are three ingredients to this book: pictures, extracts from the interviews given in 1970, in preparation for the programmes, and a historical text. Although much of this is based on secondary sources, almost two hundred interviews have been drawn on and I am particularly grateful to those who gave them, not least to those who have preferred to remain anonymous. This book could not have been written without their help.

Much of this book derives from the programmes and my thanks go to the team who made them: the Producer, his two associates, David Elstein and Andrew McNeil; to Shelagh Cutner, Cate Haste, Alexis Findon and Nigel Maslin, whose painstaking research contributed so much to the series; to Edit Arki and Sarah Boswell who were invaluable in

assembling and preparing much of the documentary material; to the consultant historians, John Barnes and Bernard Donoughue, whose sense of the period pushed us towards a deeper interpretation; and the Controller of Features, Jeremy Isaacs. Robert Kee wrote six superb commentaries.

I must acknowledge more particular debts in the writing of this book. John Barnes continually prompted me and tried to induce some measure of perspective into the text, and worked absurd hours to grapple with my interpretation. With Phillip Whitehead, he made it possible for me to meet my deadlines. To Paul Watkins whose skill has made it possible for the material in this book to influence for the good the presentation of history to a much wider public. His care and consideration have been inexhaustible. Finally to Sarah Boswell and Christine Watchorn who patiently deciphered my handwriting, typed many drafts and checked innumerable tapes of interviews.

For any mistakes that may have occurred in my text I am alone responsible.

The author

Alan Thompson. Born 1943, educated Magdalen College School Oxford, King's College Cambridge and St. Antony's College Oxford where he worked on a thesis on the British Left in the 1930s. He helped Randolph Churchill on Volume 2 of *The Life of Sir Winston Churchill* in 1967. He then went as a producer to BBC Radio Current Affairs. After a short period in BBC Television's Further Education, he went to the Features Department at Thames Television to work on *The Day Before Yesterday*.

Produced by Sidgwick & Jackson
Managing Editor William Armstrong

The historical consultant

John Barnes. Born 1937, educated Plymouth College and Gonville and Caius College Cambridge, where he subsequently held a Research Fellowship in history. He is now a Lecturer in Politics at the London School of Economics. He contested Walsall North as a Conservative in the 1964, '66, and '70 General Elections. He is co-author of *Baldwin: a Biography* (1969). His biography of Earl Beatty will be published in 1972 and he is currently at work on a biography of Harold Macmillan.

First published 1971
Text © Thames Television 1971
Design © Sidgwick & Jackson Limited 1971

ISBN 0 283 48476 4

Printed in Belgium by Les Presses Saint-Augustin s.a., Bruges
for Sidgwick & Jackson Limited, 1 Tavistock Chambers,
Bloomsbury Way, London W C 1.

Contents

Who's who

Biographies (1945-63) of personalities interviewed

Robert Allan   Former Conservative M.P. Parliamentary Private Secretary to the Prime Minister 1955-58. Parliamentary Under-Secretary, Foreign Office 1959-60. Treasurer of the Conservative Party Organization 1960-65.

Lord Alport   Worked in the Conservative Research Department before becoming an M.P. in 1950. Member of the One Nation Group. Under-Secretary of State, Commonwealth Relations Office 1959-61; High Commissioner to the Central African Federation 1961-63.

George Ball   Leading American Europeanist; was Under-Secretary of State at the State Department during the Polaris crisis.

Menachem Begin   Israeli lawyer and politician; in Siberian concentration camp 1940-41; Commander of the Irgun, one of the Jewish terrorist organizations in Palestine.

William Bevan   Welsh miner; brother of Aneurin Bevan, Labour Minister of Health.

Reginald Bevins   Formerly Conservative M.P. for the Toxteth division of Liverpool. Parliamentary Private Secretary to Macmillan at Ministry for Housing; Postmaster General 1959-64

Lord Boothby   Conservative M.P. for East Aberdeenshire 1924-58. An early protagonist for European unity.

Arthur Bottomley   Labour M.P. Parliamentary Under-Secretary of State for Dominions 1946-47; Secretary for Overseas Trade, Board of Trade 1947-51.

Lord Boyle   Conservative M.P. 1950-70. Made a quick reputation as a leading champion of the 'New Conservativism' that emerged after the war. Economic Secretary to the Treasury 1955-56; resigned over Suez. Later, Financial Secretary to the Treasury 1959-62; Minister of Education 1962-64.

Lord Butler   (formerly R. A. Butler) often known as 'Rab'. Presided over the Conservative Research Department after the war; was responsible for the 1944 Education Act, the Industrial Charter in 1947. Chancellor of the Exchequer in 1951; Leader of the House 1955-61; Lord Privy Seal 1955-59; Home Secretary 1957-59; First Secretary of State and Minister in charge of the Central African Federation 1962-63; Chairman of Conservative Party Organization 1959-61. Twice tipped as leader of the Conservative Party: in 1957 and 1963.

Lord Chandos   (formerly Oliver Lyttelton) Member of the War Cabinet 1941-45; Conservative M.P. until 1954. A confidant of Churchill's; Secretary of State for the Colonies 1951-54.

Canon Collins   Canon and Precentor of St. Pauls' Cathedral; Chairman of Christian Action; Chairman of C.N.D.

Jock Colville   Joint Principal Private Secretary to Churchill for a period during the war and from 1951-55.

Lord Crathorne   (formerly Sir Thomas Dugdale) Minister of Agriculture and Fisheries 1951; resigned in 1954 over the Crichel Down affair.

Anthony Crosland   Oxford don 1947-50; entered Parliament in 1951. Published *The Future of Socialism* (1956) which had a profound influence on Labour Party thinking. Close friend of Hugh Gaitskell.

Richard Crossman   Pre-war Oxford don; served with Macmillan in Algiers during the war; Labour M.P. since 1945; member of Anglo-American Palestine Commission 1946; persistent critic of Bevin over Palestine; supporter of Bevan. Notable political journalist on the Left, long associated with The New Statesman.

Sir Knox Cunningham   Ulster Unionist M.P.; Private Parliamentary Secretary to Macmillan 1959-63.

Maurice Edelman   War correspondent with *Picture Post*; Labour M.P. from 1945. Playwright and novelist.

Lord Egremont   (formerly John Wyndham) Private Secretary to Macmillan 1957-63.

Robin Esser   Journalist. Served as a public relations officer attached to the invasion fleet which sailed to Port Said.

Jack Foord   Prominent member of Hull Labour Party for 20 years.

Michael Foot   Prominent member of the Labour Left, supporter of Aneurin Bevan. Labour M.P. until 1955, then again from 1960; political journalist and author; Managing Director of *Tribune*.

Lord Franks   British Ambassador to U.S.A. 1948-52; academic and banker; member N.E.D.C. 1962-64. Was beaten in 1960 by Macmillan for Chancellorship of Oxford University.

Lady Gaitskell   Widow of Hugh Gaitskell, leader of the Labour Party. Created a baroness in 1963.

Patrick Gordon Walker   Labour M.P. Private Secretary to Herbert Morrison 1946; Parliamentary Under-Secretary of State, Commonwealth Relations Office 1947-50; Secretary of State for Commonwealth Relations 1950-51; close supporter of Gaitskell.

John Grigg   (formerly Lord Altrincham) Political journalist.

Averell Harriman   Democrat. U.S. Special Representative in Europe 1948-50; Special Assistant to President Truman 1950-51; Senior diplomatic posts in Kennedy Administration 1961-63; U.S. negotiator on Test Ban Treaty 1963.

Denis Healey   Secretary of International Department, Labour Party 1945-52; Labour M.P. since 1952.

Nicholas Henderson   Diplomat. Assistant Private Secretary to Ernest Bevin 1945-47; British Embassy in Washington 1947-49. Permanent Under-Secretary's Department in the Foreign Office 1950-53.

Etienne Hirsch   Devoted European. Confidant of Jean Monnet; distinguished career in French economic planning; did much of the ground work for the European Coal and Steel Community.

Alec Horsley   Prominent member of Hull Labour Party.

Councillor Huzzard Hull Labour Party and Borough Councillor. Supporter of C.N.D.

Douglas Jay Labour M.P. since 1946. Personal Assistant to Attlee 1945-46; Economic Secretary to Treasury, 1947-50; Financial Secretary to Treasury 1947-51. Close friend of Hugh Gaitskell.

Selwyn Lloyd Conservative M.P. since 1945. Minister of State 1951-54; Minister of Supply 1954-55; Minister of Defence 1955; Foreign Secretary 1955-60; Chancellor of the Exchequer 1960-62; abruptly sacked by Macmillan.

Len Llewellyn Victim of a serious mining injury before the war which left him paralysed.

Commander Marten Dorset farmer, leading figure in the Crichel Down affair 1954.

Donald McLachlan Author and journalist; Deputy Editor, *Daily Telegraph* 1954-60; Editor *Sunday Telegraph* 1961-66.

Sir Alexander McCall Ernest Bevin's doctor.

Edmund Murray Detective Sergeant. Personal detective to Winston Churchill.

Sir George Mallaby Under-Secretary, Cabinet Office 1950-54

Christopher Mayhew Labour M.P. since 1945. Parliamentary Private Secretary to Morrison 1945-46; Parliamentary Under-Secretary of State for Foreign Affairs 1946-50. Leading campaigner against the introduction of commercial television.

Sir Robert Menzies Australian Prime Minister 1946-66.

Robert Murphy Senior American diplomat. Political Adviser to U.S. Military Government in Germany 1945-49; Deputy Under-Secretary of State 1954-59.

Edmund Murray Detective Sergeant. Personal detective to Winston Churchill.

Dr. Stark Murray Labour candidate in 1945. President of the Socialist Medical Association.

Max Nicholson Secretary of Office of Lord President of the Council 1945-52. Morrison held the Lord Presidency until 1951.

Nigel Nicolson Conservative M.P. for Bournemouth East 1952-59. One of the eight conservative back-benchers who voted against Eden's Suez policy, which brought him into serious conflict with his constituency.

Anthony Nutting Conservative M.P. 1945-56. Parliamentary Under-Secretary of State for Foreign Affairs 1951-54; Minister of State for Foreign Affairs 1954-56. A protégé of Eden's until he resigned over Suez.

Lord Orr-Ewing Conservative M.P. 1950-70. A leader of the pro-commercial television lobby; Parliamentary Private Secretary to Monckton at the Ministry of Labour 1951-55; Secretary to the 1922 Committee – the Committee of Conservative back-benchers – in 1956.

Amihai Paglin Chief of Staff of the Irgun, a Jewish terrorist group in Palestine.

Enoch Powell Conservative M.P. since 1950. Parliamentary Secretary, Ministry of Housing 1955-57; Financial Secretary to the Treasury 1957-58, when he resigned. Minister of Health 1960-63. Refused to serve under Sir Alec Douglas Home.

Lord Redmayne Conservative M.P. 1950-66. Government Chief Whip 1959-64.

Lord Robens Labour M.P. 1945-60. Parliamentary Secretary to Ministry of Fuel and Power 1947-51; Minister of Labour 1951; Opposition spokesman on Foreign Affairs during the Suez crisis.

Bill Robins Post-war advocate of private enterprise.

William Rodgers Labour M.P. from 1962. A leading pro-Gaitskell revisionist. Prime mover in the Campaign for Democratic Socialism.

Lord Rhyl (formerly Nigel Birch) Former Conservative M.P. Economic Secretary to the Treasury 1957-58, when he resigned. An influential back-bencher, particularly during the 1963 Conservative Party Conference.

Ken Samuel Welsh miner; victim of serious working accident and subsequent compensation pay wrangles.

Arthur Schlesinger American historian and university teacher. Special Assistant to President Kennedy 1961-64.

Sir John Shaw Chief Secretary, Palestine 1943-46; was in the King David Hotel when it was blown up.

Lord Shawcross Labour M.P. 1945-58. Attorney General 1945-51.

Lord Sherfield (formerly Sir Roger Makins) Deputy Under-Secretary in the Foreign Office 1948-52; Ambassador to U.S. 1953-56.

Lord Shinwell Former Labour M.P. Minister of Fuel and Power 1945-47 where he had to weather the Fuel Crisis; Secretary of State for War 1947-50; Minister of Defence 1950-51.

Mrs Stickings Prominent member of Orpington C.N.D.

George Strauss Former Labour M.P. Minister of Supply 1947-51. Piloted the Bill to nationalise iron and steel.

Lord Stuart Opposition Chief Whip 1945-51.

Pierre Uri Convinced European; confidant of Jean Monnet; Director of the European Coal and Steel Community 1952-59.

Nathan Yalin-Mor Political head of the Stern Gang, a Jewish terrorist group.

Bar Zohar Prominent Israeli journalist who has consulted many private papers on the Suez crisis.

Sir Philip de Zulueta Foreign Office official appointed Private Secretary to Sir Anthony Eden and Harold Macmillan.

The commentary to the text, unless otherwise identified, has been taken from filmed interviews conducted for the Thames Television series *The Day Before Yesterday* **in the summer of 1970.**

Goodbye to all that

The people come into their own

The British people have never been so organized as they were between 1939 and 1945. The Second World War, as far as Britain was concerned, was total war. The degree of human mobilization was far greater than in America and greater even than Nazi Germany dared attempt. So staggering was Britain's was effort that no one could remain unaffected. The Government was taking three-fifths of all production and controlling directly the flow of goods. One-third of personal expenditure was controlled by rationing. Unemployment disappeared and it was soon clear that there would be a desperate manpower shortage.

This provoked the introduction of a 'manpower budget' unthinkable before the war, and by early 1943 the Government discovered there simply were not enough people to go round. By the end of the war there were five and a half million men under arms and 40 per cent of the working population was directly involved in war production. It was illegal to change jobs without Ministry consent and even strikes were supposed to be against the law.

It was the first, and presumably the last people's war in our history. The government had to consider their needs. Gone was the waste of the twenties and thirties, the unemployment, the desperate poverty, and the apparent refusal of central government to cure social ills. The government had to abandon *laissez-faire*, had to talk to organized labour to an extent previously uncontemplated, had to institute clothes and food rationing which gave many their first experience of acceptable clothes and a balanced diet.

The legacy of the Second World War was overwhelmingly collectivist; joint effort in planning was not only in vogue but vital, and it was impossible to ignore calls for fair shares. And underneath hundreds of thousands of personal tragedies, the horror of the Blitz and the V1s and V2s, people were getting a larger slice of the national cake. From 1938 to 1944 the cost of living rose by 50 per cent; weekly earnings over the same period were up by 81.5 per cent. People were becoming wealthier in real terms and their expectations grew. If war is a great leveller, that meant from 1939 and 1945 raising the level of the working class. However marginally, the people were coming into their own, despite restrictions and shortages.

And remembering the aftermath of 1918, they were determined not to be cheated. Serious talk of what would happen after the war began in 1943,

Previous page: the Jarrow Hunger March – part of the folk memory of the poverty and unemployment of the '30s. Below: Churchill greets a victorious people. Beside him the architects of victory on the home front: Sir John Anderson (left), Chancellor of the Exchequer, and Ernest Bevin (right), Minister of Labour.

Left: sharing out the fair shares. Below: to build a land worth fighting for – expectant faces at an Army Bureau of Current Affairs lecture

following the publication of the Beveridge Report which outlined schemes for social security 'from the cradle to the grave'. A plethora of white papers followed, but suspicion grew that the Conservatives, at any rate, would not act on them. This applied particularly, if unfairly, to Churchill himself.

Nothing of course could be done until the war was over. But spontaneous political discontent grew throughout the war, notably with the success of the Commonwealth Party, an idealistic socialist group who won three by-elections while the major parties held to their political truce. Industrially, particularly from mid 1943 to mid 1944, 'national unity' was under stress with numerous strikes. During the eighteen months or so delay before victory in Europe (May 1945), various proposals for reconstruction were fully talked over in the pubs, in the papers, and in army camps all over the world. Here were men who in the inevitable delays of war had little to do but talk about the future.

Ironically, information that was to change post-war Britain was spread by a government agency – the Army Bureau of Current Affairs. The weekly A.B.C.A. lecture carried Beveridge round the world after some official delay, which confirmed to many the impression of dilatory concern for social matters; it carried too, the notion of change

As in all wars, there were phases of violent action punctuated by long periods of boredom and apathy during which people had time to read and argue and discuss. In those days the troops were much concerned with what Britain was going to be like after the war. There was a great deal of discussion going on about war aims, much discouraged, incidentally, by Winston Churchill. But the people and the organizations that were stimulating the discussions of war aims were men like J. B. Priestley, Tom Hopkinson, editor of *Picture Post*, and the Army Bureau of Current Affairs which had a very enlightened Secretary General. With those sponsoring organizations and inspiring individuals, the troops were really discussing what Britain was going to be like after the war. Also, of course, there was the *Daily Mirror*, which certainly had the very educative influence of making people think in simple and popular terms.
MAURICE EDELMAN

The soldiers of the Left

Although the 1945 Tory conference had a naturally exalted mood which came from having Winston Churchill as the leader, among the rank and file there was a traditionalist carry-over which seemed to me to be completely out of tune with the times. There were very few new ideas at that conference. There was the great mystique of Churchill: one of my very great memories is seeing Churchill get up, literally with tears streaming from his eyes, to the tune of 'Land of Hope and Glory' and receiving a very great ovation. But the national mood, as personified by Winston Churchill, was certainly not the mood of those people who had been thinking about what Britain would be like after the war and who had ideas as to the political future.

When I went to the Labour Party conference the thing was very different, there was a different kind of exaltation. You had many soldiers who had come back from the war. Instead of all the white-haired bald-headed pacifists of the past, there was a new breed of Labour supporter. The young Labour officer who at one time would have seemed like a contradiction in terms, but here suddenly you had very striking, good-looking young men like Denis Healey, John Freeman, Roy Jenkins, Jim Callaghan coming to the rostrum one after the other – speaking as servicemen who had fought for their country and who had a vision of a new Britain after the war which would be based on socialist principles. Somewhere in the middle you had men like Bevin, a great trade union leader, a man who commanded a big trade union battalion, side by side with the original pragmatist, Herbert Morrison, a man of the moderate centre, a traditional socialist yet opposed to extremist leftism; to classify him socially, of the lower middle classes, who yet was of the core and essence of the Labour Party. The whole thing of course was presided over by Clem Attlee. Now Clem Attlee himself, though he was a suburban solicitor from Stanmore, a man who had been to a minor public school, a person whose passion was cricket and sherry, here he was – the leader of the party whose interests were soccer and beer, and certainly rather different from the traditional attitudes which Attlee as a middle-class bourgeois represented. The great binding element was a passion for change.

Quite by chance at a reception one evening I met Councillor Pearl Hyde, a great war hero from the Coventry blitz. She was talking to me about the problems which they were having in Coventry of finding a candidate and she said to me, rather lightly, 'What about you?' And I answered 'Well, certainly, try me', and the next thing I knew was that I was invited by Coventry to come down to a selection conference where there were about six other potential candidates, and very much to my surprise, I must admit, I was selected as the candidate by an overwhelming majority.

MAURICE EDELMAN

I do remember very well indeed the numbers of men home on leave who came on to platforms in their uniforms, quite against the regulations, who were saying they did not want to resume civilian life under the conditions they had had before they went into the services. There's no doubt about this impact of life in the thirties upon these young men. It was also very interesting to see the very large number of what I suppose one could call progressive Conservatives who were also disturbed. I had a number of people in my constituency who were members of the Conservative Party, and in some cases leading members of the party, who were in fact helping me in my campaign because they themselves were fearful of their own party.

LORD ROBENS

It was a tremendous crusade, everything was going to be changed. In a strange way, it wasn't only going to be society that was changed, we ourselves were going to be changed. It must sound naive now, and maybe it was only the younger candidates and our younger supporters who felt that, but it was a definite feeling at the time. We did do great things, we changed a lot, a lot for the good, but perhaps we underrated the persistency of human nature a bit.

CHRISTOPHER MAYHEW

and the question – who could be trusted to obliterate the thirties? Much middle-road opinion turned to Labour as the only reasonable answer.

On 11 November 1918, when the Armistice was signed, Lloyd George hoped he could proclaim 'an end to all wars'. On 8 May 1945, Churchill made no such claim for the future. Crowds danced in the streets as they had done after the Great War, but there was less commandeering of buses and random coupling in doorways than in 1918.

Perhaps people showed more restraint because they had a greater stake in their own future. No one wanted to go back to 1939. The 'people's war' was to become the 'people's peace'. Pressure from below had already shown itself at the Labour Party Conference of 1944, where there was widespread impatience to get reconstruction moving.

Labour's problem was whether or not Attlee and his colleagues should continue in coalition with Churchill and the Conservatives until the Japanese War was over. It was expected to last at least nine months. On the other hand a general election was long overdue – the last had been in 1935. Attlee and Ernest Bevin, the Coalition's Minister of Labour and a major figure in the party, were in favour of waiting, at least for a while. The dangers of Churchill being swept back to power as a triumphant war hero were obvious.

As the party leadership contemplated their tactics, Labour held their annual conference in May 1945. The atmosphere of the conference was euphoric. It demanded that the whole shape of the post-war world be changed. Scattered about the conference hall were young men in battledress, not only with sergeant's stripes but captain's pips and major's crowns. Among many others, Captain Roy Jenkins and Major Denis Healey were there. Officers of His Majesty's Armed Forces had not been noted for leftward leanings in other wars. Denis Healey proclaimed: 'The upper classes in every country are selfish, depraved, dissolute, and decadent.' It was a sign of the times.

The strength of feeling from the floor convinced important Labour figures like Herbert Morrison, Emmanuel Shinwell, and Aneurin Bevan that Attlee should break loose from the coalition. The leadership arrived at a compromise and offered to stay with Churchill until October. Churchill refused and as the leader of the largest party in the House of Commons, formed a Caretaker Government. In the closing stages of the Labour Party Conference,

26 July was announced as the day when the results of the election would be known. A delay of three weeks between polling and declaration was necessary to allow the service vote to be collected and counted. The delegates were ecstatic; and constituency associations all over the country were stampeded into finding candidates.

Churchill misjudged the mood of the country badly, most notoriously in his 'Gestapo' broadcast. He described socialism as a philosophy 'inseparably interwoven with totalitarianism', and declared that if the Labour leaders were to fulfil their pledge of establishing a Socialist Commonwealth 'they would have to fall back on some form of Gestapo...' The charge didn't make sense when Churchill had spent the last five years in government with men like Attlee, Bevin, and Morrison. But Churchill on the stump produced crowds who cheered him to the echo. A large number of people on the Labour side

thought they would vote for him too. Indeed, if anyone had paid attention to the Gallup poll they would have seen Labour's lead diminishing.

The unquestionable dominance of Churchill led some senior Labour politicians to question Attlee's ability to compete with him and with the 'big' men among Labour's own leaders – Morrison and Bevin. Although Churchill had at times given him virtual control on the domestic front during the war, Attlee's position in his own party was never as secure as it seemed. He had been elected Leader of the Parliamentary Party in 1935, to replace George Lansbury. So sweeping was Labour's defeat in the General Election of 1931, that there were few prominent Labour men left in the Commons, and there was a widespread feeling, particularly among Morrison's supporters, that Attlee was a stopgap leader until Labour's parliamentary position improved.

The people's vote

AND NOW—
WIN THE PEACE

VOTE LABOUR

The campaign itself – don't think I'm exaggerating – was really like an act of love. The candidates were treated like pop idols. Everywhere we went there were hands outstretched to shake our hands, to get our signatures. Outside the factory gates there were great crowds of workers who came to hear the Labour candidates. One of the striking things was that the agents and the supporters would go about, literally, with a bedsheet held at the four corners and the workers would throw their pennies into the sheets – filling them with the great weight of copper coins and very often silver coins, which in those days represented a considerable sacrifice. I have fought seven elections but I've never known anything comparable with the mood of 1945.
MAURICE EDELMAN

We thought we were going to win, most of us; but by that margin? I doubt if anyone dreamed that we would win like that. I shall never forget those Forces' votes being tipped out from their tins. They were all for me. Really almost every one for me. It was astounding. I remember too the enthusiasm – there has never been an election like that since – the passionate conviction; sometimes, you know, we Labour candidates, we thought we were being loved by our supporters. It was unique.
CHRISTOPHER MAYHEW

Questions over Attlee's competence as leader gained currency after the party conference and led Harold Laski, who was Chairman of the National Executive, to write to Attlee: 'The continuance of your leadership of the Party is a grave handicap to our hopes of victory in the coming Election.' 'Thank you for your letter,' Attlee replied, 'contents of which have been noted.'

But it was not to be as easy as that. Morrison let Attlee know that if he were re-elected to Parliament he would stand for the Labour leadership. To block Morrison, Attlee would need some powerful support.

On polling day few people had any real idea of what the outcome would be. From the Caretaker Cabinet, 'Rab' Butler in particular had serious doubts about a Conservative victory. But most were ready to rely on the Churchill magic. So, apparently, was Churchill himself, who, though he

regretted his fall from national to party leader, mischievously confided to Bevin: 'They know they can't win without me.'

On the Labour side, Attlee was doubtful about winning and Bevin thought they would just win. Morrison was more optimistic. But it was generally agreed that it was going to be close. While the votes were being counted, Churchill, as he had promised, took Attlee off to Potsdam to talk to Stalin and Truman about the future shape of the world. They returned together, in mid-negotiation, to await the result.

They were waiting for the Service vote, and as soon as it had been counted, it became clear that Labour had an overall majority of 146. Among all parties there was a strong feeling of shock and surprise. The swing towards Labour was strongest in London and the large provincial cities – in Birmingham it was 23 per cent. The Service vote

Is Clem the man?

went strongly to Labour and, more significantly, about 30 per cent of the middle classes had shifted to the Left. For the first time, Labour had an overall majority in the House of Commons and was no longer the sectional interest group of past propaganda.

On the afternoon of 26 July, Attlee, Morrison, and Bevin gathered in Transport House – Labour's headquarters. Churchill informed Attlee that he would be going to the Palace to hand in his resignation at seven o'clock and would be advising the King to send for him – the perfectly proper constitutional course. But there was one chance left to those who wanted to challenge Attlee's position.

The Parliamentary Labour Party leader is elected before each new session of Parliament, but there was not time to put Attlee's claims to the vote. Should Attlee wait? Morrison, supported by Cripps, said that he should, and a substantial section of the party would have upheld this course. But Attlee was sure of Bevin's support because relations between Morrison and Bevin were bad. Bevin had long regarded Morrison as untrustworthy and disloyal in previous manoeuvrings over the leadership and had no desire to see Morrison as leader, yet he was not at all sure that he himself could command the overwhelming support of the party.

His view was borne out by Morgan Phillips, the Party Secretary, who said to Bevin that he might win on a split vote. With that Bevin turned to Attlee and said: 'Clem, you go to the Palace straight away.' Attlee arrived at the Palace on time, looking, the King said, 'very surprised indeed'. Meanwhile, many new Labour M.P.s were gathering for a victory rally in Central Hall, Westminster. Some were even approached in the lavatory by the pro-Morrison faction with the proposition that the time to get rid of Attlee was now; but Attlee's arrival and his declaration that he had accepted the King's Commission took the wind out of their sails. Harold Laski, chairing the meeting, was apparently as surprised as everyone else that Attlee had already been to the Palace.

Attlee's next problem was the formation of his Cabinet. Morrison promptly laid claim to the Foreign Office. Attlee dissuaded him and made him Lord President, Leader of the House, and gave him overall control of the economy. Thus Morrison had an extremely important planning job to direct

new legislation and the Government's domestic programme. Two other major figures had to be placed: Ernest Bevin, who wanted to be Chancellor of the Exchequer, and Hugh Dalton, President of the Board of Trade for part of the war and previously a lecturer at the London School of Economics, who wanted the Foreign Office.

Although the King, when he commissioned Attlee, had advised that he thought Bevin would be preferable as Foreign Secretary, Attlee told Dalton the following day that he would almost certainly get the job. Then he had second thoughts. If Bevin and Morrison shared the home front, there would be constant bickering. Bevin had already shown his capacity to bully people he disliked and Attlee was not prepared to jeopardise his domestic programme.

There was another more imponderable difficulty. Attlee suspected that somebody tough would be needed to deal with America and Russia in two days' time at Potsdam. Bevin went to the Foreign Office; he did not conceal his disappointment. With a deft touch, Attlee asked Morrison to take charge and rushed off with Bevin to catch their aeroplane for Potsdam. Just before he left he asked all the Conservative caretaker ministers who had not been replaced to stay on at their desks a few days longer. There were many more of them than the appointments so far made – Attlee left behind him a front bench of four for the first meeting of the new Parliament. They listened dutifully as their crowded back benches sang the Red Flag. The new age had begun with lightning speed.

I had literally never been to the House of Commons before my election. I went into this great chamber and I was sitting down, then the Speaker came in and we had Prayers. Then, before anything could develop, a Welsh miner called Griffiths, a very short vigorous man with blue scars on his nose, got up and started singing 'The Red Flag'. Spontaneously about 300 Labour members all rose up and started singing, or at least trying to sing, 'The Red Flag', because many of the new intake simply didn't know the words. Most of them knew the tune but they didn't know the words. And there we were – all bellowing away. The Tories on the other side, they looked at us absolutely aghast, they'd seen nothing like it before and to some of them it was as if their fears had been realized and that revolution had arrived, at the Palace of Westminster.
MAURICE EDELMAN

Hope: Labour's domestic policy 1945-7

The state of Britain in the summer of 1945 contrasted sharply with the euphoria of the Labour voters. War was expensive: peace supposed to cost nothing. But debt cast a long shadow over Labour's hopes. Britain was the largest debtor nation in the world. Her exports were only 40 per cent of the pre-war figure and Government expenditure abroad was five times as great as before the war. Britain's 'invisible income', earned from shipping, insurance and overseas investment, which was crucial for the balance of payments, had been halved. The Merchant Navy was smaller by a third.

Coal – by far the most important source of energy for British industry – was badly run down in production, manpower, and investment. The railways were undermanned and rolling stock was urgently needed. The overwhelming need was to push up production. In particular, exports had to rise to 175 per cent of the pre-war figure to enable Britain to pay her way. It was vital to demobilize rapidly; in comparison with 1918, this remains an outstanding achievement of the 1945 Labour Government.

No sooner had Attlee's ministers got to grips with the formidable economic situation, than Keynes, Britain's greatest economist, warned them that they faced 'a financial Dunkirk'. Without American aid, the country would be 'virtually bankrupt and the economic basis for the hopes of the public non-existent'. American aid was cut off just three days later when Japan surrendered. The Americans had little concept of how badly Britain's competitive position had suffered during the war and it was doubtful whether Congress, determined on a swift retreat from Europe, would vote more money.

The formidable Keynes and a team of advisers were despatched post-haste to Washington to plead for cash. Keynes brought back a loan, but there was a time-bomb buried in the agreement. One of the conditions of the loan was that by the middle of 1947 sterling should be made fully convertible against other currencies including the dollar. In other words sterling would have to be strong enough to hold its own in the international exchange market. If it were not, Britain faced trouble. The time limit was very short.

It was against this background that Labour set out to establish 'a Socialist Commonwealth of Great Britain'. The first and absolutely firm condition of this was to secure and maintain full employment.

To run the economy by centralized direction and planning, the Labour Government had the wartime apparatus of controls, perpetuated by the Supplies and Services Act of 1945. They were maintaining a war economy for peacetime purposes and in the prevailing scarcity, people were not only prepared to accept this, but they were even proud of 'our controls' and 'our rationing' system. Not only were they revolutionising minimum standards of living, but justice could be seen to be done. 'Fair shares for all' built up expectations which were to profoundly influence post-war politics.

The first step to socialism, but a long one, was to be taken by Labour's plans for public ownership. By the end of 1946, the Bank of England had been nationalized and plans were well advanced for the nationalization of road transport, rail and air

People used to think Attlee small or weak, and of course he had no physical presence at all, no voice; but he was a tough man, strong and a big man. I've seen him knocking down cabinet ministers in a sort of waspish kind of way – very effective. 'You really ought to have found out the answer to that question before coming to cabinet, you know.' That kind of thing. And that was really effective. He was big in the sense that he went for the issues. He wasn't a tactician, he wasn't a politician in the small sense, he went for the issues, the big issues; his judgement was extremely good on big things and he stuck to it. A man of real integrity. He had his special loyalties, he was loyal to the party, he was very loyal to the army as well. He was an excellent soldier. He was loyal to his old school, Haileybury. He was very shy. I can remember when he used to be coming down the corridor in the House of Commons, and I'd see him in the distance and we'd get closer to each other and I could always see him screwing himself up to say good morning to a junior minister, a personal friend of his.

CHRISTOPHER MAYHEW

Attlee, when he presided over the cabinet, said very little. He collected the voices and went all round the table and then he summed up. He was always very precise, you know, very reticent and very precise, but very formal also. An excellent chairman, pretty shrewd. He must have been shrewd, because he managed to escape from three conspiracies to throw him out.

LORD SHINWELL

Attlee was completely reliable, always carried out any undertaking given. He was completely trustworthy so that people's confidence steadily increased in him. I think this gave him a moral authority which nobody else, with the possible exception of Ernie Bevin, had in that government. But Ernie was a great *prima donna*, and therefore people didn't absolutely know where they might be with him. Attlee was the most impressive character I have ever met or ever worked with, because he never pretended to intellectual eminence or scholarship sublime, but he had extraordinarily clear vision of the facts and he knew just what he understood and what he didn't understand: this was so much better than other people who understood quite a number of things and believed they understood more, which they did not. He saw perfectly clearly, and when he didn't understand he took advice. Of course his capacity for saying nothing was absolutely pre-eminent and he avoided all the traps which other people fell into. We used to say that he would never use one syllable when none would do.

DOUGLAS JAY

travel, and the entire structure of the fuel and power industries. Coupled with this were programmes for vastly increased welfare: by the end of 1946 the National Health Service Act, the National Insurance Act, the National Assistance Act, and the Industrial Injuries Act were on the statute book. Most of these welfare proposals were not fully established and working until 1948. The age of the 'New Jerusalem' was designed to dawn on 5 July of that year. But much of the ground work was laid with great rapidity over the first two years.

The nationalization proposals emphasized the social ownership of basic industries, and not their day-to-day management. Management continued much as before. Workers' control was ruled out. This was to cause trouble later, when the rank and file discovered that their new masters did not seem

Export or die

A lot of people envisaged the Labour government's victory as going to build a new world at long term. A lot of other people envisaged it as an opportunity to get back on the results of a great deal of Tory rule. But, in fact, by far the most pressing and dominant item on the agenda was to reconstruct the war industry of this country: to redeploy the labour force to enable us to earn our keep in the quite hideous situation which arose from the sudden cut-off of American aid. We had sold most of our foreign investment. We had no export products nor export markets to replace these overseas earnings; and suddenly, almost overnight, by Congressional decision all this aid, which had been enabling us to live while we were fighting for the allied cause and while we were taking a disproportionate share of the war burden, was cut off. We were in a most extraordinary position then, but theoretically we were one of the most powerful countries on earth. As time went on it became clear that whatever grandiose ideas people might have, it was the bread and butter jobs of getting those demobbed people into industry earning our keep in exports, export or die, all this productivity campaign, this bread and butter stuff, that was more, much more, important. In the early part of the Attlee administration, there were problems of just taking to bits various war-time controls, of finding out what controls, what rationing, for instance, would have to continue, so as to enable us to make a transition to peace time. All this was occupying the foreground of the agenda for ministers and the Civil Service in a way which I think was never perhaps fully understood in other circles. It was a dominant issue just to live day by day in order to come out of it in a position where Britain could have the rewards which everyone felt that, having won the war, they were entitled to.

MAX NICHOLSON

Keynes's brilliance rather alarmed the Americans. I think they were wary of it; and in a curious sort of way if he'd been a less brilliant negotiator, we might have had a better result. On the American side there was not at that time the realization of the extent to which the war had impoverished Europe and had drained the resources of the United Kingdom. That realization didn't come until later, when the Americans turned from giving priority to their relations with the Russians, to giving priority to the reconstruction of Western Europe. Therefore, since they were not aware of the full extent of the problem, the loan which was eventually negotiated was really too small, and the conditions were too stringent – for example, the condition that sterling should be made convertible. On the British side there was a great reluctance to accept the loan, particularly on these conditions. Of course, the American negotiators had to keep a very wary eye on Congress, which was also very reluctant to give even this degree of assistance to the United Kingdom.

LORD SHERFIELD

different from the old. But the actual and emotional significance of this first step was considerable. No British government before had ever set out to alter more the shape and purpose of society.

The man responsible for co-ordinating this colossal legislative task was Herbert Morrison, for long the champion of the public corporation. He was the only Labour politician of cabinet rank in Britain with practical experience of nationalization. He set up the London Passenger Transport Board before the war and it proved a great success. His experience of large organizations like the London County Council was unrivalled in the Cabinet. He was a superb parliamentarian and his sense of political tactics was legendary. He was convinced that the party should not lose sight of that section of the middle class on whose allegiance Labour's power depended. Nor did he overlook the institutions of the party itself, and his reading of its political pulse was unmatched. Furthermore, his procedural reforms in the Commons made the House far more efficient.

No one worked harder than Morrison in the early years of the Government, pressing the programme forward and coordinating it at an enormous number of committees; yet many Labour politicians regarded him as a 'Tammany Hall' boss, devoid of idealism, and with too many fingers in too many pies. But someone had to do it; Morrison did it, and by being the linchpin between party and government, he took over part of the leader's role. This did not make him any more content with his secondary position. But by the beginning of 1947 he had worked himself to a standstill and suffered a major heart attack. He was never the same man again.

Individual ministers had charge of the respective nationalization schemes, with Emmanuel Shinwell in charge of coal, the centrepiece of Labour's post-war reconstruction. In most cases ministers had very little to work from. The objective was clear enough; how to achieve it was not. This caused surprise in some quarters where it was felt that the Civil Service ought to have an answer for everything. Labour had never studied the subject in detail, having put too much faith in the slogan alone. Nevertheless, most of the nationalization proposals went through Parliament with little real opposition. With the exception of iron and steel and road transport, most Conservatives were ready to give Labour a fairly free hand.

A Tammany Hall boss?

Herbert Morrison was Deputy Prime Minister and he was in effect the Prime Minister for all home front matters other than the Treasury. He probably got more and bigger Bills in a very short time through the House of Commons than, I should think, any other minister before or since. He was also in charge of the party machine; responsible for the Labour Party organization in the constituencies; and an exceedingly powerful man. Morrison was, in my judgement, the key figure. I was his senior official, his Civil Service adviser, Secretary of the Lord President's office – and I used to see him sometimes several hours a day. Morrison had a public image which was very different from his private image. The public regarded him as a rather – what the American might call 'ornery' – a rather touchy, rather aggressive character, who was always leading attacks. But personally he was the most considerate of men. He sometimes said that he would rather be a Permanent Secretary than a politician. He had great professional interest in how things were done, in what surveys were made and how decisions were reached. He, of all ministers, and I've had a good deal to do with fourteen ministers – of all the ministers I've ever worked for, he was the one who, if there were a profession of being a minister, would qualify top in my view.

MAX NICHOLSON

Morrison was a great authority on local government, a wonderful campaign organizer – but inclined to be a bit of a pontifico, you know. He was very pompous: he regarded himself as a person entitled to instruct people. He was a bit didactic. I remember on one occasion he came into the room, when I said – not intending to be offensive, it was just a bit of fun on my part – I said 'Here comes His Holiness the Pope'. Of course that was what Morrison was like. He was the ruler and he held the reins very firmly.

LORD SHINWELL

There was a lot of tension between Ernie Bevin and Herbert Morrison. No one can deny that. I was Herbert Morrison's Parliamentary Private Secretary to begin with, and then I went on to be Ernie's Parliamentary Under-Secretary, so I saw both sides to it. I think I would say Bevin was really the aggressor, and it was Herbert Morrison who was always rather scared and wishing to patch things up. The real centre, in my time, of the tension was a thing called the Overseas Information Committee, which Ernest Bevin thought should come under the Foreign Office and which Herbert Morrison, in charge of Government Information, thought should come under him. I remember Ernie saying to me once 'Chris, I want you to represent me on the Overseas Information Committee and the one thing you must do is keep your eye on Herbert'.

CHRISTOPHER MAYHEW

There is no doubt that Herbert Morrison was the architect of the nationalization programmes. Whilst the party had had nationalization in its programme since the end of the last century, it was Herbert Morrison's drive and energy and his conception of what nationalized industries should be, how they should be designed, that led to the pattern that emerged after 1945. He was very incisive; he also had this splendid cockney sense of humour. It was quite difficult to have a different opinion that led to a row with Herbert Morrison. He could always turn what was a delicate situation; and, as the heat was rising in discussion, I can see now that quiff of hair flicking over his forehead as he would toss his head back and come out with some humorous remark that had everybody smiling and back on track again. He worked prodigiously, too, with people. He understood that nobody in a high position can ever carry out his functions efficiently without having a good supporting team or, in modern jargon, a good think-tank.

LORD ROBENS

A tide of legislation

Of all post-war shortages, housing was the most intractable. Direct action was inspired in particular by a strong Communist Party

I was asked by Attlee to go to the Ministry of Fuel and Power with a seat in the cabinet and to nationalize the mines. He also asked me to nationalize the electricity supply and gas. I went back to my department, consulted with my Permanent Under-Secretary and other officials, and they said to me 'Well, you'll have to prepare the headings, Minister'. Naturally, I looked around for some information, for blue-prints, but there were none in the department. I went to the Labour Party; there was very little there. There was a pamphlet written by Arthur Greenwood, who was a very prominent member of the Labour Party. There were several resolutions passed at the Labour Party conference, no blue-prints, so I had to tackle it as if it was something quite new. It was very difficult indeed to do it.

The coal industry was pretty bad at the time because it had been neglected during the war. Thousands of men had left the pits either to go into the Forces or to enter the munitions industries, and the industry was completely neglected; it was in a terrible state. Meanwhile, industrial production was increasing at a rapid rate and demands were made for more coal as there were more demands for more electricity supply. You can imagine the nature of the problem. I couldn't say very much about it. I was very optimistic about the situation: the miners' leaders had promised to produce the coal. When we had nationalized the industry, of course, all sorts of problems presented themselves (shortage of labour, shortage of equipment) and so there was trouble. In addition to which we had trouble on the railways. Then there was some trouble about production and we weren't able to produce the stuff. We found that we couldn't get it to the people who wanted it. So nationalization, although it had been advocated over so many years and regarded as one of the most substantial items of the Labour Party programme, wasn't altogether a success.

LORD SHINWELL

The Labour movement made a fundamental error when, from time to time, almost with monotonous regularity at its annual conference, it moved resolutions to nationalize something or another but did nothing about it; there was no real research done on how you would organize a publicly owned enterprise of this size. The result was, by and large, that the nationalization acts were based upon work that had been done very largely by others and in the main by people who did not share the ideas of nationalization. The coal industry, for example, was based on the work of Sir Charles Reed, who was in fact employed by the coal owners and paid by the coal owners to do a complete survey of the coal industry and produce a scheme for rationalization. Indeed Sir Charles Reed became an original member of the National Coal Board.

LORD ROBENS

Dalton, the exuberant Chancellor, called 1946 the Party's '*Annus Mirabilis*'. Indeed it was, and Labour made sweeping gains in the local elections. They were totally secure, and the first act of nationalization, symbolically that of the Bank of England, was celebrated quietly over sherry at No. 11 Downing Street. The legislative tide swept forward. Crowds surged around the House of Commons and sales of Hansard reached all-time records. Dalton said he had 'A song in his Heart'. Sir Hartley Shawcross, Labour's Attorney General, was more serious: 'We are the masters at the moment, and not only for the moment, but for a very long time to come.'

Optimism among politicians was at its height. The political programme forged ahead with little thought to cost. The underlying problem was that of scarcity: shortages of food, money, materials, men, and houses. Shortages kept rationing on and help up production. Everything was a priority; too many things were first priorities. There was simply not enough to go round. Shortage of grain was world-wide in 1946; in the British zone in Germany, there was virtual famine which the Government had to alleviate. This meant keeping the British people short and using valuable dollars from the American loan. Resentment ran high. On the day after the Bill to nationalize the coal mines was given the Royal assent, bread had to be rationed. That had never happened during the war.

House building, desperately needed after the war, was boosted by the use of 'prefabs'. But the demand for factories was too pressing to allow a large housing programme. Squatters took over army camps and fashionable blocks of flats, but however much the Government was tampering with property in other spheres, it did not relent easily here. Eventually squatters were allowed to stay in the camps – but nowhere else.

Nevertheless, as winter approached in 1946, Labour had achieved a great deal. Some would argue, with hindsight, that Morrison had gone too fast. A programme designed for five years had had its groundwork laid in less than two years. There were risks of a hiatus before Labour's term of office was up. It was all very well to obliterate the past, but had the problems of the future been faced? There were certainly growing and pressing anxieties; yet the achievement of so great a programme, in under two years, with such widespread general consent, was fit to rank with the triumphs of the war.

Power: Labour's foreign policy 1945-7

In 1945, Britain had obligations all over the world. The British Empire was no smaller than in 1914 and now, additionally, there were onerous policing duties in Germany, Greece, and the Far East. British prestige was at its height. Churchill was a figure of world acclaim, which helped to conceal reality. The British had certainly stood alone and triumphantly prevented Hitler's invasion plans by a unique and spectacular effort. But it was the Russians who had, face to face, worn down Germany's strength. 1943 marked the turning point in British power: she was fully extended and increasingly dependent on American help.

When the war was over, Britain was expected to fulfil her obligations much as before. The threat of Germany was to be neutralized forever; Russia was meant to retreat eastwards; and the Americans to return to that faraway place whence they came. Future disputes would be dealt with by an international peace-keeping organization, where, unlike the old League of Nations, the great powers would be able to say 'yea' or 'nay'.

To many on the Left, Labour's election in 1945 presaged well for this scheme of things to come. America wanted to get out of Europe; that was good. She could take her capitalist intentions and her brash materialist citizens home. Socialist 'revolution' was rife in Europe; that was good. With the help of Soviet Russia, Labour would encourage the formation of a socialist Europe. Russia herself would be welcomed into the comity of nations from which she had been excluded for so long, and together, this Leftist bloc would root out forever the seeds of German nationalism. This view seems fantastic now, but in the summer of 1945 it was commonplace.

On to this stage waddled the squat, massive figure of Ernest Bevin. Bevin was a strong man. Incomparably the toughest member of Attlee's Cabinet, he could bully and threaten. He talked about Britain's foreign policy as *his* policy; about negotiations as *his* negotiations. Bevin had made his name coming up through the Transport and General Workers' Union, where he had fought employers through the twenties and thirties. His roots were solidly working class and he never lost sight of the welfare of the working man. Whenever he felt this endangered, whether from the Left or the Right, Bevin dug in. He distrusted the Right instinctively, but he had also learned to distrust sections of the Left, especially Communists.

He could be crushing to idealists; at the 1935 Labour Conference, he had launched a savage attack on the pacifist George Lansbury, helping to bring about his resignation from the leadership. During the war, Bevin had been a conspicuously good Minister of Labour, combining the carrot and the stick when manpower was a crucial commodity, and it is a lasting tribute to Bevin that he brought the unions into daily contact with government. By the end of the war, in two major statements on foreign affairs, he had both warned and soothed the Left.

In 1944 he had supported the Government's actions in Greece, where British troops were attempting to prop up a right-wing regime, much to the fury of the British Left. Within a year he used the famous phrase, 'Left understands Left, but the Right does not.' Although this was not a reference to Russia and the future, but to France in the thirties, it appeared to augur well for the establishment of a social democratic Europe.

A few hours after he had been to the Palace to see the King on being made Foreign Secretary, Bevin and the Prime Minister boarded an aeroplane for Potsdam, where Stalin and Truman were awaiting the return of Churchill after the election. Stalin was surprised, not altogether agreeably, by these two socialist arrivals.

The most important subject of their talks was Germany, core of the post-war problem. Germany lay ravaged and desolate; all food and medical supply services had virtually broken down. Nevertheless, German recovery could not be allowed again to threaten world peace. Stalin in particular felt a profound hatred and fear of Germany; he had come within an ace of being beaten by Hitler, and the German army had done incalculable damage to Russia. At least 10,000,000 lives had been lost and Russia's economic programme had been set back ten years.

At Potsdam the three powers agreed that no central German government should be established prior to a Peace Treaty and that the administration should be decentralized. The division of Germany into four zones – British, French, American, and Russian – when it was finally agreed, was to be made workable by the establishment of a Control Council. This would comprise the four powers and would be responsible, particularly, for finance, transport, and reparations. Joint control over an *undivided* Germany was thus agreed. Some-

Ernie Bevin was a really powerful figure and if he thought something was right, well, it didn't matter that the cabinet was against it, or Parliament or the public or anything like that. He stuck to it, he pushed it through. He was very powerful and ruthless. He knew his position in the cabinet and the country was assured. He was very much applauded by the Conservatives in Parliament for his anti-Stalinist line, but this didn't always please a number of our left-wingers who were much more powerful then than they are now. They were led by Dick Crossman, I remember. This all used to madden Ernie and he used to slap them down as hard as he could and as often as he could. And when it was my turn to do my best, to do the same thing, he was always behind me – on the front bench cheering me on. There was no doubt about it, he was a strong man. He was passionately anti-Communist and he was maddened by the attacks from the Left.

CHRISTOPHER MAYHEW

He was a very bad House of Commons man, he just never understood the House, he was hopeless at it. He wasn't a very coherent speaker. He was one of these extraordinary men who are able to make magnificent public speeches. It was rather like Eisenhower: if you took his sentences down verbatim they were completely unintelligible. The sentences ran into each other – and yet, it came over as a big idea. Intellectuals, who despised Bevin because he was illiterate, he thought very badly of. But the House of Commons doesn't like people of that kind lecturing them at the despatch box, and Bevin was, therefore, hopeless there. He was very bad, also, at handling the Foreign Affairs Committee of MPs upstairs. He quarrelled with everybody because he just couldn't have time for that kind of clap-trap and nonsense. He was a big trade union boss and didn't want to waste time with those damned Parliamentarians. And he didn't only dislike intellectuals, he disliked Herbert Morrison who was hardly an intellectual: he was called a third-rate Tammany Hall boss by Ernie Bevin. He disliked, really, all professional politicians except Clement Attlee. Clem he adored; he used to call him 'my little man'. Slightly condescending, but it was true. He stuck to Clem when they tried to throw Clem out, and of course Clem stuck to Bevin. After Bevin's death I always thought Attlee never was the real man again, because he really needed Bevin to keep him going, just as Bevin needed Attlee to steer him through professional politics.

RICHARD CROSSMAN

'If we don't let him work, who's going to keep him?'

LOW

Potsdam, August 1945. Truman (centre) a new,
self-assured President. Anglo-American friendship
seems as warm as ever. Stalin is less sure. Molotov
(standing right) already looks to the future.

Bevin, behind Attlee and Truman, looks less far
ahead, while American Secretary of State Byrnes
cosies up to Molotov

Mr Attlee of course had been at Potsdam as an adviser, but he went back now with Bevin to take command of the delegation. I remember that flight very well. We took off from Northolt. Bevin arrived rather late and puffing a great deal. He had never been in an aeroplane before in his life and he found great difficulty first of all in getting into his seat, and even more difficulty in fastening his seat belt round him because it wouldn't go. But he relaxed into his seat saying 'I never thought I would be here, but I've had a lot to do this morning. Sorry to be late. I had to go to Transport House and then to the Palace. But as you know I was never expecting to go to the Foreign Office'. Soon after we arrived, I, as the most junior person present, asked Mr Bevin what he would like to do that evening for dinner. Mr Eden had been accustomed, being rather selective, you might say, and careful in his choice of food, to say in advance who was going to have dinner with him. In that tradition I said to Mr Bevin 'Who would you like to have dinner with tonight and is there anything particular you would like to eat?' Bevin said 'I don't care a tuppence who you ask and I like sandwiches'.

I think it would be wrong to say that it came as a great strain or novelty to Bevin dealing with the Russians, although of course he had never dealt with

them before in an official capacity. But he'd had a lot to do with Russians in his trade union life and I think he felt that he knew the way they would react and that he certainly could cope: that was the feeling he had. He exuded extreme confidence, both in his dealings at the meeting and in his attitude to us officials.

NICHOLAS HENDERSON

When Mr Bevin and Mr Attlee arrived, Mr Stalin seemed to lose interest in the proceedings. I think he had a great suspicion of Mr Bevin as a Labour leader and didn't know quite how to evaluate this newcomer. I think he enjoyed his encounters with Mr Churchill to a great extent. They were very productive sometimes, and I think there was mutual respect between the two. But Attlee was a complete mystery for Mr Stalin, and they were just suspicious of Mr Bevin, so that the atmosphere changed completely at that point. Bevin, I think, made a real effort to persuade the Russians of the sincere intention on his part to achieve an understanding on a constructive basis. He wasn't giving things away. At the same time he was certainly reasonable.

ROBERT MURPHY

Left talks to Left

time later, when denazification was complete, the future of Germany under one government was to be agreed. Its survival as one country depended from that day on the continued agreement of the four powers.

During the Potsdam meeting, as Stalin was preparing to help the Americans in the Far East, Truman announced that he was about to drop the atomic bomb on Japan.

From 6 August 1945, when the first atomic bomb was used in war, the United States became indisputably the greatest power on earth. Much has been made, with hindsight, of the effect of this on Stalin. Certainly it took the Russians four years before they too could test one. But it is almost impossible to believe that Stalin thought the Americans would use it against the Soviet Union, unless first provoked. After the war Russia was internally very weak indeed, but this did not prevent a cautious policy of expansion in response to the chaotic conditions in Europe. Roosevelt had led him to believe that America would withdraw from Europe and Stalin had already won important concessions over Poland. The Red Army was all over Eastern Europe; elsewhere in Europe he could use his influence through the large Communist Parties of Czechoslovakia, Italy, and France. It would have been foolhardy to intervene further west, as some later alleged was his plan. No one knows how far the Soviet expansion was a defensive response to presumed threats to the survival of the Communist world.

The heart of Europe was Germany; it was there that the microcosm of relations between the four powers was enacted. It was over Germany and the lesser Axis powers that Bevin confronted Molotov, the Russian Foreign Minister. From 1945 to 1947 there was a seemingly endless series of talks centring on a German peace treaty. Negotiations swung backwards and forwards. Were the Russians taking too much in reparation from Germany? They were. Was not the Anglo-American Agreement in 1946 to introduce some common elements into their two zones (Bi-Zonia) a breach of their undertaking to keep Germany dismembered four ways? It was.

Bevin was under pressure from everybody. Molotov was pressing him hard and made him suspicious. The Americans were preaching about British imperialism, persistently underestimating the economic condition of Britain, and were slow to grasp the nature of Soviet expansion. At home, critics

Roosevelt's anti-colonial, anti-imperialist tradition was very simple, very ingenuous may I say, and of course repudiated by later American governments. It was all part of the anti-imperial line of the Americans of 1945 to '46 – still vaguely believing that they were able to get friendship with the Russians. It's a period of twilight between the end of the real war and the beginning of the cold war.

We'd fought the election saying Britain should not be a member of either bloc, we mustn't have the world riven into rival blocs – Communists and Capitalists; Britain should be a mediator between Capitalism and Communism, just as Socialism was going to be a wonderful half-way house. We were great half-way housers and we were to lead a third force in Europe. This was the concept. Now to be fair to us, this was what we'd fought the election on. This was exactly what the whole party, including Ernie Bevin, had said at the party conference in 1945. So when it became clear that the government's policy was to continue exactly as the Coalition government had done, that the Anglo-American alliance based on the special Anglo-American connection was to lead Europe and build us up strong, and that we were to police the world on behalf of the Americans because we had the army and they didn't – we simply said this wasn't what we'd fought the election on. We had a united policy saying 'Bevin is wrong and we don't want to stand with the Americans. We want to stand with Europe, between America and Russia'.
RICHARD CROSSMAN

We had started out on the basis of what Mr Roosevelt called his great design of co-operation with the Soviet Union. I happened to have had a chance to discuss that with him and to listen to him several times: it was simply thought that these were the two super-powers that would emerge from a war-time situation and that if we failed in an effort, and he wanted an all-out effort made, to co-operate with the Soviet Union to test it out – that if it failed, then certainly in his opinion war was inevitable. He and later Truman felt that every effort should be made then – I'm talking about the period '45 to '46 – to demonstrate to the Soviet Union that we wanted to co-operate, and this led to unilateral disarmament on our part and many concessions which in retrospect probably we should not have made.
ROBERT MURPHY

The stab in the back

Bevin started me. Bevin promoted me. Attlee hated me always and Bevin said 'No, give him a chance', so Attlee said 'He's a terrible intellectual and he's troublesome at home with his Conservative mother and father'. You know, I was hated by Attlee. I was given my chance and disgraced myself by being – I'm sorry to say – prematurely right about Palestine, by saying so, very loud and clear, in a way perhaps one oughtn't to. Bevin was curious because he never could resist having a drink with one in a highly friendly way. He'd waddle into the smoking room, sit down beside you and before you knew what, you were having a fairly interesting discussion with him. He was an extraordinarily friendly man.

I remember there was a terrible conference in which Bevin made the great 'stab in the back' speech and I had done the stab in the back. That evening there was a great dance and there were people crowded around and I was standing across the floor. He saw me and he came right across the room, took my hand and said 'No ill feelings, Dick?' I never know whether I was right: I said 'There are some' and turned away. In a way I think he respected me more for not taking it, because this was what the big boss always did. When he mopped you up he tried to roll you up as well.

RICHARD CROSSMAN

The stab in the back incident. I know it upset Bevin much more than anything else because he told me this himself. Molotov apparently said to him at one stage when they were on very good terms 'Yes, well you can't speak with much authority, you haven't even got the support of your own party'. And I know Ernie was very upset about that and felt pretty bitter about the whole affair.

ARTHUR BOTTOMLEY

on the Left attacked him for being anti-Soviet. Richard Crossman and fifty-two other Labour M.P.s sponsored an amendment to the King's Speech in November 1946 which instructed Bevin to provide 'a democratic and constructive Socialist alternative to an otherwise inevitable conflict between American Capitalism and Soviet Communism'. That very day Bevin was in New York negotiating with that same 'American Capitalism' to keep the bread ration from being cut. Later in the day, Bevin waited in his hotel for the daily telephone call from London to come through. Hector McNeil, his Under-Secretary, was on the line:

McNeil: 'There's been some trouble in the Commons today, Minister. An amendment was put down on the King's speech criticizing the conduct of foreign policy and...'

Bevin: 'Who are they?'

McNeil: 'Well, Minister, there are rather a lot of them...'

Bevin: 'Who are they?'

McNeil: 'Do you want...'

Bevin: 'Who are they?'

McNeil: 'Richard Crossman.'

Bevin: 'I'll break him.'

McNeil: 'Michael Foot.'

Bevin: 'I'll break him.'

And so it went on: right through to the fifty-third name. This incident produced a public outburst at the next party conference when Bevin, shaking with rage bellowed out that he had been stabbed in the back.

Although Bevin's suspicions of Russian obduracy were growing, he was not prepared to give up: he was determined not to let Molotov's belligerence blight a settlement. Churchill's famous intervention at Fulton, Missouri, when, as early as March 1946, he said: 'From Stettin in the Baltic to Trieste in the Adriatic, an iron curtain has descended across the Continent', was regarded by Bevin as unhelpful. He had certainly not given up hope at the end of 1946, whatever his critics said.

Bevin's left-wing critics, many of them members of the Keep Left Group, were worried by what they thought was the drift of his policy towards Russia. They were too ready to blame him for failing to settle the German problem with Molotov. But they were much more shrill over his policy where fighting was still going on, in Greece and above all in Palestine.

In the summer of 1945 Jews all over the world welcomed the arrival of a Labour Government that was pledged to do all it could to create a Jewish state. At the same moment, the substance of what had happened in the death camps became generally known. A moral obligation to find a secure home for the Jews was overpowering.

Before 1939 the Arabs and Jews had been in conflict in Palestine, and only the British occupation averted civil war. The Jewish defence organization, Haganah, had been enlisted in the Allied cause during the war. Even the extremist reprisal group, Irgun, declared a truce and many of its members fought for the British, while a few extremists broke ranks to continue the struggle as the Stern Gang. Irgun called off the truce in 1943, in protest against British restrictions on the entry of

SEE FOR YOURSELF. IS IT NOT OBVIOUS THAT THEY ARE "DEMOCRATIC GOVERNMENTS WHICH ENJOY THE CONFIDENCE OF THE OVERWHELMING MAJORITY OF THE PEOPLE OF THESE COUNTRIES"?

If Labour win the election in Britain, then the Jews will be rewarded: the Labour Party will implement promises made during its conferences. Suddenly the Labour Party started to give blows on the head to the Zionist movement. This was a big disappointment. Not only a disappointment, it was maybe the last straw which broke the camel's back. When we talked to our opponents from the Haganah, they always said: 'Well, we still hope. If the Labour Party comes to power and will not implement their promises, then we shall be with you'. This was the case. Haganah had no more excuses. They had to go out fighting. At that time the so-called movement of Hebrew resistance was formed and it started a period of co-operation between the Haganah, the Irgun, and the Stern group.

You see, according to our philosophy, it was good that a man without a mask came to power in Britain. If the Foreign Secretary had been a great gentleman, and could hide his intentions by very nice phrases, the situation might be worse. Bevin was straightforward. He talked very plainly. He sometimes used phrases which could be interpreted as anti-Semitic and this was good for our cause because it disillusioned the people. It made clear to them where we stood. Therefore we owe a lot of things to Bevin because he made the situation ripe for a confrontation.

NATHAN YALIN-MOR

In your country, I suppose, Bevin is considered a great Foreign Secretary, but in our country opinion about him is different. I suppose he thought that we were going to be easily subjugated, frightened. He didn't realize, probably, that a new generation rose in this country. The Jews in this country were ready to fight, to die for their cause and for their people. He probably also didn't realize the depth of our feelings after what had happened to our people in Europe. We, for instance, here, understood that if we didn't fight and if we didn't have our own home, then our people were doomed for destruction. I don't think that we would have achieved independence in 1948 without our armed fight. I think also, historically, it was the last moment to achieve it because of the international situation, the relations of America and Russia. I think the fight in the forties until the raising of our flag as an independent nation was not only an historic necessity, but, as far as timing is concerned, it was in our generation the last moment.

Bevin made several grave mistakes which brought about national unity. I will give you one example. He ordered a ship with Jewish refugees from Europe, from the holocaust, to be sent back to Germany. That was a specific act. I wouldn't like to characterize it now, but it really brought about the unification of all groups in our people. Retrospectively, I would say, we would have preferred not to have such an opponent on the other side.

MENACHEM BEGIN

What price the Jewish vote?

I was in the United States with Bevin in 1946 when
demonstrations took place, indeed I've still got a bit
of paper which has on it 'Go home, Limey'. I don't
think Bevin took them that seriously; after all, there
had been many demonstrations in which he had
engaged himself. Bevin was genuinely concerned
about getting a settlement for the Palestine question.
At one time he was confident that he was going to do
so. Ernie told me that he had been talking to Jimmy
Byrnes, who was the then United States Secretary of
State, and with Molotov, and he thought he'd got
them to agree upon a partition of Palestine – and
probably the partition of Palestine was the best way
in which a settlement could be achieved. Now I know
that some of these State Department officials the
following morning came along and said 'We're afraid
we can't go through with this arrangement. The
pressure from the Jewish population in New York is
so great that it is doubtful whether we can get an
arrangement on the basis that had been arranged'.
Now I don't know on what basis the arrangements
had been made, but I can only say that I know Ernie
Bevin was terribly upset and disappointed about this
reaction.
ARTHUR BOTTOMLEY

It is hard to believe now, but Palestine, you know
was a side-show for the Labour government. I mean,
the important things were whether or not to give
freedom to 500,000,000 Indians, the Marshall Plan,
the formation of NATO, and so on. Palestine was the
kind of thing you left to Mayhew for an adjournment
debate in the House. It's unbelievable, but it wasn't a
major issue.

People say Bevin was anti-Semitic – that's wrong –
but what is right is that he was passionately
anti-Zionist. He was maddened by the Zionist
pressures brought on him in the House of Commons,
from other sources in Britain, and then above all
from the United States. We used to get messages like
'If only you could see your way to helping the
President with this or that demand of the Zionists it
would make it so much easier to get your Marshall
Aid appropriation through Congress'. Bevin had to
listen, and, frankly, it maddened him. And I must
say, looking back, you see, to have the fate of
hundreds of thousands of Arab people decided in
this way by votes in New York, for a mid-term
election, was wrong, and Bevin and I both felt
passionately that it was wrong. People say he came
unstuck on Palestine – even his friends say that
sometimes – and of course he made a number of
tactical mistakes. But his big point was that the Jews
were asking for more than the Arabs either could or
should be asked to accept peacefully. This was the
big point. And he was right on this big point.
CHRISTOPHER MAYHEW

The British Mandate in Palestine was trying to do two irreconcilable tasks: that is, to establish the national home for the Jewish people in Palestine without prejudice to the existing inhabitants of the country, namely the Arabs. There was no solution. We played for time, if you like. It is a characteristic British method of doing things and sometimes it is a very effective one. We played for time and hoped for the best: something would turn up, and all that sort of thing, which of course didn't and couldn't and never looked like doing so. We were like the ham in the sandwich – we had immense pressures brought to bear on us from both sides. Everything we did was wrong to one or the other.

SIR JOHN SHAW

The Americans simply said 'You take all those Jews to Palestine and you look after them, and you take all the consequences from the Arabs. That will reduce the number of Jews who will come to America'. I've never seen a more selfish attitude than the American government adopted. I must say, here I sympathize with Bevin because it was insupportable. The American government's attitude was self-righteous. They said 'It's your job to look after all the survivors of the concentration camps, you take them all into Palestine. After all, when you ask the Jews now at least as many of them wanted to go to the States as wanted to go to Palestine'. But there was a quota into the States and did the Americans lift the quota? Not one iota. So there was fury – I can understand Bevin and Attlee being angry with Truman for lecturing to them. They had to do all this without American help because the Americans would not help us at all at the time, and were not concerned to go into the Middle East. The other American attitude, of course, which made it particularly irritating to the British, was that the Jews were seen as being true Americans fighting George III and that this was the American revolution all over again. Ernie Bevin was regarded really as George III incarnate today, with all his wickedness. Now it was a bit irritating to a Labour government to be treated in this way by an American Democratic President.

RICHARD CROSSMAN

It's often thought that Bevin was anti-Semitic. Far from it, he was pro if anything. He was a Foreign Secretary who was new to the job and he wasn't even an established Parliamentarian; he didn't know the skilful way in which civil servants could perhaps lead, and one had to remember that the civil servants at that time were predominantly pro-Arab, no doubt because they thought it served Britain's interests best. So that when Ernie found that his own supporters were letting him down because they hadn't got the knowledge of the facts, it was much easier for those in the Civil Service to have an influence on him than might otherwise have been the case.

ARTHUR BOTTOMLEY

I think, frankly, at the beginning there was no anti-Semitism. At the beginning, Ernie Bevin was a natural Englishman, and therefore of course a natural anti-Semite. But Bevin only became anti-Semitic when he found that the Jews were frustrating him. By the end of his life he was, in one sense of the word, ravingly anti-Semitic, dangerously so. But it was something which grew on him as the result of the situation. The Jews wouldn't fit in with his plan to hold the Middle East, to hold the oil. For that he needed a Suez base. For the Suez base he needed a friendly Palestine, a friendly Palestine meant to him an Arab Palestine with an acquiescent Jewish minority and the Jews said they wouldn't acquiesce, so they had to be broken. I must say he was pretty rough from the start. You will remember when he said, right at the beginning of 1945, that 'you shouldn't shove to the head of the queue'. But to poor people who'd just had 6,000,000 people murdered in concentration camps, it wasn't the most tactful way of addressing the survivors, to say this kind of thing. But it was only, as I say, something coming out of him. He was a very primitive man in certain ways, enormously powerful, able, but with a simple brutality at the bottom which was combined with a great buoyancy and a great kindness, so you had both brutality and kindness in him. He simply couldn't stand his sense of frustration. The Jews were deeply shocked by this brutal and simple man and they under-estimated him. They saw him at his worst – at his bullying worst.

RICHARD CROSSMAN

Jewish refugees into Palestine. This pressure mounted as the war went on; as did Jewish determination to secure a homeland. President Truman endorsed demands to open up Palestine to Jewish refugees and the flood of illegal immigrants increased dramatically.

Bevin had to do something: he agreed to an Anglo-American commission on Palestine. In May 1946 it recommended that 100,000 immigration permits be issued and that a state be established under international guarantee, with neither Jew nor Arab dominant. Bevin was reportedly furious that the Arab community in Palestine stood in danger of being swamped; he also disliked the implied threat in Irgun's offer of a truce, should the 100,000 permits be granted. Bevin was under strong Foreign Office pressure not to sacrifice traditional British interests with the Arabs in the Middle East, and was acutely conscious of the need to keep the oil-producing countries well-disposed.

He refused to budge. The security operations in Palestine continued; British troops arrested leaders of the Jewish Agency – the representative body of Jews in Palestine. But these strong-arm tactics misfired. On 22 July 1946, the King David Hotel, headquarters of the British Security Forces, was blown up. More than one hundred were killed.

Bevin was also under growing pressure from Jewish communities in Britain, and more especially from America where mid-term elections were in progress. Simple electoral arithmetic showed that President Truman, if he was to get a sympathetic Congress, needed the Jewish vote in the big states, particularly in New York. Bevin fulminated about the public and private hustling that he believed this situation produced. During his visit to America in November 1946, he was met by demonstrators and by Jewish-American dockers refusing to handle his luggage. For the man who had done so much for the British docker the irony was complete.

In Palestine the atrocities continued. Several Irgun leaders were forcibly freed from Acre jail, but three of the rescuers were caught and sentenced to death. Irgun captured and threatened to hang two British sergeants if their men were not released. The three Irgun were hanged and so were the two sergeants. There were anti-Jewish demonstrations all over Britain and settlement seemed as far away as ever.

Bevin was also in trouble with his own supporters over Greece, where there was civil war. Attempts

to get the Communists to partake in elections in April 1946 failed, and the war went on between the Communists and a confusing array of monarchist and centre right parties. The sight of British troops propping up right-wing regimes did not look very attractive in the immediate post-war world. But Bevin could not let the situation slide completely for fear of a Communist take-over.

In neither Palestine nor Greece could he see any middle-ground opinion strong enough to negotiate

with in a deal, but at the same time he was not prepared to see British interests surrendered. His frustration was compounded by attacks from the Labour Left. A man of Bevin's temperament could not bear to be cornered.

More serious than the two civil wars in Greece and Palestine, however, was the growing threat of a gargantuan one in India, between Hindu and Moslem. Some measure of self-government had already been given to India but the nationalist movements were in full cry. Attlee for more than two decades had been a supporter of Indian independence and his Government shared his moral commitment. They hoped for a peaceful transfer of power, but in any case a speedy exit was necessary. Mountbatten was commissioned to attempt to secure it. The very nub of the whole imperial tradition was being questioned. Without India, imperial politics could never regain their old central importance.

A terrorist explains

The King David Hotel was both a military command and the centre of administration for Palestine in those days. I went on with the preparation of the operation. In the cellar of the hotel there is a restaurant which serves the officials. There was an entrance on the left side of the building to deliver merchandise and food and other things to the kitchen. We knew that the hotel staff were dressed in Sudanese uniforms. At 10 or 10.30, about half an hour before the Arabs were supposed to come with the food supplies for the hotel, a truck covered with canvas pulled in to the hotel supply entrance. A group of six or seven of our people dressed like Sudanese servants, with their sub-machine guns under their dresses, slipped into the hotel. Another group of six or seven people who were dressed mainly like Arabs started to bring milk containers into the cellar which contained our dynamite. On the way, there was an exchange of fire. One man was killed and one wounded. But they took control of the basement of the hotel and immediately they transferred the containers of milk which contained nearly half a ton of explosives. When our men knew that the operation was successfully over, they immediately went into telephone booths and informed three different places. One note was given to the French Consulate, which was the nearest neighbour of the hotel, to open the windows to eliminate glass breakage. Another was given to the police headquarters in Jerusalem telling them that the explosives had been inserted into the basement of the hotel and asking them to evacuate the hotel. The third message was given to the *Jerusalem Post*, telling them that explosives had been placed in the hotel. We understood later that somebody from the *Jerusalem Post* called the Chief Secretary and asked if they got the warning. They confirmed they'd got the warning, so the man asked whether they were evacuating the hotel. They got the answer that the Secretariat was there to give orders and not to get orders from the bloody terrorist organizations. The result was very fatal; too many people were killed. It left us with a very bad feeling of what happened.

AMIHAI PAGLIN

At the actual moment when the explosion took place, I was in my office. It had been a disturbed morning, there had been a lot of little minor comings and goings in the street outside, with small anti-personnel bombs and petrol bombs and things like that. At about half past twelve, mid-day on that Monday morning, 22 July 1946, things died down a bit. The police stopped rushing about and the road was strewn a bit with debris and so on, but nothing very much was happening and the small crowd that had collected to watch were dispersing. I was extremely busy, always chronically overworked; and I didn't want to waste any more time. I walked along the corridor to the east end, back to my office to get on with my work, and then a few minutes later – which I think was about 12.40 p.m. – there was a

muffled explosion which was more like a crack of thunder than an explosion of an explosive. The light over my desk fell down. I was enveloped in dust and fumes and smoke and everything else, so much that for a moment I couldn't see. The place was virtually dark. My papers, of course, were strewn all over the room. I wasn't hurt. As soon as I collected my wits a bit and the atmosphere began to clear I rushed out of my office into a neighbouring room which was occupied by my private secretary. I said 'Are you all right, Marjorie?' And she said she was a bit shocked and shaken. The dust was still so thick you could hardly see. Then I rushed along the corridor outside, also through this almost impenetrable darkness, to see what was happening. By some miracle so far as I was concerned, I was pulled up short on the edge of a colossal abyss: the corridor had disappeared, in fact the whole of the rest of the building had just disappeared like that, there was a precipice. Then I met another woman, a member of my staff standing just on the edge of this abyss where there was a little bit of flooring left. You've heard the phrase of people's hair standing on end – well, her hair was

standing on end, and it was completely powdered white with this plaster dust from the building, and it was standing on end. She was in a very disturbed state. At the time it was impossible to ascertain what the loss of life was because dead bodies were not lying about all over the place in the open, they were buried under hundreds of tons of masonry which was lying as rubble in the courtyard, in the street and everywhere else. I lost 70 to 80 of my own staff. The army lost a few: they only had a corner of the top floor and hadn't many people in it.

Jerusalem in July is hot, and it took us the best part of a week to get those bodies out. Before we had got the last one out with sappers and miners, magnificent workers, working day and night and other people assisting too, the whole place began to be permeated by the smell of decomposition of bodies, which is an extremely unpleasant smell; it's very pervasive and it sticks in your nostrils for a considerable period. My wife says she can still smell the smell of the King David when she thinks about it.
SIR JOHN SHAW

After the operation on Acre Jail four of our fellows remained in the city. They didn't hear the retreat signals, and were caught by the British. They were sentenced to death. We were going to do anything we could not to let these people hang. We succeeded in getting hold of two British sergeants and we had the feeling that they would release our people and we would release those sergeants. It was never the policy of the Irgun to kill people as people, but I'll say that the hanging of the two sergeants did more to get the British out of this country than any other operation. I personally believed in those days – I still believe – that hanging is one of the basest and most contemptible deeds that one human can do to another. I also believe that one who does it loses the image of God, but we were forced to do it by the attitude of the British administration here.

The British government in London failed to understand the roots of the conflict and thought by breaking the necks of a few of our members they could break the neck of the underground. So it happened they hanged our people and we had to hang the two sergeants. We declared before that we were going to do it. We didn't believe we'd have to do it, but when the British hanged our members we had to do it. I was personally involved with the decision. I think that the Irgun had no choice, because releasing the two sergeants after everyone in the world knew that our people were hanged is to give up, so we also felt it was our first, our essential duty, almost our responsibility, to our comrades who were fighting

The British didn't realize the roots of the conflict, they didn't understand what the Irgun was fighting for, they tried to handle us just like a bunch of killers. The policy was never to kill people as people, and I will say that the Irgun in the beginning of the war against the administration tried to eliminate killing as much as possible, even by risking our own people to eliminate casualties; but they treated us as a bunch of murderers and we learned from declarations from some of the main officials in the country that, in closed circles, they would say they believed that after a hundred Jews were hanged this business would be over. They didn't realize that everybody was prepared to risk his life and to give everything that he had in order to get the freedom of independence which we were sure was so vital and so urgent.
AMIHAI PAGLIN

The King David Hotel: the afternoon of 22 July 1946

Hope deferred

In the latter part of 1946, despite the promises of the miners' leaders to produce the coal, there was a great shortage. It is a mistake to assume that the Civil Service can help much when it comes to the matter of production. Indeed, as regards the electricity supply, and potential consumption, their estimates about these matters led me astray. I had to direct the attention of the government to a shortage of coal. The result was that Attlee decided to form a Coal Committee and he made Hugh Dalton Chairman of the Coal Committee. The trouble about Dalton was two-fold: first, he wasn't the kind of man whom one could co-operate with easily, and secondly, he was opposed to open-cast coal production on the grounds that it would spoil the amenities of the countryside. One of the essential features of coal production at the time was open-cast coal production, because it was much easier to produce than deep-mine coal production. That was one difficulty; another thing was this: there was trouble with the railways. The railwaymen wouldn't work weekends to remove the coal. When the so-called fuel crisis occurred there was actually more than a million tons of coal at the sidings. Transport couldn't get it to its destination. Not only because of the inclement weather, but because of the condition of the railways. The permanent track of the railways had not been repaired and maintained in proper condition during the war. So we had all sorts of problems: shortage of miners, shortage of coal; shortage of wagons, and then on top of it serious weather – perhaps the worst weather we've had for many years. And that was the situation. I advised the government over and over again about this, but nevertheless – I make a confession – I had to make optimistic speeches outside, because if I failed to do that it would have been used as an argument against nationalization. We had decided to proceed with nationalization; the miners wanted it and the public had accepted it and the coalmen had even accepted it: they really provided no stern opposition to the mines becoming public property. But there I was faced with the situation. Difficult to get the coal, yet I had to say to the country 'No, it's coming on all right'. I was optimistic about it. Attlee took the opportunity at a meeting in Lancashire to point out that this was not the fault of the Ministry of Fuel and Power, it was a matter for the cabinet itself. They had to accept responsibility. But I got scores and scores of letters, and newspapers. I have in my possession about half a dozen books full of cartoons about myself, caricatures of myself. They had a rare time with me, what they said about me, even when I was living down in south London, on the walls of my house all sorts of inscriptions, amusing inscriptions. Oh, I had a rare old time, but I survived. Nevertheless, and I'm prepared to admit this, although the fuel crisis was not my responsibility, the mistake that I made was in being too optimistic about the success of nationalization.

LORD SHINWELL

1947 was a turning point in British history which was in many ways more fundamental than that at the end of the war and the return of Labour in 1945. Britain's place in the world shifted dramatically between the beginning and the end of the year; and life for the British people got worse. In 1947 foreign and domestic policy fused and never quite parted company again. The agent of this change was hard cash.

On 1 January 1947, a fifty-year-old dream came true. Every coal mine in the country displayed the sign 'This colliery is now managed by the National Coal Board on behalf of the people.' Two months later power supplies across the country had almost broken down. Over 2,000,000 people were thrown out of work; people worked in offices by candle-light; fires and traffic lights went out; lifts stopped; the national newspapers were cut to four pages; and

periodicals did not appear for three weeks. Exports were disrupted and firms like Austin were forced to close. No one was allowed to cook on an electric stove from 9 a.m. to 12 p.m. and from 2 p.m. to 4 p.m.

These miseries were partly caused and certainly exacerbated by the longest and coldest winter this century. Ice floes were seen off Norfolk, and the sea froze off Margate; snow ploughs cleared the London streets, while the rest of the country was mostly impassable.

At the root of the problem was coal which, due to the cold weather, could not be moved. But there was not enough coal anyway. This was not entirely the fault of the Minister, Shinwell. He had made an error in forecasting both the amount needed and the productive capacity of the mines, which had been badly eroded by the war; and he made matters

An act of God

I think the real cause of the 1947 fuel crisis was undoubtedly the abnormal weather conditions coupled with the fact that there was an overall shortage of coal. I think that these two things put together created a crisis in which Mr Shinwell finally left the Ministry. In the first place there was this great overall shortage of fuel. Ernest Bevin, who was Foreign Secretary at the time, was pleading for more coal for Europe. I remember, in the absence of Hugh Gaitskell, who was my Minister, on one occasion, Ernest Bevin sent for me; he'd just come back from discussions in Germany with the French and the Americans and the Russians. He said it was essential that we should be able to provide Europe with the fuel that it needed and if he could have two or three million tons of coal it would make all the difference to his management of foreign affairs. It would enable him to influence the whole future of Europe in political terms. I remember saying to him, there is no reason that you shouldn't have as much as you like for Europe, one, two, three, four, five million tons of coal; but what you must decide is what part of British industry are you going to starve? The answer was that the coal never went to Europe in the quantities that Ernest Bevin wanted. In fact subsequently we actually imported coal from America at a net loss of £70 million, in order to enable some exports from this country of coal to get to Europe. If Manny Shinwell made a mistake at all, it was that he tended to suggest that there were other factors working against him personally, that there was some sort of conspiracy. This was the sort of image that he gave when in point of fact he had a perfect case. No man on earth could possibly have got coal through.

LORD ROBENS

The best period of all was the autumn period of September and October of '46 which Dalton called 'a golden autumn', when he was able to make big increases in social expenditure. It's astonishing how well the country did in '46. It wasn't really until '47 that the magnitude of the post-war balance of payments problem began to impinge on everybody's mind. The balance of payments was, to Dalton, a tiresome complication; he was really interested in the distribution of wealth and the distribution of incomes within the country – overcoming unemployment, curing the old depressed areas and so forth. He was very energetic, very intelligent, very successful on those fronts, I think, but this wretched balance of payments kept impinging on him, and in the end he couldn't really fully cope with it, indeed nobody else has been able to since the war.

DOUGLAS JAY

The Greek domino

worse by optimistic statements. Hugh Gaitskell, his Parliamentary Private Secretary, had warned him of the shortage of coal stocks, but, as Shinwell said, 'We do not produce coal at the Ministry of Power.' The results were horrendous: over £200 million in exports were lost and national recovery was seriously set back.

Against this background, Dalton was preparing his third budget. The American loan was being eaten into at an alarming rate. Because of the convertibility clause, sterling would have to stand on its own feet by July, and inflationary pressures were building up at home. Something had to be done to cut expenditure. But Dalton was more worried about manpower. According to his estimate the country was going to be short of 600,000 men in 1947. There were 1,500,000 men in the Armed Forces. The expenditure overseas on them was £200 million per annum. Germany, in aid and defence alone, was costing £60 million. Across the street, Bevin realized that Britain could no longer sustain her foreign policy. She must cut her commitments and America would have to be persuaded to share Britain's load.

It all seemed to happen at once. In the third week of February, the Cabinet decided to give India and Burma their independence. Palestine was no longer to be a British responsibility. The United Nations was to be involved and an attempt was to be made to institute an international force to keep the peace there. The Americans were told officially that British support in Greece would be withdrawn in six weeks, as would financial support from Turkey.

In Greece and Turkey, British departure would leave a large vacuum. The power best able to influence events in these areas was the Soviet Union by its proximity and with the aid of a large Communist party in Greece.

Within a fortnight of the decision, President Truman addressing both Houses of Congress, announced: 'I believe it must be the policy of the United States to support free peoples who are resisting attempted subjugation by armed minorities or by outside pressures.' This was the Truman 'doctrine' and it marked a fundamental departure in United States policy. It was not popular; it was symptomatic of American feeling when Representative Buffet said, 'Here is British Imperialism in friction today with Russia. We walk over to Britain and say: "Here we are on your team. Here is a new shot-gun." ' But Dean Acheson, Truman's

The Americans were surprised and irritated by the suddenness of the British decision to withdraw from Greece and the speed with which we proposed to withdraw our troops and stop aid.
LORD FRANKS

During the early years after the war, what the British government was more conscious of than anything else was the fact that Britain was desperately over-committed. She was the only European power still having armed forces in being and her economy, of course, was exhausted by the sacrifices of war. So all the time they were looking for new sources of power rather than new sources of responsibility. There was only one possible source of power in the world as it then existed and that was the United States of America, which, don't forget, had committed itself by act of Congress to neutrality nine years earlier in 1936. I think that Bevin saw the Greek crisis as a burden which would break Britain's back unless he could get rid of it. The only possible country to take it over was the United States. He took a calculated risk is saying we must get out. The Americans did in fact respond and took the burden over, and this was really the beginning of America's involvement not only in Europe but in the world.
DENIS HEALEY

Aid to Greece was really the first basic change in American foreign policy. It was almost revolution. We'd never thought, nor had it even occurred to us, to take responsibility in the area of the world which wasn't under our direct responsibility. It was quite clear that Greece would go under without any help, but we had to recognize that Britain was not able to carry the load any more. The plan to aid Greece and also Turkey, which was under attack at that time too, was later christened the 'Truman Doctrine'. That principle, of course, led to the Marshall Plan on a much wider and more ambitious initiative.
AVERELL HARRIMAN

Deep freeze in Moscow

The conference in Moscow in 1947 went on for quite a few days. I think we were there three weeks. Bevin was determined that we'd achieve some sort of agreement. I remember the temperature was 25 degrees below zero outdoors. We were all stuffed into this room. Mr Bevin at a point when adjournment had been suggested said 'Oh . . . let's give it another whirl, another day'. Everybody groaned at that time; it was perfectly futile. We went through an additional twenty-four hours trying to arrive at some form of practical basis of understanding, but it just wasn't on the cards. Nobody can say that an intensive effort was not made by the British to arrive at an agreement which would have carried on with the Potsdam outline, but the Russians just weren't having it.

ROBERT MURPHY

Bi-Zonia emerged by a process of trial and error, I suppose. The question occurred to me often, why did Mr Stalin sign that Potsdam agreement providing for a four-power control and economic and political unity for Germany, when, the day after it was signed, they proceeded to demonstrate that it was not going to be implemented. I still don't quite understand why he did that, except on the notion that I think was a conviction he had at the time: the United States was so obviously eager to get out of Europe, send its men back home, to reduce its military establishment to almost zero on a unilateral basis, that the Americans would soon tire of the German problem and voluntarily leave the scene. Molotov used the expression several times: 'As goes Germany, so goes Europe', and that was their objective. And then to their shock and amazement, perhaps, they found the Americans were staying on rather permanently. So that, from the early stages of rather complete four-power co-operation in the administration of Germany, the situation deteriorated to a point where there wasn't any co-operation at all. It wasn't going to work, and that led to our decision with your government, of course, to establish Bi-Zonia. I think financial reasons were important. I think that your people were harassed right along by lack of financial means. That was true during the active fighting in the last war period and it was true when everything was happening in Germany during the occupation: reduction in Forces, lack of means to carry out objectives – that was a very definite practical consideration.

ROBERT MURPHY

There's quite a school of historians now who take the view that the causes of the Cold War are difficult to fathom and that the British and Americans were just as much responsible for it as were the Russians. I don't think this could possibly be held or believed in by anybody who sat through any or all of those meetings, in which that great effort was made to get the Russians to co-operate on some kind of basis. I happened to be with Bevin when Mr Churchill made his Fulton speech in the States. Bevin's immediate reaction was to wonder whether it was wise to come out so categorically, before making more of an effort to try and reconcile the difference.

Bevin hoped for a long time that it would be possible to reach some understanding with the Russians over the most difficult and most important problem of all, the future of Germany, and I think he really thought that this should have been possible, if only there had been some goodwill. But I think it was a very long time – December 1947 – before he did decide that it really was going to be extremely difficult, with Stalin and Molotov, to come to any kind of agreement that was acceptable to the West.

NICHOLAS HENDERSON

"I should like it to be clearly understood that th is to be only an illusion

Bevin was powerfully anti-Communist and anti-Stalinist. 'Molotov, Stalin, they are evil men', he used to say. It was a good thing to say because not everyone was saying it at that time and it was really round this rather major assessment that a great deal of his policy was based. I think, though, in spite of that, he went on hoping for a deal with these 'evil men' rather too long after it was reasonable to do so. I think the real disillusionment came with that Foreign Ministers' meeting of 1947. There they sat – Molotov, Bidault, Marshall, Bevin – and Molotov much the cleverest of them I thought, and terribly skilful, terrible to listen to, frustrating, maddening. I remember Bevin coming away from one of those meetings: we went back to the Foreign Office with his senior officials and he slumped in his chair and he said 'Can anyone tell me what to do? Can anyone tell me anything to do?'
CHRISTOPHER MAYHEW

General Marshall made his speech in June 1947 at Harvard and the very next morning Bevin picked it up listening to the BBC. He went to the Foreign Office at 8.30 that morning. Bevin had quite a temper. No one was there. His officials arrived at about a quarter to nine and they went over this speech, what it meant, and it was obvious that Britain and France would have to take a lead together. Bevin despatched his officials that very same afternoon to Paris. That led to the meeting of representatives of European countries in Paris. Bevin thoroughly understood what General Marshall had in mind: that Europe should co-operate together in a plan of mutual help. The Soviet Union would have none of it. Molotov would have none of it. He kept insisting: find out from the United States how much they'll give; we'll divide it on the basis that the country that's suffered the most should get the most. Obviously, this was the Soviet Union. That, of course, was not General Marshall's idea. The idea was to have a co-operative plan; that through co-operation Europe could be reconstructed and perhaps be made healthier than ever.
AVERELL HARRIMAN

Under Secretary of State, argued forcibly that Greece, in particular, was vulnerable to Soviet influence. What, after all, he argued, had happened to Rumania, Bulgaria, Yugoslavia, and Albania? Communist parties had in effect taken over the governments of all these countries and they threatened democratic states like Czechoslovakia, Italy, and France. Congress accepted by a large majority that Greece and Turkey should be helped.

This change in direction of American policy from the end of February 1947 to the middle of March 1947 was indeed remarkable. On the American side Acheson helped, perhaps decisively, in getting Congress to accept the commitment. But how had Acheson, and other State Department officials become convinced of its necessity? Although it was in the United States' own interest not to see Europe slide, the point was put over forcefully by Ernest Bevin. British administrators dropped strong hints of withdrawal to an American mission in Greece in January, and the fact that Bevin did not press Dalton as hard as he had done for funds for Greece suggests that Bevin had more than an inkling of how the United States would respond.

Shortly after the Truman doctrine was announced, Bevin met Molotov again in Moscow. It is an indication of Bevin's continuing hopes of a settlement that he tried to prolong the conference. But Germany again provided the stumbling block. The Anglo-American development of Bi-Zonia which came into full force in January 1947, generated Soviet fears about Western intentions toward Germany. The economic council in Bi-Zonia took on increasing importance, correlating aid and economic planning on a bizonal basis. The Russians sensed the political implications while at the same time their grip hardened over Eastern Europe. Molotov got one thing out of the conference: Bevin taught him to sing 'The More We Are Together' at Moscow railway station.

After the Truman doctrine, Americans at home became much more conscious of the real condition of Europe. The winter of 1946-7 had been no milder in Europe than in Britain. Starvation was widespread, Communist parties flourished, and rioting was commonplace. Europe was failing to pick itself off the floor. Bevin was acutely conscious that British aid programmes were not enough. Dalton complained that Britain was paying interest on the American loan, although it was in part

A dose of austerity

being used to feed Europeans, particularly Germany. Britain simply had not the wherewithal to help out, and stories of Europe's plight began to be listened to in America. The gap in resources could only be made up by America, and Bevin knew this well.

One morning he heard on the radio that the American Secretary of State, George Marshall, had suggested that further aid for Europe would be forthcoming, so long as they organized themselves for recovery: 'The initiative must come from Europe.' Bevin was surprised and delighted. By the end of the day, he had his representative in Paris to correlate a European reply, and from July to September a European conference arranged the details of Marshall·Aid. Bevin had seized his opportunity with both hands. It was just what he had been waiting for.

The Marshall Plan was an extension of the Truman doctrine; it marked the profound concern of America for the survival of democratic Europe. Marshall's offer had drawn no distinction between East and West. Molotov came to Paris for the conference. Hindsight has encouraged the assumption that he came to wreck it, but in fact Molotov changed his attitude during the conference from cautious participation to theatrical rejection. He walked out of the second session. Stalin had changed Molotov's tune. In doing so, he turned down vital aid for Russia, to avoid economic and possibly political interference in the Eastern bloc. Further, he made sure that Czechoslovakia, which had initially accepted the offer, did not take part in the Marshall Plan, though the Czech Communists were not in full control. Through the establishment of the Cominform, an updated version of the old Communist International, Stalin instructed Western Communist parties to do their best to wreck Marshall Aid.

Bevin was driven to desperation by this turn of events. The initial glimpse of a relaxation in international tension was gone, but he made one last attempt to find common ground with the Russians in London, in November. His efforts were met with almost total failure. The stumbling-block again was Germany. Bi-Zonia had become much more integrated during 1947. Within the economic council, two 'houses' had emerged: a lower 'house' based on popular representation and an upper 'house' representative of the constituent states. With the growth of representation came trade unions and

political parties. Germans became increasingly active in administration and to the Russians, at least, it looked as though the British and Americans were handing over, albeit by stages, to the Germans. A new German state was in the making. The die was now cast. To the Russians, the British and Americans were trying to revive an economically powerful Germany; to the British and Americans, the Russians were subjugating Eastern Europe. Even the short-term future showed both sides to be right.

Events at home, too, shook the optimism of 1946. Resources of men and machinery were scarce; the need to produce and export more was overpowering. Dalton had obtained the concessions he wanted on overseas spending, but as the 1947 Economic Survey stated: 'We have not got enough resources to do all that we want to do. We have

take time to get on our feet again and that was why we bought time by borrowing from America and Canada. But that time has proved too short.' Indeed it had; had it not been for Marshall Aid, which was on its way, the Board of Trade estimated that bacon, cheese, sugar, and butter rations would have been cut by one-third, and the shortage of raw materials would have put 1,500,000 people out of work.

The serious difficulties of the Government led to fundamental doubts in the cabinet about Attlee's leadership. Attlee looked small, unimpressive, and shy; on appearances, Churchill was right when he said, 'An empty cab drew up, and Mr Attlee got out.' But Attlee knew that he alone was essential for the control of the unruly talent in his cabinet, even if this control could only be exercised by playing one off against the other. The prime movers against him in 1947 were Dalton and Cripps – an oddly contrasting pair.

Dalton, exuberant and noisy, had some sworn enemies. But he was quick to spot rising talent in the party; the capable crop of middle-class socialists elected in 1945 owe much to Dalton's help and tutelage, Hugh Gaitskell and Anthony Crosland among them. Dalton was shameless to the point of absurdity in his scheming; no lover of Attlee, he frequently said so in a voice that could be heard across a crowded room and further.

Cripps was altogether different. A highly religious man, he appeared to have unusually intimate knowledge of the Almighty and His intentions. He was ascetic, a vegetarian (although only on grounds of health), and always got up before six in the morning. But he was used to mixing it vigorously with the leadership of his own party. Of the twenty years he spent in Parliament, eight were spent fighting the party's policy from the Left and he was only re-admitted to membership in 1945. His political touch was erratic. He felt that when certain things had to be done, they should be done regardless of their political repercussions. He had a slightly heroic stance; a rigidity reinforced by the belief he was doing right. 'There', said Churchill, 'but for the grace of God, goes God.' Cripps saw the way ahead with great clarity: Britain had to export more or go under. Money from the Americans helped bridge gaps but it wasn't the answer in itself.

barely enough to do all that we must do.' Government policy was preoccupied with the problem of diverting too few resources to too many places. Rationing had to continue.

In the summer of 1947, sterling became convertible against other currencies – as had been agreed by the terms of the American loan. In the prevailing world-shortage of dollars, the pound was bound to become weakened in the rush to convert pounds to dollars. An absurd situation developed where dollars from the American loan were being converted into sterling to bolster the pound, while at the same time, as people lost confidence, pounds were being sold for dollars. Convertibility had to be stopped in a hurry and on 6 August 1947, a stiff dose of austerity was announced by Stafford Cripps, the President of the Board of Trade. Attlee defended the measures: 'We knew it would

Dalton, with his subordinate George Brown, and Cripps, were joined in their bid to overthrow

End of a big noise

Cripps had two sides to his character, he could be pretty saintly but he could be very vicious. When Attlee suggested that I should leave the Ministry of Fuel and Power and go to the War Office it took five days to make up my mind whether I should go, or resign. I discovered later that Cripps had suggested that I should be thrown out of the government because there had been some failure, according to him, at the Ministry of Fuel and Power. There was in fact no failure on my part, as Attlee admitted himself in public. He said it was a matter for the cabinet itself. At the same time as Cripps actually wrote to Attlee – 'Get rid of Shinwell' – he sent me a letter sympathizing with me and speaking about the fine work I had done at the Ministry of Fuel and Power. I have got both Attlee's book with the record and I have got the letter from Cripps written in his own hand, in red ink. He always wrote in red ink.

LORD SHINWELL

I remember Ernie Bevin asked me in and said 'Who do you think has been to see me, Chris? 'Hugh' – that was Hugh Dalton – 'Stafford' – Stafford Cripps – 'and Strakey' – he always used to called John Strachey 'Strakey'. 'They asked me if I wanted to be Prime Minister: what do you think?' Well, I gave him what I think was good advice, looking back. I said that I thought the party was too divided on this East–West thing, on the NATO–Stalinist thing, for him to keep it together, and really I didn't encourage him at all. He said 'I think you're right, and what's Clem ever done to me? Clem is a little man but sometimes you need little men as Prime Ministers.' That was typical of Ernie Bevin; of his egoism and also of his fundamental loyalty and decency.

CHRISTOPHER MAYHEW

I don't think anyone loved Hugh Dalton. He lacked charm; he had a certain amount of goodwill about him. He was very anxious always to help younger people in the party. But he was an awkward character. Domineering sometimes; he would lose his temper in committee; and towards the end, shortly before he left the cabinet, his health deteriorated through worry. He could be very, very difficult to work with indeed, he thumped the table. Not a popular figure, but highly respected. He had a habit of writing daily notes to the Prime Minister, Attlee, making his comments about the activities of other ministers, usually very critical comments, a most peculiar thing to do.

GEORGE STRAUSS

Dalton always kept what he called a prod sheet beside him, which was a little bit of paper on his desk with the things he particularly wanted to remember and push at that moment: they could pop out on any subject. He was a good party man in the sense that he always kept his Labour Party aim very much – I might almost say loudly – to the forefront, even in all his departmental dealings, I think he had two defects, really. One was that he didn't suffer fools gladly. He got very impatient with people who were slow or stupid and sometimes really abused them, to a point which did harm rather than good: because really in government departments as elsewhere people do their best work if they are praised rather than if they are abused. He never quite understood that. His other fault, of course, was that he couldn't keep quiet. Sometimes he could, sometimes he couldn't, but there were occasions when he could not keep quiet when it would have been better to do so.

DOUGLAS JAY

Cabinet told: I let you all down

By WILSON BROADBENT,
Daily Mail Political Correspondent

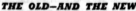

MR. HUGH DALTON, CHANCELLOR OF THE EXCHEQUER, RESIGNED FROM THE SOCIALIST GOVERNMENT EARLY LAST NIGHT.

The King was informed without delay, and accepted the nomination of Sir Stafford Cripps, formerly Minister of Economic Affairs, as the new Chancellor.

These developments marked a day of considerable excitement and agitation in the House of Commons, following charges that there had been a leakage of Budget proposals published by the London evening newspaper the *Star*.

The moment these charges were brought to the notice of Ministers, Mr. Dalton admitted responsibility and declared his intention to take the full blame.

His attitude was that he had unwittingly let down his colleagues.

This happened just before noon yesterday, and Mr. Attlee and other Ministers were astounded, first, when they heard of the leakage, and, secondly, when the Chancellor of the Exchequer frankly admitted his part.

'I WAS INDISCREET'

Conferences started at once, and Mr. Dalton was urged to consider seriously all the consequences of his departure from the Government before formally tendering his resignation. But clearly Mr. Dalton was intent on making a clean breast of his part in an unprecedented situation.

After more than two hours' talk, Mr. Dalton insisted on the formal statement he would make to the House of Commons when the matter was raised by a Conservative back-bencher, Mr. Victor Raikes. This statement read:

"I very much regret to tell the House that publication arose out of an incident which occurred as I was entering the Chamber yesterday.

"In reply to questions put to me by the

THE OLD—AND THE NEW

Dalton? The most wicked man in politics I've ever known. Intrigue, conspiracy, always whispering about people. His whispers were very audible: they could be heard hundreds of yards away. We had a Labour Party conference at Margate, and one of my colleagues was staying in a particular hotel on the fourth floor. He was looking out of the window – gathering the ozone, enjoying himself – when suddenly he heard somebody saying 'Between you and me . . .' He looked down four floors, and it was Dalton speaking to somebody.

He wanted to be Foreign Secretary, of course, but he was prevented from being so by Attlee. Dalton was one of the county people, one of the aristocrats; he didn't belong to the proletariat at all although he was a member of the Labour Party. I don't know, I think he wanted power. I think Dalton regarded himself as the ablest man in the Labour Party, or in politics for that matter. He wanted to be the boss, he would have liked to have been Prime Minister, and in order to become Prime Minister he had to denigrate everybody else. I remember hearing him in the corridor in the House of Commons, speaking of that 'bloody little man'. I didn't know at first whom he was talking about but then I understood it was Attlee. That was the type of man Dalton was. Nobody was right with him.

LORD SHINWELL

You can't say that Dalton was incapable of intrigue: I mean no one could maintain that, although the intrigue had something of the innocent quality about it. He was enormous fun to be with and this gave his intrigue a certain quality of innocence and humour. I think history will give him a much more favourable verdict than the contemporary verdict. First, he was very ingenious in matters of taxation; all his budgets had a very high level of ingenuity. Second, he carried through the nationalization of the Bank of England, the establishment of peace-time exchange control for the first time, very smoothly, with great confidence. Thirdly, he gave a strong push to certain things very near and dear to his heart – I think, of great intrinsic importance – help for the development areas; a very high degree of help for the universities; and, of course, he did an enormous amount for the Forestry Commission, for preserving the countryside through the Land Fund and the rest of it. And lastly, despite what was said at the time, I think in terms of covering inflation he has as good a record as Cripps. It's a great illusion that there was some sharp change of direction when Cripps took over from Dalton. The fact is that everybody thought that Cripps looked and sounded like deflation and Dalton looked and sounded like an inflationist. But whether he could have gone on in view of his physical condition, I'm doubtful. He was very, very done-in indeed by the summer of '47.

ANTHONY CROSLAND

Attlee by John Strachey, the Minister of Food, another former left winger who felt that there was not enough forward direction from Attlee. The plot failed mainly because there was only one possible successor – Bevin. Morrison, who might have played along, was recovering from a stroke. Bevin may have wanted the job but he realized that he could not hold the party together. In any case it suited Bevin for Attlee to hold the ring. It gave him a free hand overseas where he was master in his own house. Attlee was again saved by the strongest man in the party and from then until the Government fell, he was safe. And he again showed he was the shrewdest politician of them all: soon after the plot, Cripps was appointed Minister for Economic Affairs, where he could exercise his visionary zeal to the full.

There was one final twist. The indiscreet Dalton committed one indiscretion too many. In many ways it was so in character that it was surprising it had not happened earlier. On his way to make an emergency budget speech in November 1947, he indicated its contents to a journalist in the lobby. An outline of these proposed measures appeared in the London *Star* as Dalton was announcing them in the Commons. His subsequent resignation provided a convenient scapegoat, but it was more than a little harsh.

Dalton is sometimes remembered for his skilful financing of social reform, more often as the advocate of cheap money at a time when this was thought inappropriate. In this final budget, he took a firm grip on inflation and set the pattern for the next three years. If he deserves some share of the blame for underestimating the damage done by the war and for overrating the pace of recovery, he should be praised for his courage in raising taxation to combat inflation, thus easing the task of his successor at the Exchequer, Stafford Cripps.

1947 was the year of reckoning. It became clear economically that for some time to come Britain would be dependent on American aid. Shortages were inevitable while the country pursued its export target – a 75 per cent increase on the 1945 level. In foreign affairs, too, Britain needed to act in concert with the Americans. 1947 brought America back to Europe: it also dashed hopes of a deal with the Russians over Germany. By the end of that year, Eastern Europe looked like a Russian bloc to Western eyes; but to the Russians, Western Europe looked like a client state of America.

"*Psst!*"
"*What?*"
"*Nothing—only psst!*"

*Right: Stalin and the western leaders. 'Your play
Joe,' says Truman*

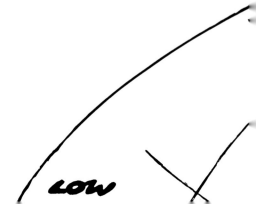

4 Cold comfort and cold war

The con man cometh

I think the public was getting extremely fed up with the system of controls, of rationing, of licensing and so forth. This system was in many ways inevitable at the time, but when you have a system of that kind then it's also inevitable that people will try and get round it. The other significant – the really significant – thing about it was that the government at the time, like any other government at any other time, I think, was determined once rumours of possible corruption amongst members of the government or civil servants had got about, to have the thing proved in depth to make quite sure whether or not corruption had in fact occurred, and if it had, to expose it.

Sidney Stanley was a very remarkable person. He was almost a caricature of a confidence trickster. He had a great sense of humour, I think, and he was completely irrepressible. I remember once in the course of a cross-examination I conducted of him which went on, I think, for several days, he said 'Sir Hartley, you're trying to trick me with the truth'. Well, of course, what could one do but burst out laughing? He was completely irrepressible and had a certain charm of manner, and one can understand that rather unsophisticated people not used to meeting characters of this kind were taken in by him, I suppose.

LORD SHAWCROSS

A spiv was somebody who was on top of the world in those days – the wise boy. He got stuck into anything, a real sharp character who was really playing on his wits. You had to go round saying 'She wants tea, she wants sugar, she wants butter and she wants stockings'. One of the best commodities I think we had a run on was the nylon stocking – God bless America, you know. A lorry-load of these things came in and they came in via the public bar. We picked these up quite reasonably, had two fights to keep them. Nylon stockings then, women would . . . there was no price for them, you could just go on and on and on, it was just unrestricted, completely, no end at all. You could pay 8/- for a pair and sell them for £4 in the right place, as simple as that. We sold to 80 per cent of respectable people, about 20 per cent of so-called crooks – you can work that out for yourself. In those days everybody was basically crooked otherwise you just couldn't sell it. Without the respectable housewife, there was no market. I think the housewife, in those days, had a bigger war than the soldiers did, and they kept things going. There was a sort of understanding with the police. I mean coppers' wives had to live just the same. I mean they were rationed, so any copper those days, every bloke he nicked he diminished his source of supply.

Petrol – always dodgy, that was the only thing that the police had really wrapped up. They had all this litmus paper. If you got straight petrol, people never believed you. People used to pour it through bread and things like that and this was supposed to take the chemical out. We tried this and it never did work: so after that you could have a thousand gallons and a bloke would only take it off you if he was prepared to take a chance. In the end you got every bloke that you were going to sell petrol to – he was a scientist, he was a bloody crook. You could go to sell him the petrol and he whips out a strip of limus paper, whacks it in and you'd carry ten gallons for nothing because it turns blue. So it was never really a thing; there weren't many cars on the road and they all got nicked anyway. So it wasn't a thing that we went in for, really.

BILL ROBINS

Sidney Stanley: a product of austerity

Labour was decimated in the local elections of November 1947. Life was not getting any better. Expectations, so high in 1945 and 1946, had not been fulfilled. Most wartime controls remained, and by 1948 daily rations were below wartime levels. August 1947 to July 1948 (when bread came off the ration) was the high point of austerity. Snoek, a sort of barracuda packed in tins, was in; foreign travel was out. There were few eggs; cigarettes had gone up a shilling to 3s 4d for twenty, and beer was 10 per cent weaker. It was a criminal offence to turn on a fire in summer, and it was almost impossible to get petrol for private use.

In such conditions, the black market flourished. The spiv came into his own: whether it was butter, eggs, chocolate, whisky, or nylons, the spiv had it. A quick morning's work could bring in £12 – a very good weekly wage. Much of the forbidden fruit was stolen which, in many cases, gave room for more profit by blackmail. The crime rate became a wave. The spiv, a sort of popinjay, stood out against depressing uniformity. The rising comedian of the age, Arthur English, made him the contemporary Lucky Jim. In the strait-jacket of the time it was quite reassuring to know that some people were corruptible.

To the Government it was not so funny, particularly when it appeared that the tentacles of this sleazy world reached out as far as Whitehall. In October 1948, rumours abounded of scandal in Whitehall. The name of John Belcher, Parliamentary Secretary to the Board of Trade, was linked to industrialists and black marketeers. It was not clear that corruption had stopped there.

The Government decided to act at once and appointed the Lynskey Tribunal for which the Attorney General, Sir Hartley Shawcross, tried to elicit the facts. A football pools firm, flats in Park Lane, bouncing cheques, and the rather absurd figure of Sidney Stanley, a con man who twisted the regulations and who was a 'benefactor' of people in high places, made the headlines. The Lynskey Tribunal's 50,000-word report, which at 1s 6d became a best-seller, cleared Belcher of the worst allegations, but he and a director of the Bank of England were forced to leave public life. Stanley was deported and the British wallowed in the thought of how evil some people were.

By the beginning of 1948, only iron and steel of the 1945 programme remained to be nationalized. The Cabinet was divided over this. Any proposals for a takeover would be extremely complex, given the number and diversity of the firms involved. Additionally, the industry was again becoming profitable as economic activity increased. In 1947, Morrison and John Wilmot, the Minister of Supply, both argued for a compromise on complete nationalization. Attlee went so far as to ask Morrison to sound out the steel masters and the unions. Morrison reported to the Cabinet that both sides were ready to do a deal.

Dalton and Aneurin Bevan, the Minister of Health, were appalled. Bevan threatened to resign. The news was leaked to back benchers, already restive because no plans had appeared, and Attlee gave way. He left Morrison vainly defending the compromise in Cabinet, and relations between them deteriorated sharply. A few weeks later Morrison's responsibilities for economic affairs were taken over by Cripps, and John Wilmot was replaced by George Strauss.

A nationalization Bill was prepared, but before it could be introduced, the power of the Lords to hold up the bill had to be weakened. Late in 1947, a Bill to reduce the power of veto from two years to one was introduced, and, after an abortive attempt at an all-party compromise, it was forced through. The way was now clear to bring in the Steel Bill, the first act of nationalization to arouse really concerted and heavy opposition. It was ably attacked by the Conservatives, particularly Oliver Lyttelton and Harold Macmillan. The Lords were still prepared to give the Bill a rough ride. In the end, there was an agreement between the parties that the Bill should be passed, but the date for making steel nationalization effective would be postponed until after the next general election. Steel had become a political football.

Against the gloom of austerity there were, however, immediate and real improvements in the help individuals could get. In that 'Annus Mirabilis' of legislation, 1946, the National Insurance Act, the Industrial Injuries Act, and the National Health Service had been put on the statute book. In 1948, the creation of the National Assistance Board completed the work. For the first time insurance became universal and comprehensive. Family allowances, death grants, sickness, unemployment, and retirement benefit all increased.

In many ways this was a development and rationalization of what had been done before the war, and it had in fact to some extent been planned by the

Breaking the mould

Iron and steel had been talked about a great deal and I suppose some preliminary thought had been given to the nationalization of the industry before I went there. But there were no concrete plans there whatsoever. A great deal of the effort of my predecessor, John Wilmot, had been devoted to trying to effect some agreement, some arrangement between the steel masters and the cabinet, particularly Herbert Morrison, which would bring about a compromise plan – government—public control without complete ownership. But detailed plans for nationalization were practically non-existent.

Morrison had taken a rather strong line in the government against full nationalization and in favour of some compromise solution. He was a bit upset when his view was overturned and I was put into the Ministry of Supply to carry out nationalization. And his personal relationship with me for some time was very cool indeed. Now that doesn't mean he didn't help as Chairman of the Nationalization Committee. In formulating the plans which I brought before the Committee, in suggesting this and suggesting that, he was wholly co-operative. But our personal relationship during that period was a bit cool.

The Conservatives loathed the Bill. They accepted, rather grudgingly, the nationalization of services, gas, electricity and even the railways. But here we were nationalizing an industry – the biggest, the most important industry in the country – and that they thought was wicked. It was going to lead to Communism and all that sort of thing. This was the heart of industry and once we had nationalized that, where were we going to stop? We might proceed to nationalize all sorts of other industries, and they loathed the idea.

Some of the Conservative speeches from the front benches were almost hysterical in their hatred and loathing of the Bill. We had difficulty, of course, with the House of Lords afterwards, and we had to compromise with them about the date of implementing the Bill. The Lords, loathing the Bill, did not like to veto it completely because that would obviously lead to a demand for the abolition of the Lords. So they devised a method by which we couldn't implement the Bill fully until after the next General Election, and it was only under these conditions that they passed the Bill.

GEORGE STRAUSS

The nationalization of a key industry like steel, cuts right away the profound doctrinal belief of the Conservatives: that industry should be a free-enterprise affair, and once you start centralizing an industry as complicated as steel, whose products go into thousands of other industries, you are trying to bring a million skills which go into the production of steel, and all its features, into a department in Whitehall who've never been engaged in it at all – a completely different concept to the nationalization of the services. But steel goes right to the root of all free enterprise and therefore cuts at one of the fundamental doctrines of Conservatism, and that's why we fought it very hard. We had the feeling, or I had the feeling, perhaps it's a very conceited one, that the government argument did not stand up to what we produced against them; it was a pretty hot Parliamentary debate, as hot as you've seen on many other subjects.

LORD CHANDOS

wartime Coalition on the basis of the Beveridge report. This, Ernest Bevin had claimed, was 'the culmination of ideas on social services over the last forty years... a co-ordination of the whole of the nation's ambulance services on a more scientific and proper footing'.

Despite the hopes of Jim Griffiths, Labour's first Minister of National Insurance, his colleagues could not face the establishment of a national minimum standard of living, only 'a broad subsistence basis'. Even this was quickly abandoned. Against all hopes, the National Assistance Board still had a large part to play. What the Labour Government did do was to ensure that the wartime plans were put into effect and improved, with none of the qualifications about economic impossibility that a Conservative regime might have introduced.

The result was a set of services truly national in operation as well as in name. They made a real difference to life when they came into force in 1948 and, coupled with the pledge of full employment given by the wartime Coalition in 1944, provided a guarantee against any slide back to the senseless destructive poverty of mass unemployment.

Above all, the Health Service was a great step forward in the completion of a Welfare State. In its final form it went a good deal further than anything the Conservatives would have proposed. It was the creation of Aneurin Bevan, who had, as a young man, been part of a local health co-operative in Tredegar, South Wales. Bevan virtually nationalized health. It was to be 'free to all,' financed by taxation, and would 'make it, in future, somebody's clear duty to see that all medical facilities are available to all people'. Cash must no longer buy better treatment, and the self-sufficient general practitioner must be destroyed. This brought Bevan into conflict with the doctors and their protectionist body, the British Medical Association.

Bevan spent eighteen months fighting the doctors. His political supporters wanted a state-salaried medical service to which the doctors were bitterly opposed. The real objects of the Bill became lost in a welter of charge and countercharge. There was talk by doctors of socialist conspiracy because Bevan, quite rightly, refused to negotiate with them. But he was forced to make concessions. The result was a draw. Bevan abandoned a salaried service but in return secured the complete integration of the hospital service under regional boards. The

buying and selling of practices was stopped, much to the fury of the doctors, and a complicated system of payment worked out which safeguarded the doctor's independence. Timely concession had stopped the row, and the service was inaugurated in July 1948. No fewer than 18,500 of the country's 20,000 doctors joined the scheme. The New Jerusalem had its most important constituent.

To finance these expensive policies – and not many people could be bothered to work out that the social services cost the equivalent of an all-round weekly wage increase of £2.75 – was Stafford Cripps's task. Cripps dominated domestic politics from 1948 to 1950, and it was his fate to preside over a shift in economic management with which he cannot have been wholly sympathetic.

Dalton and his wartime predecessors had been preoccupied with manpower. Changes in the distribution of the work force were at the heart of Labour's post-war system of planning. They had even toyed with the idea of the direction of labour – the Control of Engagements Order, August 1947 – but this was clearly unacceptable to their trade union allies.

In any case Cripps had come to realize that centralized planning had wholly unacceptable totalitarian implications. Manpower budgeting was steadily superseded by more indirect fiscal controls and by their planning counterpart – a wages policy. Cripps wanted to direct the economy, but he knew he would have to use 'agreement, persuasion, consultation, and other free democratic methods'. His powers of persuasion were couched in moral imperatives: it was, he said, necessary 'to submerge all thought of personal gain and ambition in the greater and deeper desire to give our all to secure the future prosperity and happiness of our people'.

Cripps made the moral imperative work. He managed to inspire businessmen, trade unionists, and the man in the street with some notion of a common good. If controls would not work, some such agreement on what was to be done had to operate instead. It was Cripps' great gift that he could bring moral and patriotic emotions to bear in a way which made men behave in a way that they would not otherwise have contemplated. It had something of the same force and appeal as a latter day Ignatius Loyola or Savonarola and his certainty and personal austerity gave him the temporary ascendancy of a saint. He knew where

The New Jerusalem

I got up at 5 o'clock in the morning on the 26th of June, 1939. I had to run to work because I was late. My particular job was cleaning and greasing machinery. It came half past ten, time for my break. On this particular day part of the machine was making a row, it was dry and squealing. I went to grease it. I had to stand fifteen feet off the floor on the concrete slab, cock my leg round, and hold on while I greased it. To turn out the grease caps I had to turn the grease cap and fill it up tight. Now once you've filled them up, once you turn them up tight, all the grease would go in because the bearing was hot, therefore you had to refill it. In the meantime I must have got grease on my hand. When I went to turn it, my hand shot in and it ran up my arm from my wrist up to my shoulder and I had to pull myself up off this machine while it was still in motion. I was standing on the top of this concrete slab screaming, my arm badly crushed.

After I left the Cardiff Infirmary I was at home for roughly about six months. I was having 19/6d compensation. I started back to work and I thought, and everyone else thought, that I would still get the 19/6d. I goes into the office on Friday to receive my compensation. 'Oh . . .' he said, 'there's no compensation for you', he said, 'you're already getting your wages'. So I said, 'Don't I get anything?' 'No', he said 'you are having the wages that you had prior to your accident, so therefore you can't claim it'. He said, 'It's only based on loss of wages'. I had very bitter feelings over it. I was suffering from a 'phantom' limb, the feeling that your hand is still there, so therefore I had to stop work, and I was home then roughly about seven years. We had in them days a gentleman coming round, he would knock at the door and he said he wanted to offer me a lump sum – £500 – and he as good as told me that my life was finished unless I accepted the £500 and got out of the colliery. My life was actually finished and I was at that time 18. Of course now there's nothing like that, my money would have been there just like that. I would have had a real sum. Today I have a nephew who has lost his thumb and his damages amounted to £2,500, which is a vast amount as far as I was concerned. I'll never get that as long as I live.

KEN SAMUEL

On Derby Day 1937 I went to work as usual, happy-go-lucky-like, hoping to have a winner. I took this other man's place. He'd failed to turn up for work that morning and about 11 o'clock I slipped under the journey and my legs came up over my back. My mate jumped off the journey and asked me if I could stay there while he got help to get me out; I told him no. I said I couldn't stay no longer because I was doubled right up in a ball. So he knocked the slack out of the journey, and the driver who had it on the brake at the time pulled up to let off the brake just a fraction, and I felt my body just snapping, my back was paralysed. I lay there as stiff as a bone. They took me to hospital where they just dumped me in the corner with only the local GP coming to see me every day. I was there for ten weeks, still with nothing done. I was anxious to have something done, but they sent me home in August. The district nurse said do the same thing again, send 10/- to the Cardiff Infirmary, as it was run on contributions and appeals then. So I had a letter back thanking us and awaited till towards Christmas, and the district nurse said do the same thing again, send 10/- to the Infirmary, and see what it will do. On the 3rd of January they sent for me and I went in and had an operation, and they put me in plaster. From August until the 3rd of January they hadn't done a thing. If you have an accident like I had then now they have police escorts to rush you straight to hospital where they do these jobs. A couple of months after I left hospital the Compensation Inspector came; he just asked me if I would like to take a lump sum and he offered me £400 to £500 and said that that was the maximum, you couldn't get no more. A bit later he turned up again and he'd jumped up to £600, thinking I was going to fly at that, but I told him he was only wasting his time, it wasn't worth him coming.

LEN LLEWELLYN

In 1911 a meeting was called by the people of Tregaron asking every single man to contribute to a medical service. We agreed to pay 3d in the £ – every £ that was earned by us there was 3d deducted and put into the pool for the medical aid service. That paid the doctor, and it paid the hospital; so whenever anyone in Tregaron had an ailment of any kind it didn't cost him a penny. Never mind if a man had a wife or seven, eight or twelve children, that was covered by this 3d in the £ and that is the basis of the present Health Service. When my brother Aneurin went to the Ministry he came with a background of this comprehensive cover. He said, and has always said, that a man or a woman should not pay to be ill or to go to hospital and anybody at any time or part of his life should volunteer to pay for the benefit of the medical aid service. Now that experience, and my brother who was a member of the medical aid service was a member of the committee at 17 years of age, was a very early experience of the administration of a medical aid service. And that has developed now, as everyone knows into the National Health Service. There was no doctor in Tregaron who required a penny to start a practice: they came out of their training and could start to have an income straightaway. The Tregaron medical aid scheme was very, very important to Aneurin. I think he based the whole of his political life on the medical aid scheme, realizing how important it was to society generally that one could be sure of getting medical treatment, hospital treatment, without being controlled by any income whatsoever. He said very often, 'Spend the money on the railings for the top of the quarry and not a lot of money for the hospital at the bottom – prevention is better than cure'. A lot of people couldn't afford to have a doctor or couldn't afford to go to hospital. That's why he put the expenses on the Treasury, so that there would be a fair distribution of the cost of the administration of the whole of the Health Service in this country. A man paid his contribution to the hospital and his health through his income tax. The National Health Service started in the town of his birth.

WILLIAM BEVAN

Bevan said a good Health Service was one which to be poor would not be a disability and to be rich would not be an advantage. He wanted medicine put on a quite different basis, not this market-place type of medicine and therefore to get rid of buying and selling people. I can remember him on one occasion speaking of the buying and selling of patients as if they were cattle. Bevan objected to human beings being subjected to any sort of barter between other human beings. Right from the start Bevan knew that the biggest battle he would have to fight would be with the medical profession; his fight with the British Medical Association had to be very well engineered because he knew he would have to make compromises. There was no reason, from his point of view, for having a head-on clash if he could

avoid it. He thought the BMA was always fighting battles that were not going to begin anyway because he was prepared to go along with some of the points they were going to make.

The BMA was not a united body, it represents the bulk of the Medical Association so far as they are members; but there are general practitioners, there are the specialists, and their interests aren't the same. Bevan, of course, knew this very well; he saw that within the BMA there was a possibility of a split – if he could interest one group and they split off, then the other group would be weakened. So I think he really set about the specialists first, and he was aided at this time by a report that suggested that one of the difficulties in the National Health Service would be that you still had to preserve some plums for those at the top. When Bevin was told that if he instituted a system of merit awards for consultants, a bonus as it were, they would come in. He said to me, 'I'm told this will cost me £300,000 a year – so what? If I can get them in we'll have them in'. I didn't like the merit award system, but he thought this was a worthwhile compromise. It costs us a lot more today, but that is by the way.

Coupled with that he agreed that private practice should be inside the National Health Service. Again I objected, but he said 'We would rather have private practice inside the National Health Service so that at least we have some measure of control'. When Bevan came to argue with the general practitioners the terms and conditions under which they would come into the new Health Service, they wanted to stay on the old basis, called contractors, involving a very complicated system of payment. Bevan conceded that point, but he took from them the other point that the buying and selling of practices should be stopped. There were elements in the BMA that saw this as an end of medical practice – a man was no longer going to be free to buy himself in where he wanted to buy himself in. So Bevan made the one concession and gained the other point and was able to get rid of this buying and selling.

All sorts of complicated systems were suggested to make sure the doctor didn't become a salaried officer. Bevan said, 'All right, I'll not attempt at this juncture to bring in a salary service and I'm not going to have any of this kind of nonsense about paying for it. We will pay for it out of taxation except in so far as there is a contribution to come from the social security side', (which there still is today). This was his decision, this was the way to do it. It carried out the principle that the rich and poor were to be treated alike and it would be paid for by the nation as a whole.

STARK MURRAY

Sir Stafford Cripps preparing his 1949 budget. Apostle to some; leader to others

Britain was going and how to get her there. What was more, he was prepared to tell her people the unpalatable truth: 'Our own consumption requirements have to be the last in the list of priorities. First are exports, second is capital investment in industry; and last are the needs, comforts, and amenities of the family. Marshall Aid would buy time to fill the export gap, but the export drive was the necessary condition of Britain's survival. Although imports were only three-quarters of their pre-war volume, the balance of payments deficit was nearly £700 million, and Britain's reserves had fallen by £1,000 million. The year 1948 was one of steady, even spectacular, progress. Production rose rapidly, exports were up by nearly a third, and the balance of payments was about to go into surplus.

Cripps' most dramatic stroke was his deal with the unions, and the parallel discussions with employers. Both were persuaded to exercise restraint. It was designed to get inflationary pressures under control and make it easier to get the balance of payments right. It was extremely successful: weekly wage rates had gone up 8 per cent in 1946, and 5 per cent in 1947; in 1948 they went up 4 per cent and in 1949 only 2 per cent. But this preoccupation with the balance of payments, very much a post-1947 phenomenon, led to another step which undermined and eventually destroyed the wages policy.

Between the spring and summer of 1949, the deficit on trade conducted in dollars doubled. All the progress made in 1948 was temporarily wiped out and there was speculative pressure on the pound. Import cuts in June and July did not halt the drain and a Commonwealth Conference was called in a crisis atmosphere. Cripps refused to contemplate devaluation, but at this crucial moment he was taken ill and retired to a Swiss sanatorium to recover. The Economic Secretary at the Treasury, Douglas Jay, together with Hugh Gaitskell, then Minister of Fuel and Power, came to the conclusion that devaluation was inevitable. They tried to get the help of the President of the Board of Trade, Harold Wilson. He was unwilling to commit himself at this stage. But they convinced Attlee; Cripps returned on 19 August to make the formal decision and finalize arrangements for 'D-day'.

Cripps, when the decision was finally announced on 18 September, was savaged by the Conservatives for his earlier denials that devaluation was about to take place, while his own left wing called it a

I think the really outstanding thing about Cripps – which may be peculiar in politicians, slightly less peculiar in British politicians – was that he really believed in literal Christianity in every word and deed. He believed that the direct revelations of the right course were made to him by the Almighty. It took one some time to realize this. The conviction that his decisions were directly dictated by Almighty God gave him great strength of purpose but made it difficult for him to do justice to the motives of others. When he was convinced that something was right, nothing would stop him; but he did think, having made up his mind, that anyone who disagreed was an agent of the Devil. And this did give him strength, but at other times it created difficulties. But of course there's no doubt that the main lines of his policy were right in trying to keep down consumption in the country, to build up exports, to build up investment. Looking back on it one can see that this was really, I think, the most successful period in British policy since the war.
DOUGLAS JAY

The public image of Sir Stafford Cripps, that of a very severe rather self-disciplined person, was not really at all an accurate picture. He was full of fun and wit and an immensely personal man in his relationships. I used to go for walks with him when he was Chancellor of the Exchequer; the only time that one could ever see him was at about 6.30 in the morning when he used to leave promptly for a walk round St James's Park and one had to get up and join him on the walk, then you'd have him alone. He was a man who believed very, very much in his Christian faith, but he wasn't very interested in Christian dogmas as such. He was interested in the practice of his faith and particularly keen that Christian insight should be brought into politics and the whole sphere of life. One of the occasions, I remember, when he wanted the Christian faith to be brought into the political arena was when he persuaded me to organize a pre-election service in St Paul's Cathedral.

CANON COLLINS

capitalist remedy that was bound to fail. The devaluation was perhaps too large: the dollar exchange rate was cut from $4.04 to $2.80, but part of the effect was lost when other countries followed suit. Prices of imports – and this meant food – went up and by the latter half of 1950 wages could no longer be held. The trade union leadership was forced by rank and file pressure to abandon its bargain with Cripps.

The parallels with 1967-9 are striking, although each situation had different components. There was, however, one constant: Harold Wilson, on both occasions, was reluctant to take the plunge into devaluation.

The long-term effects of the 1949 devaluation are still controversial, but its immediate effect was for the good. By April 1950, Britain had made good her loss of reserves and she was well on the way to a balance of payments surplus of £300 million. She had reached that elusive and staggering goal: exports were 175 per cent up on the pre-war level. It was a major and substantial achievement. Certainly, it was helped by the growing level of world trade and by Marshall Aid. But given the expensive social policy Labour had set up, the economic state of Britain in early 1950 looked distinctly promising.

Cripps, more than any other, could take the credit for this. He had assumed responsibility during the worst post-war economic crisis and for someone who is remembered as more socialist than his Labour successors, he had severely pruned government expenditure. The expenditure abroad, on the Armed Forces, which Dalton had so loudly complained about, had dropped from £200 million in 1947 to £98 million in 1949. He had cut food subsidies as far as he dared, but not as far as he wanted. His 1948 budget had cut direct taxation, and the general trend of his budgets was towards more indirect taxation. Redistributive taxation, Cripps argued, had reached its limit. 'There is only a certain sized cake,' he told the Trades Union Congress in 1948, 'and if a lot of people want a larger slice they can only get it by taking it from others.' This was the essence of Cripps's message: Britain had to cut her cloth to suit her coat.

The change in domestic policy was matched abroad. Bevin brought the Americans in while Cripps made Britain pay her way: it was an intelligent response to a dangerous situation, but for some, not socialist enough.

Devalued

The decisive point of the 1949 devaluation was the meeting with the Commonwealth Finance Ministers in the first week of July, when it became quite apparent, if you compared the export price of British goods with those of American goods in all the main export markets of the world, that American prices were 25 per cent or 30 per cent on average below ours, which really was conclusive evidence that you couldn't maintain that rate of exchange. Strangely enough, the man who really produced the clearest and most decisive evidence was Sir Edgar Whitehead, the then Finance Minister of Southern Rhodesia and who later became Prime Minister of Southern Rhodesia.

There was a seething ferment of disagreement within the Treasury: broadly, the economists were convinced that it was necessary. I was economic secretary, and the senior civil servants naturally took the more cautious view. I think they were quite right to do this, it's a very drastic step. Stafford Cripps, characteristically, took rather a long view of the whole thing: that this just wasn't the sort of thing that one did, and he didn't really, quite frankly, fully understand the argument for it. This went on, I would say, for a couple of weeks. I came to the conclusion on the third Sunday in July that devaluation was necessary. Hugh Gaitskell and I and Harold Wilson had been made responsible for economic policy under the Prime Minister when Stafford Cripps was away. He was leaving for Switzerland on the Monday. I therefore went round and saw Hugh Gaitskell on the morning of that Monday. I told him the conclusion I had come to and that we must get on with it. He at once said that he had come to the same conclusion on exactly the same day, for exactly the same reasons. So I told Stafford Cripps just before lunch before he went that I wasn't arguing the thing but I ought in fairness to tell him I had come to this conclusion. He said 'What – unilaterally?' and was, I remember, very shocked. That was all he said. And then there were discussions in the remaining week – the last week before the dispersal of Parliament and usually the last cabinet meeting until September – between Hugh Gaitskell, myself, Harold Wilson, the Treasury officials, and Attlee and Morrison. And by the end of that week they were convinced that there was no alternative. I mean Attlee's view was always that he didn't profess to understand all these things but that it was the fact that the gold was disappearing. Therefore he rather left it at that and the cabinet was then asked to give authority to deal with the whole dollar problem, as we called it in those days, to the Prime Minister during the recess. And I remember that far from displaying any objections to this possibly rather authoritarian proposal, everybody heaved a sigh of relief. They were then told not to make any speeches about dollars or sterling throughout August and September. It was left at that. We then dispatched a very secret letter to Stafford Cripps in Zurich, which I drafted, as a matter of fact. Hugh Gaitskell and I took it down to Chequers, it was signed by Attlee and taken overnight to Stafford Cripps. Stafford gave a rather reluctant assent. Preparations then went ahead. I think it was the most successful operation I've ever seen carried out in Whitehall, because there was no leak of any kind. The date was set and Stafford Cripps and Ernie Bevin went out to the international monetary fund meeting in September just the day after.

DOUGLAS JAY

In the end we had to send over Hugh Gaitskell – Cripps had retired sick to Switzerland at the critical time – and Hugh Gaitskell was the only member of the government who had the technical economic proficiency and the courage to go over and reason with Cripps in his retreat in Switzerland, and it was through Hugh Gaitskell's courage that something very much worse was averted. We must remember that in the Attlee administration ministers were always looking over their shoulder – we must never again have a Ramsay MacDonald – we must never have a national government – we must never have mass unemployment. The negative aspect was terribly important. There were certain things, liable to jump out of a bag when you weren't looking, which had to be avoided at all costs. And so this devaluation thing was very fraught with painful memories of 1931. One must understand that this rather dominated the views of the cabinet. I think the cabinet would have been willing to devalue in July had it not been for the advice of the Treasury, and I think if Stafford Cripps had not by that time been a very sick man, it's possible that he would have got the message sooner.

This very sad episode of devaluation ended with Stafford Cripps telling a downright lie – that we were not going to devalue. And then of course a very short time afterwards we did devalue, and not only the pound: considering Stafford's almost saintly reputation, it did a good deal to devalue the ordinary man's faith in government. I thought it was rather sad that the facts took so long to sink in, that the decision-making processes of the old Treasury and of the Civil Service proved so incapable of adjusting themselves to the facts of life post-war.

MAX NICHOLSON

The arrangement was that Bevin and Cripps would go together to Washington to conduct the operation and the discussions. It so happened that the two ministers only met when we got on the boat. Cripps used to get up early in the morning, four or five o'clock, and after taking a lot of exercise around the deck he would then engage in discussions with the officials. But Ernie Bevin had a different habit. He didn't really get up until about four o'clock in the afternoon, so we had great difficulty in bringing the two ministers even to meet, because there was only about half an hour in the day at which they could get together.

LORD SHERFIELD

["Even if we had then had some future intention of altering the rate of exchange, which in fact we had not, no responsible Minister could possibly have done otherwise than deny such intention."—*The Chancellor of the Exchequer in the House of Commons.*]

Czechmate

The Marshall Plan was put up by the Truman administration to the Congress with the strong support of President Truman. Senator Vandenberg played a very important role. He was a Republican, but he was then Chairman of the Foreign Relations Committee of the Senate. I think historians should give him parallel marks with Truman for his support of these principles. The *coup d'état* in Prague was right in the middle of the argument over the Marshall Plan and it was not very clear which way the vote would go. We were all hopeful that we would carry it, but perhaps, by a rather small margin. But the *coup* in Czechoslovakia caused such concern that the Marshall Plan went through a few weeks later with a very large majority.

The blockade of Berlin really broadened the scope of NATO. Certainly the Berlin blockade played a terrifying role, it concerned people very deeply. Of course there was an argument as to whether stern measures were to be taken. General Clay wanted to force the tanks through. We had at that time still a monopoly on nuclear weapons and Truman, undoubtedly with our approval, decided to go ahead with the air lift and Britain played a very important role. We played in the beginning a parallel, an equal role, but then we gradually took a large percent of it. I've forgotten just what position Mr Bevin took, but I'm sure Mr Attlee was on the conservative side of that decision.

AVERELL HARRIMAN

By the end of 1947, Bevin's patience with Molotov finally ran out. Perhaps it was only his belief in himself as a negotiator that had made him try so long and so hard. But he had few sanctions he could realistically apply: British power was too limited and too limiting.

Nowhere was this more apparent than in Germany. The Anglo-American Bi-Zonia had by 1948 created widespread apprehension among the Russians. Were the Americans and British not laying the ground' for German economic revival, which the Soviet Union had sought to prevent by exacting heavy reparations after the war? By the middle of 1948, Marshall Aid was pouring into Western Europe – the American, British, and French zones in Germany included. Furthermore, this prospect was appealing to other countries left with the remnants of an industrial base, particularly those states whose economies had been intimately tied to Germany. Stalin had already excluded Czechoslovakia, whose main industrial centres abutted the American zone in Germany, from receiving Marshall Aid; but his control over the Czechoslovaks was incomplete.

Czech Communists took that control in February 1948. To Bevin, the situation was crystal clear. Communists had wrested control from socialists without full democratic appeal – a situation he had seen countless times in his union days. With the exception of Austria, the last hope of a social democratic Central Europe had gone. With Communist-inspired general strikes, and the approach of an Italian general election, which the Communists had a good chance of winning, it was time to look to what one had.

Within three weeks of the Czech *coup d'état* Bevin had brought together Britain, the Benelux powers, and France in a West European union

I think it's important to distinguish between two American approaches to the problems in the post-war world. I think the professionals in the State Department – of whom the outstanding example was George Kennan, who was at that time head of the policy planning staff and wrote the famous article by Mr X in *Foreign Affairs* – didn't believe that the Russians were out for world conquest but did believe that it was necessary for Western Europe to hold the line roughly where the armies had stopped at the end of the Second World War. And, should this happen, the Russian regime would ultimately mellow and come to terms – as I think was right. But of course this was a very sophisticated view to put to a people which had, only a few years earlier, become conscious of the fact there was a world beyond the oceans. And one of the problems, I think, was that those Americans who did become interested in foreign affairs in the post-war period tended to see Communism as an absolute evil, very much in the same way as we in the Labour Party in the 1930s – and still – saw Fascism as the absolute evil. And in some ways, I think the tragedy of this period was that, in order to get the Americans committed to a very prudent and necessary strengthening in Western Europe against a spread of Soviet influence, the Americans were easily persuaded by Soviet behaviour in Czechoslovakia and Berlin that the Russians were really out for world conquest in the same sense as Hitler really was out for the conquest of Europe.

DENIS HEALEY

treaty. Ostensibly, the Brussels Treaty was a development of the Dunkirk Treaty signed in 1947 between Britain and France and directed largely against renewed German aggression. In fact it was part of a wider design to safeguard Western Europe from Soviet disruption. In December 1947 he had already secured a promise from the American Secretary of State to do what he could to help Western union, subject to Congress's approval. Bevin had told Field Marshal Montgomery on 23 December 1947 that Western union was only a beginning: he hoped to draw in Scandinavia, Italy, and the United States. The Czech *coup* reinforced his determination.

American economic commitment was not enough. Marshall Aid was preventing Europe from sliding into a major slump, but Bevin had some sense of the arithmetic of 1950. Because only a quarter of Marshall Aid was left to go into capital investment, the programme of European economic recovery was expected to be slow. Strong Communist parties in France and Italy were well placed to take advantage of any break in economic progress. There had already been widespread strikes and Bevin felt Europe needed a security umbrella to prevent any Soviet invasion in the meantime.

The Czech *coup* helped the Marshall Aid programme through Congress but it was the crisis over Berlin that finally swung American opinion behind a security commitment to Europe.

Throughout the late spring of 1948, the Soviet authorities, increasingly worried over the trend of Western policy, had made trouble on the access routes to Berlin. The former capital of Germany, itself under four-power control, stood in the middle of the Russian zone and could be reached on land only by defined rail, road, and canal links.

The Western powers were not to be deterred.

After the Berlin blockade, it became obvious that one of the big problems was fuel. I think we needed right away about 2,000,000 tons of coal, because there was just a tiny bit of coal available in the city, in the western sectors of Berlin at that point. And the question was how to get that coal, and the next item – food. And this ran into considerable tonnage. In the absence of determination to meet the issue on the ground where it should have been met – mind you, this was a period when we had the atomic bomb and the Soviet Union did not have the atomic bomb – I believe that any thought of the Soviet Union going to war with us over this issue of Berlin was in the realm of fantasy. They couldn't possibly; they were in no condition because of circumstances back home where the destruction had been so terrible. Their population was in no physical or mental condition to permit them going into a war. I find fault with our American joint Chiefs of Staff on that point because they insisted that they had to have eighteen months to prepare because this might lead to an all-out confrontation with the Soviet Union and that was one reason or *the* reason why we did not meet the issue. All we had, you see, about the blockade of Berlin, was a note addressed to us by the Russian Military Governor, saying that the highway would be closed to traffic, because it was in need of repair, for the indefinite future, and then they put a pole across the road with two Mongolian soldiers – and that was a blockade. It didn't cost them a penny, and instead of politely sending them a note and saying thank you very much, but as you are not in a position to give prompt service on the maintenance we will undertake it ourselves, and putting a division with some combat troops and some engineers ready to undertake the maintenance of the highway, we backed away from the issue and resorted to the air lift. Now the air lift was technically a beautiful job, achieved under great difficulties and at great expense. I think we spent over 2,000,000 dollars a month on that thing. The trouble was that we would not stand up on an issue which was very serious, where we had all the cards in our hands – this was the sad feature of that history. General Clay was our Military Governor at that time and we were having a meeting in his office and discussing the question of delivery by air of whatever was needed. The Commander of our Air Force at that time was stationed at Wiesbaden, and his name was Curtis Le May. General Clay picked up the phone and called him and said – 'Curtis, can you deliver coal by air?' And Le May at the other end of the phone – we could hear the extension – said 'Would you repeat that question?' And Clay repeated the question, and he said that the Air Force could deliver anything. It was on that basis that the air lift started. The German population co-operated tremendously. That was one of the most astounding features, they worked day and night, sometimes with very little pay and under bad weather conditions and bad food conditions especially. You know, that first winter in Berlin I think probably 20 people a day died from the cold and malnutrition.

ROBERT MURPHY

There were a lot of people who imagined Nye Bevan thought that if we pushed an armed brigade up the corridor from the west of Berlin, the Russians would let it through. I believe they were probably right but Bevin thought, and I must say I agreed with him, that we could not really rest the future of humanity on a 60 or even 70 per cent gamble. The essence, I think, of the post-war situation has always been that neither side was prepared to initiate the use of force directly against the other. The Russians were able to close the corridor by land without using force; we could only open that corridor by using force. On the other hand, we could use the air route and the Russians couldn't close that without shooting down our aircraft, and by choosing to break the blockade by an air lift of food, and coal, and supplies into Berlin we in effect called a Soviet bluff. The Russians, in the end, despite one or two dangerous incidents, allowed the air lift to work. Berlin was saved and the position which many people at that time thought was totally untenable for the West remained solid to this day.

DENIS HEALEY

The Berlin air-lift. The Americans took a progressively larger share of the load

All Shape and no arms

Mr Bevin, during the early part of 1948, had been very anxious to get the Americans interested and, if possible, involved in the defence of Western Europe. With this in mind earlier in the year, he had formed a European alliance (the Brussels Treaty). During 1948 I had been told to try and make progress with the Americans and I made no progress at all. Then quite suddenly, at the beginning of July, I remember Mr Lubbock, the Under Secretary of State of the State Department, saying to me 'Why aren't we making faster progress, it's time we got on?' And the reasons were there had been a Communist *coup* in Prague in February and then after that, in June, the Berlin air lift. The mood in Congress had changed and in particular Senator Vandenberg, the most important Republican in foreign affairs, had come to see that America could no longer go on in isolation, and therefore Congress and the administration would have won, so negotiations for a North Atlantic Treaty could begin, and they did.

LORD FRANKS

In 1949 there's no doubt at all that the prime importance of NATO was to commit the United States to the defence of Western Europe. It used to be a joke in those days that NATO was like the Venus de Milo, all shape and no arms. It was only really during the fifties that NATO began to build up conventional forces in Western Europe. The political importance, I think, was absolutely paramount in the early days, it was only later that it acquired some military muscles.

DENIS HEALEY

I can't exaggerate to you the personal contribution Bevin made to try and get America involved in giving economic help and then in joining in some sort of military alliance. I think that there is no doubt that history will show that he was the main architect, apart from General Marshall himself. Bevin was the main architect for the European side and certainly the visionary. It was his vision that led to both the economic recovery programme and NATO.

NICHOLAS HENDERSON

Bevin had, of course, enormous moral and physical courage and he didn't let his poor health interfere in any way with his work, and although at times he appeared to be rather slumped and exhausted, he always, in my experience, managed to pull himself together. I remember going to see him one morning and I said to him 'Well, Secretary of State, how are you feeling this morning?' and he said 'My behind is like a dartboard', because, of course, poor man, he'd had so many injections.

LORD SHERFIELD

The London Agreement of 1 June 1948 set out the main lines of a constitution for a West German state and its full association with the economies of Western Europe. Moreover the plan involved a new West German currency which superseded the money previously circulating in all four zones. This confirmed every Russian fear and they retaliated where the Western powers were weakest – Berlin. The Russians cut all land access to the city.

To save Berlin there were two courses of action: break the blockade on the ground by risking a fight, or even war; or bring supplies in by air. The Russians would then be forced to shoot aircraft down if they wanted to maintain their blockade. They would have to face the risk of provoking a world war. Despite disagreements in the British Cabinet over the response, Bevin himself preferred the air-lift. He thought it gave a better chance of avoiding war. He was right: the Berlin air-lift continued for nearly a year, when the blockade was called off as suddenly as it began. There was, however, one subsidiary feature of the air-lift whose significance was not lost on Bevin. Britain's contribution declined, and America's increased as the air-lift continued.

The Berlin blockade confirmed many suspicions and defined Europe into East and West. Bevin never faced serious trouble from his Left again. But it also raised a lot of questions, particularly over the future of Western Europe and the American role.

Bevin now embarked on a policy that was the most successful of his career. The French, traditionally and often justifiably suspicious of any Anglo-American deal, joined Bi-Zonia a few weeks after the blockade began. In Italy, the Communists were unexpectedly defeated by de Gasperi and his coalition in the general elections of 1948. But the most important prize of all, the United States – while helpful – remained militarily uncommitted.

By the summer of 1948 the United States Congress was clearly ready to make some further commitment to collective security within the broad framework of the United Nations Charter. American reluctance to become involved had now been overtaken by real fear of Russia's intentions. Talks in Washington and London filled the second half of the year, and by the spring of 1949 the State Department was ready at last to take the line so often cast before by Bevin. The Atlantic Pact, signed in March, linked the United States and

Bevin at Colombo, Ceylon. He was now so ill that he had to complete the last part of the journey by sea – a journey to his last great achievement

Canada with the Brussels Treaty powers, and as other countries hastened to join the alliance, the North Atlantic Treaty was signed on 4 April to the tunes of 'I've got plenty of nothing' and 'It ain't necessarily so.' Bevin's hook was in the second clause of the Treaty: 'An armed attack against one or more of them in Europe or America shall be considered an attack against them all.' The Americans were in.

Bevin had shown remarkable skill in using opportunities that might never recur to get the United States and Western Europe into line. Not only did he have a clear understanding of the dangers of Europe's situation, but he displayed a remarkable tactical skill in finding a remedy. If the U.S. commitment was at first more political than military, this was true of the entire Atlantic

concept. No steps were then taken to create any coherent force in Europe beyond the armies of occupation in Germany. Not until 1950 was an attempt made to put teeth into the North Atlantic Treaty by the creation of the North Atlantic Treaty Organization.

Bevin had hoped to make the Atlantic Treaty the basis for some economic arrangement linking not only Europe itself, but 'Europe overseas... It would be done with the object of making the whole world richer and safer.' Frustrated in this, so strongly did he feel that joint remedies must apply to South East Asia that he insisted, although desperately ill, on attending a conference at Colombo. This meeting launched an Asian counterpart to the Marshall Plan. It was to be the last major achievement of the 1945 Labour Government.

for family - happiness - and a home

remember?

JARROW CRUSADE

UNEMPLOYMENT

Don't give the Tories another chance

VOTE LABOUR

Where do I come in with fair shares? Labour? Not me

SOCIALISM leads to COMMUNISM

VOTE CONSERVATIVE

LA HEAD cove

Make B great

CONS

5 The interregnum

How much longer?

The 1950 election suffered from this difficulty, looking at it from the Labour point of view. The parliamentary party had exhausted itself. It had introduced an immense programme of reform – the National Health Service was only one – including the nationalization of a large number of industries. A tremendous programme. They had exhausted themselves, physically and mentally. The ministers had nothing new to offer. They devised various strange schemes – nationalizing insurance, and sugar, and so on – without really very much thought; just trying to think up something attractive. But the real trouble was the exhaustion after such a period of immense activity, and during the '50 – '51 Parliament we did practically nothing with the majority of six; we couldn't do it. One felt in a sort of hiatus. The impetus had gone which existed from '45 to '50. The excitement, the making of new laws which were going to be of great social benefit, all that had disappeared after the election, so it was rather a trying period really.
GEORGE STRAUSS

In 1950 we had a majority of six which was then thought to be an impossible majority. Later on ideas changed. The older men, Attlee I think, thought that you wouldn't be able to go on really for very long. You'd be defeated inevitably in the House and would, in his view, have to resign. I remember this came out at the first cabinet I attended, because I became a cabinet minister at the end of that election. Attlee was taking it for granted that if we were defeated that night on an amendment to the address, we would just resign and let the other side take over. I remember saying – a very brash young man – that I thought this was quite wrong, that votes should count in the House, and if the government were defeated there should be a General Election, even though there had only been one three weeks before. In the end this view prevailed because one or two other people, like Ernie Bevin, strongly supported it. We weren't defeated, of course, and it proved possible to stay in office for nearly eighteen months. Indeed, we could have stayed longer on a majority of six. For Attlee and Morrison, it was the tail end of what had been a tremendous life; they'd been ministers through the war and in '45 and '50. To younger people like myself, and one or two others who'd just got into the cabinet, it was a very exciting time; we were full of energy and indeed optimism and we expected and hoped to win the following '51 election.
PATRICK GORDON WALKER

By January 1950, Labour had fulfilled every major pledge in its programme; there was little left for the parliamentary party to do. Although Britain was still dogged by austerity, the economic indices looked healthy. The export target had been reached and Britain was well on the road to a £300 million trade surplus. In the autumn of 1948, Harold Wilson had begun the slow process of dismantling wartime controls, characterizing it as a 'bonfire'. Clothes and furniture came off the ration in 1949 and during that summer London enjoyed the bright lights for the first time since 1939. It seemed only a matter of time before further relaxations could be announced. There would be problems, but the outlook was brighter than at any time since the war.

But Labour's leaders were tired and ill. Attlee, Morrison, and Bevin had been in office for close on ten years, Cripps almost as long. Bevin was dying; subject to continued heart attacks, he refused to face the prospect of retirement. Cripps, too, was spending long periods in a Swiss sanatorium. He had approved devaluation in 1949 from his bed in Zurich. Morrison had slowed down since his heart attack in 1947.

Previous page: election posters, 1950
The Prime Minister, Clem Attlee, campaigns in the
February 1950 General Election in Stepney, his
constituency

It was inevitable that Attlee would soon have to go to the country, at any rate before July 1950, but it was Cripps who dictated when. He had been greatly upset by the deceptions he had had to practise during devaluation and was determined that his integrity should not again be questioned by the introduction of a budget that might be construed as electioneering. His argument was accepted, reluctantly in Morrison's case, who expected Labour to poll badly in winter weather, and Attlee called the election for February.

Labour went to the country on a programme of limited extensions of public ownership on sugar, insurance, cement, and water supplies. This pleased the activists as far as it went, but to everyone it looked too much like a watered-down version of 1945. The atmosphere in 1950 was very different: most middle-ground opinion accepted and even favoured what Labour had achieved. But, and it was a big but, when was life going to get better? Nationalization was no longer seen as a sure answer to this immediate question and the impact of Tate & Lyle's 'Mr Cube' campaign against nationalization could have been seen as an omen. However,

would a vote for the Tories mean a return to the means test and unemployment of pre-war days?

The neck-and-neck struggle as the results came in transformed a dull campaign into one of the most exciting post-war elections. Nearly twenty-four hours elapsed before Attlee could be certain he had an overall majority – in the event it was only six. There were 1,500,000 more Labour votes than in 1945, but the swing to the Right was strong. The closeness of the result was partly due to mechanical factors; psephologists have estimated that the redistribution of seats in 1948 and the more efficient use of postal votes by the Conservatives cost Labour about thirty seats. The Conservatives had clearly benefited from ten years of restrictions, which seemed to the middle classes to be an unnecessary privation. This showed in the suburban results with a vengeance. An increase of 2,500,000 in the Conservative popular vote put politics on a knife edge.

Attlee, when asked for his reaction to the result, replied with typical brevity: 'Carry on, of course.' But for how long? It was going to be hard enough to avoid defeat in the House of Commons, let alone initiate controversial legislation. He would have to get a firmer mandate soon.

The situation was quickly complicated: four months after the election, the Korean War broke out. To many, a divided Korea in the East paralleled a divided Germany in the West. The North Korean invasion of the South was taken to be further evidence of Soviet aggression, and with U.N. backing, United States forces went in to preserve South Korea. Britain committed herself to air and sea support, and then added a Commonwealth brigade.

The changing fortunes of war brought the Chinese into action to save their North Korean allies, and many Americans, among them the U.N. Commander-in-Chief, General Douglas Macarthur, saw their chance to reverse the Communist victory in the Chinese Civil War a year earlier. Macarthur argued that he could inflict a military defeat on the Chinese if he were allowed to bomb their bases across the Yalu river, which would mean extending the war to China. President Truman told a press conference that the use of the atomic bomb was not necessarily out of the question and the House of Commons grew alarmed. Their concern drove Attlee early in December to fly to the White House where he obtained the necessary assurances.

Wafted to Washington, Attlee leaves a sick Bevin in London

British troops arrive in Korea; and (below right) Red Hammer meets Red Star: Molotov and Mao. Will the Korean war become the Third World War?

A paper tiger?

Mr Attlee flew over to Washington in December 1950. I can remember very well at the end of the conference the problem of drafting a formula which could satisfy both the United States government and the British Prime Minister. It so happened that I had to draft the formula and there was nowhere for me to write it except for a very small table, so I got down on my knees, trying to invent it and write it out. I can remember President Truman saying to me that it was the first time that a British Ambassador had been on his knees before the President of the United States. I think Mr Attlee had crossed the Atlantic hoping for an undertaking for prior consultation on the use of the atomic bomb, but what he got was a more general understanding that the United States would in fact keep in close touch with Britain on all developments in the military situation. This satisfied him and he was able to go home.

LORD FRANKS

Attlee was really wafted there. I've never seen anything happen like it – he was wafted by the House of Commons and there was such excitement in the place, they just had to decide to do it, and in the course of two hours the decision took place. I don't believe he knew what he was going to do when he got into the plane, because he'd only just had time to inform me and off he popped. But it wasn't a stupid thing because Truman couldn't afford to see the Commonwealth Brigade pulled out, and Attlee was able to say 'Now look, you know if certain things are done by MacArthur, we will pull out'.

RICHARD CROSSMAN

As far as Truman was concerned, there was never a moment's serious thought in his mind to use the atomic bomb. Truman had a good deal of difficulty with General MacArthur and that led to his recall. It really was quite a constitutional test, whether a military proconsul should settle American foreign policy rather than the President of the United States. Truman was a man of definite action, he stepped right up to it and recalled probably one of the most popular generals in history.

AVERELL HARRIMAN

Before Gaitskell was appointed, Attlee sent for me, and he asked who I thought should be sent to the Treasury. I said, 'Well I think you ought to send Morrison there'. 'Oh, no, Morrison knows nothing about finance.' But I pointed out that he didn't require to know a great deal about finance in order to be Chancellor of the Exchequer. However, he said 'No, Morrison won't do', and 'What about Gaitskell?' I said, 'Well, I don't think Gaitskell is the man, he is too much of an orthodox economist, besides he has very little experience'. 'Well', he said, 'I think we'll experiment with him'. So I said 'Well, all right, you're the chief, you're the boss, you decide.' So Attlee appointed Gaitskell. That led to a lot of trouble in the government and in the party. First of all, Morrison disliked the idea of Gaitskell going there. He was, according to Morrison, a second-rater, but that's to say really a new-comer, although it was generally admitted that Gaitskell had a lot of ability. Undoubtedly he was a very able man. Then Nye Bevan was annoyed, because he had expected promotion.

LORD SHINWELL

CRIPPS RESIGNS

Will leave Parliament —Gaitskell is named new Chancellor

By BILL GREIG

SIR STAFFORD CRIPPS has resigned as Chancellor of the Exchequer and is also leaving Parliament because of ill-health. He is to take a year's complete rest.

He is to be succeeded at the Treasury by Mr. Hugh Gaitskell, until now Minister of State for Economic Affairs, who, at forty-four, becomes the youngest Chancellor since the days of William Pitt, in the eighteenth century.

And now Mr. Gaitskell, in his fifth year in Parliament, will fall the task of producing the next budget, with all the new problems which result from the necessity to rearm Britain.

Post Not Being Filled

'Back in twelve months'

The Korean War put strong pressures on the British economy. The strong balance of payment surplus reached in 1950 was undermined by the soaring price of imports – up by 40 per cent in twelve months – because of extensive stockpiling of strategic raw materials in the United States. Further, it seemed clear to Attlee that the Americans, and indeed the Conservatives, were right in pressing for a considerably increased rearmament programme. Rearmament became the Government's top priority. It made necessary the partial reversion to a war economy, the restoration of some controls, and a deflationary squeeze on all other private and public expenditure.

Cripps could no longer carry his burden. He had written to Attlee in October 1950 saying that he could not face another election and he was going to resign. The principal claimant for his job was Aneurin Bevan. Attlee was worried whether Bevan would 'inspire confidence', and knew that he would not contemplate any cuts in social spending which might be involved in rearmament. To many members of the Cabinet the final choice, that of Hugh Gaitskell, was a surprise. Gaitskell, as Minister of Economic Affairs, had done much of the final preparation for the 1950 Budget, and Cripps himself had recommended his advancement. Thus, it was Gaitskell's task to find the wherewithal to finance the rearmament programme.

While the budget estimates were being prepared in the spring of 1951, there was still more jockeying for position. In March 1951, Ernie Bevin was celebrating his seventieth birthday at a party in the Foreign Office. The telephone rang: it was Attlee on the line demanding his resignation. So the story goes. Whether true or not, Attlee certainly knew Bevin was dying. He had been too ill to accompany the Prime Minister to Washington in December 1950 to see Truman. He had held on in great pain, with the help of drugs. But Attlee, reluctantly, had in the end to ask his staunchest ally to go. Bevin was dead within three months.

The list of suitors for Bevin's job was long but unbalanced: Bevan irritated by his seeming demotion to the Ministry of Labour in January, and Sir Hartley Shawcross made soundings; Alfred Robens was considered, but Morrison was an obvious candidate. Attlee played safe, or so he hoped, and Herbert Morrison achieved his last-but-one outstanding ambition.

Bevan had supported the rearmament programme in January, but faced with Gaitskell's proposal to put charges on teeth and spectacles in the budget, he threatened resignation. The amount involved was small – £13 million – but the emotional significance large. Bevan felt that 'his' Health Service, which he had promised would be 'free', was being attacked. Shortly after Gaitskell presented his budget, Aneurin Bevan, Harold Wilson, and a junior minister, John Freeman

Socialist Party splits on the Budget

MPs talk of an election looming

BEVAN RESIGNS

And Wilson pays night visit to Prime Minister in hospital

By Daily Graphic Political Correspondent

...ieling last night among back - bench Socialist M.P.s was that, if Mr. Wilson joined Mr. Bevan, Mr. Attlee could be expected to go to the country within weeks, or even days.

...divided party with a majority of only five in the House of Commons cannot hope to last.

...is understood that the ...aces of Mr. Bevan and the late Mr. Bevin will be filled shortly.

...t. Attlee, I gather, does not propose to make a major Cabinet reshuffle at the moment.

MR. ANEURIN BEVAN has resigned his office of Minister of Labour and has left the Government in protest

I wasn't altogether surprised at the resignation of Nye Bevan, partly because it was well known that he was bitterly opposed to Hugh Gaitskell and he was very disappointed when Hugh Gaitskell was made Chancellor of the Exchequer and he was only made Minister of Labour. He wanted either the Chancellorship or the Foreign Office and these had been refused to him, and he was very bitter and very angry. It was fairly clear in the cabinet that he was picking a quarrel with Hugh Gaitskell.

Hugh Gaitskell had to produce a budget which allowed for this great increase in expenditure and put on taxes; charges for spectacles and false teeth under the Health Service, partly to raise money, and partly, I think, as a symbol to the country that this was a very tough time. Bevan picked on that. We had the final cabinet meeting after endless attempts to reconcile them and they were both very stuborn and obstinate and wouldn't budge. Nye Bevan suddenly opened up the whole charge as one of rearmament, not just teeth and spectacles, and resigned on that. And then suddenly – I don't think anyone expected this, I didn't myself and I discussed it with other ministers afterwards – Harold Wilson suddenly announced that he was going to resign with Nye Bevan. Nye Bevan rather laudably said 'You've been very loyal to me, I release you'. But Harold said no, he was going, and everyone was surprised and wondered what his motives were. But anyway out they both went. That, I think, led to our defeat in the next General Election.

PATRICK GORDON WALKER

It was a personal, bitter antagonism of jealousies, which were wholly disastrous and very unpleasant to witness. To a social reformer such as Gaitskell, the man who wanted to go forward with big nationalization schemes like those of Aneurin Bevan, these were all factors in the row, but basically it was very largely a personal one, in my view.

GEORGE STRAUSS

I don't think Bevan was an easy subordinate to anybody. He was the kind of man who didn't understand team spirit, loyalty, and that sort of thing. He was very much the man who ought to have been the top chap. I dare say Attlee wasn't altogether sorry when he finally decided to get out of it. Because Attlee, you see, thought of the government as being one mighty good regiment, with a chain of command which was very clearly defined from top to bottom, and this was exactly the kind of thing that Bevan couldn't stomach.

Attlee was very keen on the British Army, indeed, loved it, and was proud of it and of his own part of it. And Bevan was inclined occasionally to sneer at this and think it was a kind of establishment thing – rather high-hat business altogether. But if he did make a sneer, Attlee was very quick to fly at him and would relapse into the vernacular and adopt the language of the officers' mess. I've heard him on many occasions, and this was a bit of a shock, I think to some of his rather high-minded, socialistic colleagues. I think Bevan was the spokesman for this defection. I don't know myself about Wilson saying anything about this, but I think he left most of the talking to Bevan.

SIR GEORGE MALLABY

Bevin suffered from serious heart trouble – angina of his heart with involvement of his blood vessels, lungs, abdomen, in fact every part of his body. But at the same time his top notch was in excellent condition – sharp. He had been a sick man for about seven years but he wouldn't see a doctor, he disliked them. He was overweight and was put on a diet, and then he was treated medicinally and then by discipline – real discipline. He was a very bad patient. He wanted to be boss but I wouldn't have it. I had to cut down his drinking. He really was an impossible man to deal with and the only way you could do it was to fight him. He was getting attacks of angina of his heart. I pointed out to him that he would need to resign as Foreign Minister, which he did on his return to England from Colombo. He then asked me how long I could keep him going. I told him that was a very difficult thing, but he insisted and I told him roughly six months. He took it with his usual courage, very philosophically, and with no display of emotion at all, he was perfectly calm. He knew that it was quite impossible for him to carry on. He realized that even before he went to Colombo.

SIR ALEXANDER McCALL

I think Attlee had a curiously open mind about the Foreign Secretaryship, and in the end the choice really depended on Mr Morrison's own decision. At the time, I was led to understand, both by Mr Attlee and by Mr Morrison, that the choice really lay between Mr Morrison and myself. Mr Morrison wasn't really terribly interested in foreign affairs. I don't think he'd got any feeling for international matters. He was essentially a Londoner and first class on matters of home policy and domestic affairs. But he wanted, very naturally, to become the leader of the party and the Prime Minister when the time came for Mr Atlee to go, and the way he put it to me was that he felt that if he didn't take the Foreign Secretaryship, which was in effect at that time the number two job, people would regard this as a kind of confession of failure on his own part and that he would be put out of the running for the succession to Mr Attlee.

Mr Attlee would have had very great difficulty in not appointing him, I think, in view of Mr Morrison's seniority and the rather delicate relationship which existed between the two of them. When it was known that he wished to be appointed it would have been a very, very severe rebuff that would have given rise to very awkward repercussions.

LORD SHAWCROSS

There was the famous occasion in a train when someone said to Bevin that Morrison was his own worst enemy and Ernie said 'Not so long as I'm alive, he ain't'.

PATRICK GORDON WALKER

End of an era

resigned. The reasons for their resignations went beyond the immediate issue and were a mixture of pique, concern over Britain's capacity to pay for the rearmament programme, and worry that the Labour Government was slipping from one crisis to another regardless of its supporters' interests. Although the resignations were a bad blow for the Government, the dissidents promised not to bring it down. But greater difficulties were to come.

Morrison was soon uncomfortable at the Foreign Office. The Anglo-Iranian Oil Company was seeking to renegotiate its concessionary rights with the Persian Government. Moussadeq, the Persian Prime Minister, had just come to power on a wave of nationalist feeling and, almost immediately, nationalized the company's oil wells at Abadan. Morrison reacted violently, hoping that swift action by force would topple Moussadeq. But, apart from Shinwell, the rest of the Cabinet were in no mood for foreign adventures. Morrison was isolated.

The Americans sent Averell Harriman, a senior diplomat, to Persia to see if he could help. He could not. For the first time Britain demonstrated that she could not control her oil suppliers; an attempt to involve the United Nations miscarried, and Labour was to go out of office with the Abadan dispute unresolved.

In the summer and autumn of 1951, the going became much harder for the Government. In these months the Conservatives suspended all normal parliamentary co-operation and they fought the Finance Bill inch by inch. The Government was under threat of daily defeat. Sick M.P.s were seen being lifted out of ambulances on to stretchers to be nodded through the division lobbies. 'One final heave', Churchill had said in 1950.

The last few months of the Labour Government were dominated by a deepening balance of payments crisis with colossal pressure on the reserves. The 1950 surplus of £300 million was transformed in twelve months to a deficit of nearly £500 million. At home there was violent inflation. Gaitskell's rearmament budget had put 6d on the income tax and doubled the purchase tax on cars, radios, and domestic electrical goods – not an election-winning recipe.

Late in September 1951, without any consultation with his colleagues, Attlee decided on an election. Many of the Cabinet were badly shaken; Gaitskell and Shinwell, on a visit to America, cabled their disagreement. Morrison, Labour's greatest election

expert, was in Canada. But Attlee pressed on, determined to get a larger majority.

Although Labour polled more votes (13,500,000) than before or since, the Conservatives won an overall majority of seventeen seats on a lower popular vote. There was nothing to suggest that the Conservatives could survive a full term or that they would win the next election, and Attlee stayed on as Leader of the Opposition to wait for that day. When he left 10 Downing Street he had been in cabinet for eleven years and six months consecutively. He cannot even claim a record in this.

The Attlee Government of 1945-51 was one of the major reforming governments in British history. The corpus of legislation passed represented a major step in resolving some of the worst problems of the pre-war years. It had overwhelmingly reinforced the view that high levels of unemployment are unacceptable and moved the whole area of British politics onto a more socially just plane. Much legislation since has been devoted towards building on the foundations laid by Attlee's Government or readapting the premises of 1945-51 to fit contemporary conditions. Mass affluence changes the way in which politicians think about society; it was not until the sixties that the universality of the social services began to be powerfully questioned. Nevertheless the very achievement of the 1945-51 Government, because it had done so much to clear away the evils of the past, meant that it was psychologically rooted in the past. It was to prove a long and hard road before the Labour Party could grapple with the political problems of a mixed economy that was working and being managed with some success.

The 1951 government collapsed through sheer exhaustion. There was immense controversy in the Conservative Party as to whether we should behave like gentlemen and give them a fair run, or whether as I think Boothby said, we should indulge in factious opposition. The Labour government at the time had rather an assortment of elderly gentlemen who were liable to become sick or even to die. The Conservative Party decided in favour of factious opposition so that there were no pairs. I always remember George Chetwynd, who was Parliamentary Private Secretary to Hugh Dalton, saying to me one night 'You know we're going to the country, Reg?' I said, 'No, I didn't know'. 'It's defeat', he said. 'Why?' I said. 'Well, they are tired out, they can't take it any more'. And of course some of them had been ministers continuously for eleven years, since 1940.
REGINALD BEVINS

CHURCHILL

THE TORY TEAM

Cut out Government waste

TU

6 Set the people free

hopes
nto
mes

CHURCHIL

COMMITT

'They dismissed me'

When Churchill was defeated in '45 this was a devastating wound for him. The last thing in the world that he thought was possible, that he should be thanked, eulogized, and dismissed. This was a great blow. I used to discuss this after the war when I was here with him and say, 'But why are you worried about coming back into office, what does it matter? You can't add to your reputation in history. It can't add anything to your stature.' 'Um, um, they dismissed me, they dismissed me.' You see this had really bitten into him. It wasn't a question of how long he might be Prime Minister again, but that he should be elected Prime Minister for whatever the period might be. That really assumed a magnitude in his mind that I wouldn't have expected in so great a man, but there it was.

SIR ROBERT MENZIES

We were in a state, of course, of great disarray, because we didn't really expect that Winston Churchill would be defeated after winning the war. There was a good deal of confusion and I remember the Chief Whip, James Stuart, telling me that he thought his entrails had been pulled out of him. We had great difficulty in reforming ourselves. I took to it like a duck to water. I remember being asked to take part in the Bill on State Insurance although I knew nothing about it, which rather shows that we hadn't organized our team at all. Then we got some buildings and eventually moved into where the present Conservative Research Department is, and started to form an Opposition. But it took us many months and indeed almost two years before we really got settled into 1947.

LORD BUTLER

Immediately the war was ended the Conservative Party started to collect together a number of men, most of whom had come out of the services, like myself, for instance, who went to form the Conservative Political Centre. Those young men came with very firm ideas as to the sort of Conservative Party they wanted to see grow up out of the disaster of the 1945 election. It was to be a Conservative Party that held the middle ground in politics; it was keenly sympathetic to the problems of social reform; it was a reformist party rather than a Conservative Party in the old style that we'd known under Baldwin and Chamberlain before the war. It was a revolt in some ways against those pre-war years and we had the opportunity, which would never come again in our lifetime, of remoulding the party along our lines, which we'd had aspirations for in those years before 1939.

LORD ALPORT

To Conservatives, the defeat of 1945 was peculiarly personal: the return of Labour to power they saw as an ungracious and ungrateful act. Churchill himself was deeply wounded. Labour propaganda that the Conservatives had been solely responsible for the miseries of the inter-war years had stuck. Unfairly, because the Conservatives themselves had done something to interpose the state between economic forces and the working class. But the desire to obliterate what had gone before was strong. Electorally, the Conservatives badly misjudged the popular mood.

Once they had recovered their wind, they realised that something substantial would have to be done, if they were to regain their former political ascendancy. A fight, muted and private, but nonetheless real, had begun as early as 1943 for the soul of the Conservative Party. There was talk of the 'magic circle', the largely hidden influence of great Tory families, of the exclusiveness of policy making and the disregard for democratic processes within the party. Many people felt that the Conservative Party had been left on the shelf; that it represented a society which would never return. The age of the common man had begun in earnest.

The very slow process of adjusting the Conservative Party to a more democratic world had begun under Baldwin, but the battle had still to be fought out and won. Above all, the party apparatus – reorganised by Ralph Assheton at the close of the war – had to be captured for the 'new wave' of Toryism. The reformers' chosen instrument was the Research Department, revived under the control of Butler.

Butler had been the protégé of Neville Chamberlain, the somewhat tidy-minded architect of social reform between the wars, and he had already shown his mettle as a Tory reformer with the epoch-making Education Act of 1944. Butler and David Clarke, his right-hand man, picked a strong team including Iain Macleod, Reginald Maudling, Enoch Powell, and Cuthbert Alport.

However much the 'diehards' resisted the changing nature of Toryism, the tide was against them. Most Conservatives after the war felt that something should be done about the mines and the railways. There was more argument about Labour's plans to nationalize the public utilities, particularly road haulage, but it was only with the iron and steel proposals that the party really dug in hard. Over Labour's welfare programmes, Conservatives complained about their cost and the high rate of progressive taxation that was necessary to finance them. But their attack was handicapped by their appreciation that they themselves would have had to tackle these welfare issues. Churchill himself had planned to make welfare an important part of a post-war Conservative programme.

It was important to show the distinctive but constructive side of Toryism. 'Rab's boys' got on with the job and by the summer of 1947 they were ready with the Industrial Charter – a Conservative statement on the economic and social order emerging under Labour. It was a key post-war indicator of the movement of Conservative thought. The Industrial Charter restated the party's commitment to full employment but it also accepted the need for some central direction from the state in the economy. It criticized Labour's methods of control as conducive to the class war, and there were proposals for greater contractual security for individual workers. The Government and both sides of industry should get together to consider the establishment of 'wage fixing machinery'. Wage levels might, the document thought, 'be kept in proper relationship with productivity, and wage rates between different industries be harmonized'. There was no suggestion, however, that this policy should be anything other than voluntary.

Wage-fixing was and is strong meat to many Conservatives and the Charter certainly went beyond anything that would have been adopted in pre-war years. The *Daily Express* yelped loudly. However, the Charter also criticized the number of controls in force; argued for lower taxation; and, while accepting the nationalization of the Bank of England, coal, and railways, asserted that a Conservative Government would submit the other nationalized industries 'to the test of the highest standards of commercial efficiency'.

Churchill's reaction was not immediately enthusiastic but, after making a few alterations, he approved it and the Shadow Cabinet accepted the document without difficulty. Prominent members of it, like Oliver Lyttelton, Oliver Stanley, and Harold Macmillan, had already helped Butler on his steering committee. At the party conference in October 1947, it was approved by an overwhelming majority; Eden's speech in favour of it revealed his latent social idealism. The Industrial Charter established Butler as a key figure on the Party's social and economic front.

The idea of the Industrial Charter was to give the impression that you could be in favour of free enterprise without trying to do in your neighbour. That is to say that competition is not just a brutal thing for the economy and the idea of free enterprise, which Churchill had preached, you remember: 'Make the People Free', he said. The idea was for us to try and bring in a document which made this look like an unselfish way of conducting the economy and this was of course extremely successful; we had a leader, a first leader, in every paper except the *Daily Herald*.

This got across to the country and we had a very distinguished team, including Harold Macmillan who helped us with his *Middle Way* ideas, Oliver Lyttelton, and many other distinguished back and front benchers. David Eccles was one of them. This particular paper really took the place of what Peel had introduced a century ago in the Tamworth Manifesto and had a wonderful effect of giving a lift to Conservatives of the modern world.

Churchill was, to put it bluntly, a little bit out of touch with some of what you might call the modern tendencies in politics. He didn't exactly ever approve the Industrial Charter but he gave me a dinner at which he put me on his right, which my colleagues thought was a mark of great honour, and we took that to be a tacit approval of what I was doing, although he never vouchsafed it himself. It was after that that we decided to publish it, but it wasn't really until the autumn at the conference that he took a great interest in it. There we had a great resolution on which Maudling moved an amendment and on which I spoke for some length, and we passed that by an enormous majority of thousands. It was then that Churchill sent for me and produced some champagne and said that victory had been won and that my cup was full. So I said I quite agreed and I asked for some more. It was in that sort of tacit way that this very great genius himself acknowledged that we were doing the right thing.

LORD BUTLER

Lunches at the Savoy

Churchill let all this activity continue with apparent good humour. The daily grind of opposition bored him, he found himself in agreement with Ernest Bevin in foreign affairs, and he suffered a great sense of anti-climax after the activity of war. He had always seen himself as a national leader and he showed little concern with the detail of party policy. He clearly doubted its value. For long periods he stayed in the South of France painting, and at Chartwell he wrote *his* history of the Second World War. His friends, men like Brendan Bracken, Lord Beaverbrook, and Oliver Lyttelton, tended not to be mainstream Conservatives.

The organization of the Shadow Cabinet's opposition to legislation left something to be desired. On occasions no one seems to have known quite what brief they were to take; this was partly a consequence of Churchill's determination to keep people on their toes. When Parliament was in session, the life of the Shadow Cabinet was dominated by a fortnightly lunch at Churchill's 'advance battleheadquarters', the Savoy. These have been described as 'heavy', 'gargantuan', 'alcoholic', and 'superb'. Churchill paid for them.

Churchill's infrequent attendance at the House offended many Conservative M.P.s. At the height of Labour's legislative landslide in late 1946, Churchill had to promise stronger opposition tactics to the Conservative back-bench committee (the 1922 Committee).

There was restiveness in other quarters. Late in 1947, Harry Crookshank was host to half a dozen important members of the Shadow Cabinet. Churchill had nominated Eden as his successor in 1942 but Eden, who knew what was afoot, took good care not to be present. The Conservative Chief Whip, James Stuart, was instructed to tell the 'old man' that he should step down. Churchill refused. The 'old man' was seventy-three and, while the energy was still there, some thought him a waning asset in the party battles that were to come. But it needed more than high-level muttering to dislodge Churchill.

Churchill's abiding interest was foreign affairs, and he spent much of the late forties abroad making speeches, many of lasting import. His 'Iron Curtain' speech at Fulton in 1946 was matched by another important pronouncement later that year

Our main meeting in the Shadow Cabinet, which differs slightly today, was a gargantuan lunch at the Savoy Hotel for which, as far as we could see, we were never asked to pay. We assumed that Churchill paid, I don't know otherwise how they met the bill. I remember one day an enormous sweet coming in, which was brought in on an immense tray, and he turned to the waiter and said 'Take this pudding away, it has no theme' and we never saw it again. It evidently was completely wasted unless it was used for the people at night. As the lunches were very powerful, it was rather difficult to get business satisfactorily transacted. We tried very hard with the aid of the Chief Whip of the day to get it done, but it was very much hit and miss.
LORD BUTLER

Ernie Bevin read out a speech at great length without much punctuation and we didn't really know what it was all about. It had a sort of Foreign Office smell about it and we gathered things were very much as they had always been. Oliver Stanley began by the usual compliments: 'We on these benches would like to congratulate the Right Honourable member on the high office to which he has become heir and for the great responsibility which he will surely be able to discharge in the best interests of his country. At least, we on these benches realize that at the beginning he's understood the importance of being Anthony'.
LORD CHANDOS

Plots in Pont Street

at Zurich. There he argued for the establishment of 'a kind of United States of Europe'. A real momentum for a Federal Europe was unleashed. Under Churchill's aegis, but with the organizational drive supplied by his son-in-law, Duncan Sandys, the International Committee of the Movement for European Unity was set up in 1947. It looked as though there would be a strong British lead for one Europe.

In May 1948, the first Congress of Europe met at the Hague. Churchill again championed the European cause and the conference adopted a resolution calling for a European Assembly. A year later the Council of Europe was established at Strasbourg, and there, almost exactly twelve months later, Churchill proposed the 'immediate creation of a European Army under a unified command in which we should all bear a working and honourable part'.

On the face of it, all this added up to a formidable commitment on Churchill's part to some form of European unity. But he spoke only in general terms, and it is now clear than an association of governments was his immediate aim. More might grow

from that, but it was not the 'British way' to indulge in blueprints. In any case Britain had a role and interest elsewhere. Churchill presented that role as the centre, almost the hub, of three overlapping circles, the United States, the Commonwealth, and Europe, and he refused to give priority to any one over the other two.

In 1949, Jean Monnet, then head of French economic planning, proposed an ambitious scheme to merge the French and British economies. The Labour Government turned it down. A year later they prevented the Council of Europe from becoming a fully European parliament; they preferred it to be a consultative body. But Labour's distrust of a federal Europe did not allay French fears of a resurgent Germany. If German heavy industry could be integrated with that of France, Belgium, and Luxembourg, she could never again threaten the peace of Europe, and the link could provide a blueprint for a United Europe. Ideas for this had for some months been under discussion at the Council of Europe, and the French sounded out the Labour Government in the spring of 1950 about British participation. They received an

About six or eight of the chief people met at Harry Crookshank's house in Pont Street and discussed this awkward and important subject. In the absence of Anthony Eden, they came to the – for me – not very attractive conclusion that I was the one who should tell Sir Winston Churchill the bad news – or whatever you like to call it – that the party, the head men of the party, thought that the time had come, perhaps owing to his age, etc, etc, to make a change. I said to Churchill as I went into his room, 'I'm afraid I've got some rather difficult and awkward news to convey to you and I trust it won't annoy you because, as I've said to you before, you've done more than any for this country, and wouldn't you like to have a rest and be able to devote more time to painting?' At which he proceeded to get annoyed and said 'Oh, you've joined those who want to get rid of me have you?' And, I said, 'I haven't in the least, I'm not instigating any plot, but', I said, 'I suppose there is something to be said for the fact that change will have to take place sometime and you're not quite as young as you were', or words to that effect. At which he banged the floor with his stick and got quite annoyed.
LORD STUART

Europe unite?

I don't think Churchill was very interested in being leader of the Opposition after all those years of supreme power. He saw a lot of things being done he didn't approve of, a lot of industries being nationalized. I think he got disillusioned with the House of Commons. He flung himself with immense fervour into the crusade, it amounted to nothing less than that, of forming a united Europe. He formed the United Europe Committee which he asked me to join as a founder member. He went to Zurich and made a great speech in which he described the condition of Western Europe as desperate, and he was right and said the only solution was a European structure in which we could all live in peace and prosperity, and then said a kind of United States of Europe. Then came the Hague conference which was called, at British instigation – the Congress of the Hague in 1948, and that in turn gave rise to the Council of Europe which met in Strasbourg the following year. Churchill asked me to be a delegate, one of the five Conservative delegates. I travelled with him alone from Milan to Strasbourg, a day's journey, and I pressed him very hard on that journey to define precisely what he had meant by United States of Europe. He refused to be drawn. Then he used one phrase which I shall never forget: 'We're not making a machine, we're growing a living plant, and we must wait and see until we understand what this plant turns out to be'. Then changing the metaphor he said 'Nevertheless, we've lit a fire which may blaze or it may go out', and, 'This is most probable, it may die down, the embers may glow and then one day they may spring to light again'. He wouldn't be drawn specifically on the details, but he was very, very keen, and when we got to Strasbourg, he voted in favour of a European political authority with limited functions but real powers. And then, the following year, 1950, he himself proposed to the assembly, the consultative assembly in Strasbourg, the creation of a United European Army under a single Minister of Defence. I think he felt that he might be *that* Minister of Defence.
LORD BOOTHBY

Churchill used to draw three circles on paper for my benefit. The whole point was that one circle, the European circle, and the rest of the world circle, and another one, the Commonwealth circle, all these intersected. The point of the intersection was Great Britain. This was merely his graphic way of saying that whatever the problem was in the world, Great Britain was in it and significant in it. I think he was right.
SIR ROBERT MENZIES

After the Schuman declaration, Jean Monnet and myself went to London to explain the proposal to the British government. The one who was interested and who spoke with us was Sir Stafford Cripps. We explained the aims of this plan and tried to persuade him to join. The question was discussed within the cabinet and we were told after a few days that their decision was negative. The explanation was, they said, that it was very good for all the countries of the continent of Europe who had been defeated or invaded but that the situation was quite different for Britain who had not been defeated, who was still a country with its Commonwealth. They didn't accept the structure of a proposal with the high authority, and the power given to the high authority, nor that the British government would be quite willing to discuss the problems but not on the basis of the Schuman proposal. They added that as they decided that they would not join; they were convinced that we would not go forward.
I am not sure that Bevin and Cripps had a precise understanding of what we meant by 'community'. They certainly hated the idea of having an organization which would have powers in some instances above the national governments. I think that was the crux of the decision.
ETIENNE HIRSCH

One factor in Bevin's turning down of the Schuman plan was the belief that it wouldn't work, but the appearance that Europe was getting together without the Americans might encourage the Americans to reduce their commitment or even to withdraw it. This was a factor in those days, strange as it may seem. Secondly, I think, there was a feeling that Bevin himself had strongly thought that it wouldn't really be internationalization, it would be some sort of racket. I think Bevin himself had been depressed and disappointed by what he saw in the immediate post-war French policy in the French zone of Germany and thought that this would be an extension of it. He was, of course, quite wrong in that. Thirdly, of course, there was an element of doctrinal objection in the Labour Party at the time. The feeling was that the Schuman plan would make nationalization impossible. This proved not to be the case. I think there's no doubt, looking back on it, that Britain made a mistake in not going into the Schuman plan when the chance existed.
DENIS HEALEY

unenthusiastic response. Without hesitation the French Foreign Minister, Robert Schuman, launched on 9 May a plan to pool the coal and steel resources of France and Germany.

The world was startled and Bevin was provoked to immediate, if private, criticism. Attlee was more circumspect. After several diplomatic exchanges he announced that Britain would take no part in discussions on the plan and that they had no alternative to offer. From Labour came a remarkable statement, inspired by Dalton, which made it clear that there could be no thought of European co-operation except on a basis of socialism. Macmillan begged Churchill to give a lead; he did, and with varying degrees of acceptance, the Conservative Party followed. Eden, too, attacked the Government, recalling NATO and the other organizations to which Britain had committed herself 'without regarding them as incompatible with our sovereignty or with our position as the heart and centre of the British Empire and Commonwealth'. Edward Heath, then a young back-bencher, made a strong pro-European speech.

But the Labour Government were adamant; steel was about to be nationalized and they had no wish to see it pass under the supranational authority that Schuman proposed. When the European Coal and Steel Community came into being, the British were not included. E.C.S.C. set the pattern and the device by which Europe would move towards union: it was the first example of the community method.

Churchill himself was responsible for provoking a second European initiative. His proposal for a European army was taken up by the French Prime Minister, Pleven. Western European governments learned with relief of America's decision in September 1950 to create a defence force in Western Europe to give teeth to the Atlantic pact. But they were uneasily aware that the condition for her action was a German contribution to this force. The Labour Government reluctantly acquiesced, but the French were desperately worried.

Pleven, acting under traditional fears of German rearmament and revanchism, sought to apply the community principle to defence. E.D.C. – the European Defence Community – was the military counterpart of E.C.S.C. But as European schemes for federation gathered pace, so did electoral politics. With Labour's overall majority cut to six, the Opposition was in striking distance of victory. The pace of life in the Conservative Party quickened.

The 1950 intake of Conservative M.P.s was not only large, but most of them bore the stamp of the party's post-war commitment to a broad pattern of social concern. From the ranks of 'Rab's boys', Macleod, Maudling, Powell, and Alport made their débuts. Among other 'post-war minds' were Edward Heath, Robert Carr, Edward Boyle, Charles Hill, and Angus Maude. Many of the brighter spirits formed the 'One Nation Group' which stressed, in advance of official party policy, the positive side of the Tory alternative. They argued that it was not part of the purpose of the state to provide services that individuals could provide for themselves. Needs, and not means, was their byword. They argued that some means-tested charges should be applied, for example on hospital board and prescriptions, in order to spend more freely on the areas of real hardship that survived. At first they had scant support; an interesting indication of how far the leadership had accepted Labour's achievement.

The rank and file, too, were demanding something more positive than complaints about austerity and nationalization. At the 1950 party conference a revolt from the floor forced the platform to pledge themselves to the building of 300,000 houses a year. The experts said this was impossible because of the shortage of raw materials, particularly timber. But it was an astute political move. Labour's housing programme had reached its peak in 1948 and had then dropped to 178,000 a year. This was nothing like enough to meet the acute shortage, but Labour were forced to regard it as a secondary priority to industrial building. Prefabs were still in use long after their occupiers had been led to expect better.

The Conservatives expected an election at any moment. It only needed four Labour members to be unable to vote for the Government to be defeated, and the increasing pressure of events both inside and outside Parliament led Attlee to gamble on an election in October 1951. The fight was bound to be close. Despite the first television party political broadcast, this was the last election about the political issues of the 1930s. The campaign was a good deal tougher than the preceding year. It was marked particularly by the warmongering scare put about by the *Daily Mirror*. Their campaign, 'Whose finger on the trigger?' was directed at Churchill and his tough talk over Abadan. On the other hand, Churchill, though

One more heave

The pressure of the Finance Bill that summer did the trick. I can remember, it seems fantastic now, we had an amendment on the entertainments duty where we were beaten at 11.30 at night by 293 votes to 287. It was absolutely ceaseless pressure, literally night after night. In one or two instances we sat all through from Thursday down to Friday midday, then from Monday 2.30 down to 10 a.m. on Tuesday morning. It was that that made Attlee feel he couldn't continue any longer and, of course, from the Conservative point of view it was very important that the election did come at the end of 1951 and not a year later. But there's no doubt at all that politically it would have paid Attlee to have stayed on longer.

LORD BOYLE

We had a public meeting at Liverpool. Churchill arrived at about half past seven and he sat down, left his hat on, didn't speak to anybody, just slumped in the chair, and after about ten minutes he started to mumble. 'Even if we win,' he said, 'I don't think we can get it right.' Then we went into the stadium and Churchill made his speech, was a bit ponderous, wasn't very lively, but of course everybody loved him at that time so it didn't make much difference. And then we went back to the Adelphi Hotel for a supper party. Winston must either have had a bath or some sort of refreshment in his own private rooms and when he reappeared he was quite a different man from what he'd been before, and he started eating. He had three helpings of oysters, followed by beef steak and Lord knows what, and a fair amount of brandy. While he was consuming all this he was conducting a non-stop monologue. I remember at one point I ventured to try to get a word in when I thought the process of mastication would have to stop for a moment, but I was wrong. I think I'd said two words when he turned to David Maxwell Fyfe (later Lord Kilmuir), who was a Liverpool Tory MP, and he said to Fyfe, 'a large brandy' and then he turned to me and gave me a withering look so that was the end of me, I shut up. A little later on David Fyfe kept looking at his watch and then said 'We've only got ten minutes for the midnight train'. Churchill said 'There's a telephone here, ring them up and tell them to hold it for half an hour'.

REGINALD BEVINS

The big point to me is that the leadership was already historical, it was already divided from all of us by the gulf, not of war, we'd been in the war, but by the fact that it had been the wartime leadership, the wartime victor; and Churchill's position placed government at a distance – politically, psychologically, and personally – in the sense that they didn't know us, which is perhaps unusual.

ENOCH POWELL

bellicose about the 'excesses' of socialism, was extremely conciliatory on domestic policy. He denounced Labour leaders' claims that the Conservatives were going to turn the clock back thirty years.

Churchill was elected with an overall majority of 17. He was 76, and had already suffered one serious stroke. As in the war, his first gesture was to make himself Minister of Defence. But significantly, he had to give the job up within six months. Churchill knew he faced a major economic crisis, and he was by no means confident of his ability to handle it. He needed a Chancellor who could handle the run on sterling without resorting to harsh social measures at home.

The most obvious choice was Oliver Lyttelton, (Lord Chandos), the party's spokesman on economic affairs after Oliver Stanley's death in 1950. But Lyttelton had an aggressive parliamentary manner, was a strong advocate of free enterprise – he was a successful businessman in his own right – and, perhaps unfairly, was thought to represent the old guard of the party. He was acknowledged to be one of the few Conservatives who could stand up to Churchill, but he was not widely liked by the party in the Commons. Churchill felt that he represented too one-sided a view of economics and that he would give the impression that welfare policies were to be axed. Instead Churchill chose Butler.

Despite the distrust Churchill felt for Butler's judgement – Butler was a man of Munich, had fought Churchill over India and had been, Churchill believed, a man of peace in 1940 – he needed him in 1951. The first paper Churchill read on resumption of office was a Treasury minute on the financial situation which forecast the exhaustion of Britain's reserves. Politically, what was needed was a moderate hand. But Churchill also appointed a ministerial advisory committee to watch over Butler. The Prime Minister was anxious to heal the wounds inflicted by pre-war Toryism; he had had it made brutally clear to him in the summer of 1945 just how damaging the Conservative label was. If that were not to happen again, class antagonisms must not be provoked and Butler seemed the embodiment of moderation.

Almost as important was his choice as Minister of Labour – Sir Walter Monckton, an old friend and lawyer, a man of no obvious and public Conservative sympathy. Monckton was a conciliator *par excellence* and Churchill wanted to be quite

Oiling the works

I had been Chairman of the Finance Committee after Oliver Stanley died and I had no idea what office I was to be offered. I went upstairs to Winston's bedroom. He was in bed and he had the look of a sea captain who had just come out of a very heavy storm and was glad to be in harbour again, tired, but there he was; so he said, 'I've thought a great deal about the Treasury, but I have come to the conclusion on the whole that I will send Rab there if he will take it. I want you to be Minister of Materials and Reconstruction.' So I said 'I'll do that, if you like, but only for a short time, because it really is not a man's job and I've had experience of being Minister of Production; it means continual war with the departments. It's possible when you have the sanction of war and security but in peace time to take on the Admiralty on Wednesday, the Board of Trade on Friday and the Home Office on Tuesday is just not on, but if you would like me to do that, I will do it, but not for long.' So he said, 'Are you disappointed in not being Chancellor?' And I said 'Yes, I think I am, but at any rate I can see a short end to my ministerial life' and with that I made for the door, and he said 'Well, my dear, would you like to go to the Colonial Office?' So I said 'Well, I would because I think it is a terrific job and I think we're going to lose Malaya, a country which I know very well, unless something pretty drastic is done about the whole thing, and I'll take that on with pleasure.'
LORD CHANDOS

When I first went to see Churchill when he became Prime Minister again, he was lying in bed smoking an enormous cigar, with a cat on his feet acting as a hot water bottle. He said 'You will be very surprised to see your name opposite the list of offices.' I was very surprised, of course, to be made Chancellor in 1951 because Lyttelton was my superior both in age and knowledge of finance. And Oliver Stanley, you see, would have probably been made Chancellor, but he had died in 1950. So I came in quite young. I was only 49.
LORD BUTLER

Churchill said to me, 'In the war I knew what to do – it's not always easy to do, but I knew what to do, I can always see my way – but since I've read the Treasury's minute since we've come into power I'm appalled by the economic situation of which we are the heirs. I don't know, I can't see my way into these things at the moment, infinitely complicated and some of them on subjects which will have to be explored by experts and I don't see the way. I expect we shall find it but at this moment, this morning, I really am staggered by the size of the task.'
LORD CHANDOS

All through his life it had been Churchill's line to win and then to conciliate, and I think it was wholly in keeping that having at last beaten Labour, and by not much of a majority won the 1951 election, he then wanted to conciliate. He was genuinely very worried about the economic situation he found. It seemed extremely threatening at the end of 1951. He'd never had the experience of gold and dollar reserves falling by 300,000,000 dollars a month, really an enormous fall. And I think his whole mood was one of trying to pursue a national policy. I suspect in any case Butler would have had the Exchequer. I may be wrong there, but I think it was more likely, although Butler and Churchill were not very close. None the less, Churchill had a very genuine respect for the work Butler had done on policy after 1945, and certainly, of course, over labour matters Sir Walter Monckton was exactly the sort of appointment Churchill wanted. I think one can think of several other appointments which he made intending to give as much of a national image to his government as possible.
LORD BOYLE

We all expected that Sir David Maxwell Fyfe, who had been the Shadow Minister of Labour, would go as Minister of Labour, but this didn't turn out to be. Churchill, surprisingly, appointed Walter Monckton to go there and I think Walter Monckton's brief – and I was his Parliamentary Private Secretary – was to be conciliatory towards the unions: to try and show that the first post-war Conservative government could work amicably and efficiently and smoothly with the much more powerful trade unions which emerged in the post-war world. The very first day that I reported to his office as his PPS, I was rather staggered when he told me that he was there purely to conciliate and to keep the peace but that he was expendable, and if a real row broke out and we had a major strike, his head would fall.
LORD ORR-EWING

We believed that people should have, as far as possible, a choice of how they should spend their own money, a choice of how they should live their lives, and all these things were interfering with the liberty of the individual. The liberty of the individual is one of the Tory doctrines which cannot be pulled about by anybody and so Churchill started doing it, and you will see if you look at the regulations which were cancelled, they were as big as a telephone book.
LORD CHANDOS

sure that the union leaders would not be antagonized. Some Tories were less happy about this appointment and Monckton was privately referred to as 'that old oil can'. The tougher David Maxwell-Fyfe had been the most likely choice: he was given the Home Office.

In choosing the rest of his Cabinet, Churchill hankered after coalition and harked back to the war years. He wanted an Asquith from the great Liberal family for his Lord Chancellor, and got another Liberal, Gwilym Lloyd George, for his Minister of Food; but failed to persuade other Liberals. Familiar figures from the war, like Ismay, Woolton, Leathers, and Cherwell reappeared and there were further overtones of the war in Churchill's abortive attempt to make them supervising overlords. Churchill's chosen successor, Eden, insisted on returning to the Foreign Office rather than take up a supervisory role on the home front. Macmillan, to his gloomy surprise, went to Housing to build the 300,000 houses pledged at the 1950 conference. 'It is a gamble,' Churchill said, 'it will make or mar your political career.' There were suprisingly few orthodox Conservatives in the Cabinet: Lord Salisbury and Harry Crookshank were the most obvious. In his Private Office too, Churchill surrounded himself with old friends, with Jock Colville as his principal private secretary.

Butler bypassed 'those old battle-axes' his Cabinet overseers, Lords Swinton and Woolton, but quickly proved himself more ruthless than Gaitskell in dealing with the economic situation. Butler's most valuable weapon was his power to cut imports: import prices, artificially inflated by the Korean war, were at the root of the balance of payments crisis. With three chops in almost as many months, imports were cut back by £600 million and the foreign travel allowance was cut to £25. Hire purchase was further restricted, the bank rate was pushed up, and in a dramatic step that made nonsense of free enterprise – the Notification of Vacancies Order – employers were prevented from taking the initiative in filling jobs. Even the rearmament programme for which Churchill had pressed was severely pruned. In three months Butler had introduced a note of Crippsian austerity.

So serious was the position that the Treasury, with support from the Bank of England, had considered letting the exchange rate of the pound 'float'. Nobody was under any illusion that this would mean down – a *de facto* devaluation. The Commonwealth countries, all large holders of sterling, were ready to agree. The Chancellor, briefed by Oliver Lyttelton, put the plan up, and Budget Day was advanced in readiness for a decision. But 'Operation Robot', as it was called, never saw the light of day. Lord Cherwell had the Prime Minister's ear and the plan was quashed – shortly before the budget. Its devotees, rebuffed but unsure that Churchill's heart had been in the rejection, returned to the attack once the budget was over. Yet once again, Churchill's uneasy role as 'His Master's Voice' – a contemporary reference to Cherwell's great influence over the Prime Minister – was decisive. 'Robot' was finally buried in June.

Butler had won himself room to manoeuvre. With great acumen, he sensed that the inflationary tide was slowing and that deflationary measures would hit production and employment. Adroitly, he gave an appearance of activity, cutting back food subsidies and, balancing that, increasing welfare payments and reducing income tax. The Labour Party howled at the first proposal, but they listened in growing silence as good news followed. An Excess Profits Levy, suggested by Churchill to mitigate profits made from the rearmament boom, emphasized Conservative classlessness, and a rise in the bank rate reassured foreign bankers. The recipe proved, if anything, a bit severe, but to compound Butler's good fortune import prices began to fall.

For three years, Butler was able to indulge his preference for economic expansion. It was a remarkable turnaround. From early 1952 to the late part of 1954, the trend in import prices was on his side; they fell by a quarter. In effect, this gave Britain an extra £400 million to spend abroad each year without anyone having to lift a finger. The export drive no longer seemed necessary and increases in production were absorbed by a rapidly expanding home market. Domestic consumption rose dramatically; consumer subsidies and controls could now be eliminated without risk.

In his remaining budgets, Butler was able to take another shilling off income tax, to cut purchase tax, and to provide incentives for investment. By 1954 he was able to talk of doubling the standard of living in twenty years, although only a few months later he lengthened it to 'twenty-five'. Had the situation continued, he would have been right by a very comfortable margin. It looked and was

Rab's red box

When I was asked to be Chancellor, I was asked to do two things. One was to bring in an Excess Profits Levy and the other was to build 300,000 houses, both of which were a great strain on the Exchequer. The Excess Profits Levy was brought in by Churchill himself, backed by Eden, because they had in their minds the idea that the building of arms at that time in the post-Korea period was a very great strain on the economy and was bringing a great deal of profit to private people. Churchill was impressed by the American model of the Excess Profits Levy and he didn't remember that Maynard Keynes had warned in the years before that this was a tax on enterprise and, as Maynard Keynes said, 'a tax on you'. However, I introduced it as I was ordered to and it only lasted two years and then I withdrew it. The Excess Profits Levy and the 300,000 houses were a great strain and eventually led to a certain amount of inflation.

LORD BUTLER

I talked to Butler a lot about the floating pound. I wouldn't like to say I persuaded him or anything like that, because he's not the sort of man who takes ready-made opinions from colleagues. At any rate we were at that time more or less in agreement that we should have a floating pound. This was knocked down I think very largely by Lord Cherwell, who I had a very high opinion of and who was a great friend of mine, but frankly as an economist I think he was a disaster. He immediately assumed that a floating pound meant that your imports were going to cost more and your exports were going to be equally indemnified.

LORD CHANDOS

I think the secret of my first budget in 1952 is this: I did so much before the budget ever came in, that I was able in the budget to give certain concessions, which is rather extraordinary considering that in the autumn of 1951 the gold was draining away to such an extent that it would have ruined the British economy. What I did was to cut imports: I cut over £350 million worth of imports before the year was out and another lot in January. Now that is no longer the fashion, you are not supposed now to be able to cut imports because the idea is that you are frightened of retaliation. I did cut expenditure and the combination of cutting imports and cutting expenditure gave me a certain amount of leeway in the budget of 1952. But then in the budget of 1952 I cut the food subsidies by about £160 million. That was a great shock at the time because we were all subsidized as to our food to the tune of about £300 million and I cut over half of that in one budget. Then I gave away the surplus to income tax payers, old age pensioners, and people in need. That's what made the budget of '52 such a symphony, if I may so describe it, and one which rather perplexed the Opposition at the time.

LORD BUTLER

We were anxious certainly to give more opportunity to people in their private lives, less burden of taxation, less burden of government interferences. But it wasn't as simple as that. We were there trying to recreate an England which would be in tune with the post-war period, something which would combine government assistance, government leadership, authoritative leadership from the official circles, and a strong social policy, so that we would never have to go through what for us in our younger days was a terrible period of unemployment before 1939. And in Parliament, I think, for all of us, the principal fear, though not many of us ourselves had suffered from that particular social disaster, was the fear that we would see it again. I mean we were determined, whatever the policies might be, that this sort of phenomenon would never appear in this country while we were responsible for the political leadership.

LORD ALPORT

A taste of freedom

I had a great opportunity, which you haven't got nowadays, in that everything was war-controlled. My first task, over the first two years, was to liberate some of these controls. I remember, for example, freeing meat from the ration, and making a speech in Gloucester when I said: 'You've been burning most of your books of ration cards . . .' It was no longer usual to talk about 'snoopers' and 'spivs' because we wanted to free the economy. The other thing is that by encouraging the relief of taxation, I encouraged expansion. I had probably the best expansion that has occurred since. I don't think we ever had such good expansion in the economy as in 1953 and 1954.

LORD BUTLER

On one occasion Churchill asked that the food ration for the week should be set out so that he could see what people really had, and to his horror it was brought in on one small tray – the entire rations for one week – and it was the kind of thing he would normally have expected to have for a rather small breakfast. He was a great believer in red meat. I remember him saying that the slogan for the Conservatives should be houses and meat and not getting scuppered. And then he went on to say that perhaps under the circumstances prevailing, not going broke was going to be even more important.

JOCK COLVILLE

I remember so well the time when we were going to decontrol eggs and the popular press was saying eggs were going to be a shilling each for the poor people in the country. This was splashed about the place and Winston came to me and said 'Oh, my poor people, they cannot pay a shilling for eggs.' I said, 'They won't have to pay a shilling for eggs, Prime Minister. Let us decontrol them and you'll find the eggs will emerge out of the ground.' After a lot of argument and much discussion, both inside and outside the cabinet, the decision was taken to decontrol eggs. Well, from that moment onwards eggs appeared from everywhere, eggs were reduced in price as the months went by and there has never been a shortage of eggs since. He took an enormous interest in the food for the people of the country and one year, at the time when I was Minister, when it looked as if there was going to be a shortage of potatoes, he got into a very great state of mind about this. I assured him that there wouldn't be a shortage of potatoes and he gave me such a look that I realized if there had been a shortage of potatoes, I'd have been for it; but there wasn't and he accepted it. But his interest in the well-being of the people in the country was very real and very genuine.

LORD CRATHORNE

a period of great buoyancy. This new-found confidence in traditional 'market place economics' made a profound impression on those Tory M.P.s who had long resented the parsimony of controls.

The last rationing, symbolically of meat, finally disappeared in July 1954. The date displays the caution of the Conservatives and a certain amount of political skill. Too much, too soon would have been disastrous. Memories of Cripps taking sweets off the ration early in 1949 only to put them back on six months later were strong. Churchill was worried that the premature derationing of eggs would force up prices. There was anxiety too over sugar, but the political pressure was great and the economic situation did not justify continued delay. Nevertheless, the Minister of Food, Gwilym Lloyd George, had to be pressed hard to deration, although with world prices running in Britain's favour there was no reason to fear additional food imports. 'Conservative freedom' could be made to work and the party's political desires gratified by a surrender to public pressures, possibly too soon in the case of building controls, which, when removed, in November 1954, marked the disappearance of the last traces of wartime control.

Still closer to the political heart of the Conservative Party was the question of denationalization. They were pledged to denationalize steel and allow private road hauliers to return to business. Despite that, there were rows in Cabinet and growing pressure from back-benchers to hasten up legislation. One senior minister, with an interest in economic problems, was against any reversal: 'The high theory of the British Constitution is', he observed, 'always to put one foot in front of the other and never to take a step backward.' There were serious practical difficulties, particularly over steel.

When the idea of a quick solution was abandoned, it took all the business experience of certain members of the Cabinet committee on steel to overcome the pervading air of caution and produce a workable, if complicated, solution. In the upshot, steel was denationalized with a substantial measure of continuing government control. British Road Services, another prime target for denationalization, was dismantled. It was by no means a complete reversal of Labour plans.

Butler seemed to have found 'some golden law of progress'. Each year appeared better than the last and Labour forecasts of doom proved hope-

lessly wrong. Unemployment remained low, and cuts in taxation did not lead to reductions in welfare. Gaitskell found Butler so much his successor that the *Economist* coined the phrase 'Butskellism'. The Conservatives and their opponents had reached a substantial central area of agreement, that had enlarged steadily since 1939, and growing feelings of ideological claustrophobia were forcing both Left and Right outside the centre ground demarcated by 'Mr Butskell'. Some doubted whether it would be the same when the boom ended.

Butler's own doubts were principally caused by wage settlements. Monckton had been told by Churchill on his appointment as Minister of Labour to avoid strikes. It was not easy. Prices in the wake of devaluation and the Korean war had risen by 17 per cent between October 1950 and May 1952. The pressure for wage increases was on. Wherever possible Monckton referred the unions to a Court of Enquiry, but this became a pseudonym for concession. All too often Monckton settled direct.

In 1953 and 1955, he made a settlement with the railwaymen that forced the Transport Commission to contravene their statutory requirement to break even. He was acting with Churchill's full encouragement and behind Butler's back. The Prime Minister would brook no interference. He was out to salve his own and the Conservative Party's tarnished reputation as the enemies of organized labour. Moreover, he assiduously cultivated three right-wing leaders of major unions, Arthur Deakin, Will Lawther, and Tom William-

Walter Monckton was a brilliant choice for Minister of Labour because he had this patient legal brain which he could apply to these disputes. But one of the weaknesses of my time as Chancellor of the Exchequer was that we really had no wages policy. Wages were very often settled by Churchill and Monckton working together. I remember one morning when I came to my office, Churchill sent for me and said 'Never mind, old cock, we settled the rail strike last night without deciding to keep you up – on *their* terms.' And that is very typical of what happened at the time of Walter Monckton and Winston Churchill working together. Of course the reward was that we had very good industrial relations; the difficulty was that the inflation came in 1955, which I really couldn't avoid.

In 1954 I did nothing in the budget and was extremely cautious because I was worried about the state of the economy and Winston, of course, was very disapproving. He thought I ought to have given a lot away and said that I had no initiative or drive, but I determined that I wouldn't do anything in 1954.
LORD BUTLER

I think Butler was an outstandingly good Chancellor in the 1951 to '55 Parliament. I think the general conduct of economic policy in the '51 Parliament was extremely good. Looking back on it I think it was so successful between '51 and '54 but possibly we carried on the same line just too far. I think the complete scrapping of building control in October 1954 was probably premature, and I think there was certainly a good case for saying we shouldn't have pruned taxation again so much in the spring of '55. For the first three years I think Butler was an outstandingly good Chancellor of the Exchequer and showed impeccable good judgement.
LORD BOYLE

A pledge fulfilled

In 1951 everyone was saying – including the Tory quality papers – that all this idea of setting the people free was nonsensical and couldn't be done. Macmillan was given this job of building 300,000 houses. He did it, and trailing along were people like Lloyd George, who was Minister of Food but who had no idea whatever of food derationing until Harold Macmillan told him in a very forthright way that if he could do it with housing, he could do it with food. The thing spread from Harold Macmillan right through the government ministries.

Macmillan was a worker and he worked all the hours God sent. He inspired everyone in the Ministry to pull out all the stops. I think he saw Sir Thomas Sheepshanks, who was the Permanent Secretary, about two or three times and he used to refer to him as 'the Bishop', I don't know why quite. Macmillan decided quickly that Sheepshanks was too leisurely for him, and within no time Dame Evelyn Sharpe was effectively Permanent Secretary.

I think Sheepshanks was still in his large room overlooking Whitehall for quite some time, but nobody took any notice of him, and of course Macmillan did cut corners as well in a big way. When there was a bit of a tussle in cabinet as to whether he wasn't stretching our economic resources by building too many houses, he persuaded Churchill to leave it to him to argue it out with Rab Butler. Macmillan had, I think, about three nocturnal talks with Rab. I remember the last occasion very vividly. He had a drink with me in the smoking room at about midnight, which was rather late, and then he went off to see Rab and said would I wait for him. He came down at 2 o'clock into the smoking room and bought me a drink and said 'It's all over, Reg, I've got my own way, and I simply report to the Prime Minister that Rab has agreed with me.' Rab was tired; Macmillan had more stamina.

REGINALD BEVINS

son. They remembered Monckton as one of the best ministers they had ever had to deal with, and this was more than a tribute to his strong sense of fair play.

Butler was further upset by the demands of the housing drive. Macmillan had assured himself of Churchill's support and he prosecuted his demands ruthlessly on the Exchequer and the Civil Service. Macmillan on the move had been an almost forgotten phenomenon since his days in Algiers during the war with the Americans and the French where he became '*de facto* Viceroy of the Mediterranean'. He organized the Ministry on a war footing. He recreated the Ministry's regional machinery and set up industrial planning boards which brought builders and civil servants together. At the Ministry itself he brought in two energetic and self-made businessmen – Percy Mills and Ernest Marples – much to the horror of the Civil Service. He shunted Sir Thomas Sheepshanks, the Permanent Secretary, off to one side and gave his orders to Dame Evelyn Sharp, a more dynamic Deputy Secretary. Reginald Bevins became his P.P.S.

Macmillan got the bricks to the sites. He started to fulfill ambitious programmes for the New Towns inaugurated under Labour, and, unlike earlier experiments, he saw to it that the pubs in them were built first and not last. But it was not all straightforward: the Treasury was worried about expensive imports like timber and bricks, and despite an increasingly buoyant economic situation, there were still widespread shortages. Even so, Macmillan's organizing capacity was more than sufficient to cope, but he rightly paid tribute to Dalton for designing the smaller house which, quickly and economically built by local authorities, was one answer.

From 1 November 1952 to 31 October 1953, 301,000 houses had been built. By the end of 1954, houses were being built at the rate of 350,000 a year. This was much more than a statistic, it represented not only living space, but a home, where the frustrations of post-war overcrowding gave place to a more settled home life.

In February 1952 George VI died. He had been much more a people's king than most, sharing the Blitz and something of their post-war austerities. The accession of a new Elizabeth gave rise to hopes of a fresh Elizabethan age. From the vantage point of 1953, there was much that was good about

life in Britain: wages were rising sharply both in money and in real terms. There was little need to spend more on food; the extra went on consumer durables, symbols for a new age. Already there were complaints that more than 1,000,000 licensed new cars would bring chaos to the roads; the number of television licences quadrupled bringing the 'idiot's lantern' to a third of British homes. The Coronation service itself became the first great event of the age of television. Less dramatic but equally tangible signs of the national prosperity were to be found in the growing number of homes with a vacuum cleaner and a washing machine. The age of affluence had begun.

More symbolic events kindled a sense of national well-being and Churchill, although he could scarcely claim the credit, brooded over them like some symbol of the glorious past, transmitting present prosperity into an equally glorious future. Some remembered Melbourne guiding the young Victoria, others found Benjamin Britten's opera *Gloriana* closer to their aspirations. John Grigg, an astringent critic of nostalgia, found himself Editor of the *New Elizabethan*. Older figures seemed to take on fresh life. Gordon Richards piloted Pinza to a Derby victory; Stanley Matthews brought Blackpool from the brink of defeat to victory in the Cup final – and his only winner's medal; for the first time since before the war an Englishman won a Grand Prix. More important still, the Ashes were captured in an orgy of public participation; Denis Compton made the winning hit. The crowning glory was the announcement on the morning of Coronation Day that Everest had been conquered.

There were more concrete achievements to record, promising much, but in the end disappointing. In the air the Hawker Hunter and the Swift duelled for the world speed record. The Comet airliner led the world to a new age of passenger transport; the tragic crashes in the Mediterranean in 1954 soured its triumph. Britain led in the peaceful uses of atomic power; the R.A.F. even convinced the Americans that they should buy British with the Canberra bomber. Jaguar's triumphs at Le Mans provoked a boom for British sports cars across the world; Rover pioneered the gas turbine car. But, symptomatic again, only a few noticed Britain's failure to match the German Volkswagen in the field of popular cars.

A new age?

I think when people hope for a sort of historical repeat performance it nearly always turns out to be a false hope. That's to say when people expect a second Elizabethan age, looking back very much to the first, this is almost certain to be disappointing because one has to create something new. You can't have that kind of repeat performance, and in the particular atmosphere of the early fifties I think there was a great element of make-believe and self-delusion on the part of us all. There was a great deal of genuine and good sentiment, associated with the Coronation, for instance. A lot of that sentiment was perfectly good sentiment, but some of it was make-believe; the same I think is true of the attitude towards Churchill when he came back to power. I think there was a great deal of indiscriminate feeling towards him. He'd become an ancient tribal chieftain and people didn't bother to consider him for what he really was. He'd become a totemistic figure; in fact he'd presided over what was in many ways a very efficient and very effective government, but he wasn't judged for what he really was and the whole thing produced an artificial atmosphere.

JOHN GRIGG

NO. 17,790   THREE HALFPENCE

Dail

great day dawns—a

THE CR○

EVERE

Edward Hillary

on the top

MOUNT EVEREST has been co has flown on the 29,002ft. p tore it to shreds. Nature's grea Coronation morning.

Two attempts to reach the peak failed. The final bid was made a few days ago by Mr. Edward Hillary, a 34-year-old New Zealand bee-keeper, and the great Sherpa climber Tensing.

From their lonely camp they had abou 1,500ft. to climb, each step, each breath a agony — even to think an unbelievable strain.

They would not be denied — just a Captain Cook, Francis Drake, or Captain Scot would not be denied. What a triumphan moment it must have been to stand on top o the world.

They have returned to safety and reported t Colonel John Hunt, 42-year-old ex-Commando who lea the expedition, that Everest, unconquerable Everest, tamed at last.

'IT COULD NOT BE BETTER FOR THE CORONATION '

Their feat was achieved with only hours to spare

(second column fragments)

EATER
RY

JUNE 2, 1953.

ment

h ever rode to
n with such
ings as these
d her realms.

d and written
w Elizabethan
ng with our
's reign. The
the far-off
of an epic
gloriously in
adventurings
lizabethans.

allant men of
s have pitted
skill, and en-
st the awful
Everest. That
of the world
m all till now.

Queen's flag
ic quality of
's men that
at last sub-

n, though
nd organised,
l an Empire
d the peak
by a young
er, EDWARD
mpanied by
i d Sherpa

nd share the
and kin in
must feel in
perb accom-

here is news to make it the GREATEST

WNING GLORY—
ST CONQUERED

ants the Queen's flag
the world

ed by Britain.   A Union Jack
til the cruel Himalayan wind
ze belongs to the Queen this

**THE MAN
WHO
DID IT**

He keeps bees

500,000 WAIT
ON KERBSIDE
ALL NIGHT

London sees its most
amazing scenes

Daily Mail Reporters

LONDON was one vast camp of Coronatio
sightseers this morning, and more tha
half a million people were lining the route, fil
ing every front-row view for today's grea
procession.

Just before midnight Trafalgar-square wa
a tangled mass of traffic, sightseers, ar
campers-out.

Buses, cars, and motor-cycles were jammed roun
Nelson's Column. Five rows of traffic stretched acro
Trafalgar-square away into the Strand.

Over the noise of this multitude could be heard t
cheering, and singing of "Land of Hope and Glory," fr
thousands more surging round the walls of Buckingh
Palace. To cries of "We want the Queen" there w
added the blare of car horns.

Tradition and expectation came together in the Coronation. To triumphant fanfares the young Queen was crowned to an age-old ritual. Past greatness was reflected in the review of the Imperial fleet. To both ceremonies came a brash newcomer – television. The Coronation film with its hushed, reverent commentary became a world best seller.

It was especially popular in America, but some Englishmen there watched it with a very professional eye. Shortly before the actual crowning, the American networks had a commercial break. The figure of J. Fred Muggs loomed large on the screen selling goods. J. Fred Muggs was a chimpanzee. This juxtaposition of banal and sublime offended the B.B.C's representatives in America, who informed their superiors of this tasteless absurdity.

What prompted this sensitive eye on American television was the battle being fought in Britain over the introduction of commercial television. The question divided the Conservative Party: those who saw it as part of a free-enterprise crusade were ranged against an establishment belief that commercialism was as serious a threat to English values as socialism. Back-bench unrest and suspicion at the slow pace of denationalization and decontrol played into the hands of those who wanted the change. The way had already been charted by Selwyn Lloyd's dissenting report from the Beveridge Commission on Broadcasting in 1951. He had argued that the only safeguard on 'the brute force of monopoly' was competition. This was a gift to the impatient young turks who wanted to expand private enterprise. They had allies in high places.

Woolton, Chairman of the Conservative Party, was close to Churchill's ear. He had built his business reputation as a salesman, believed in the free market, and was politically suspicious of the B.B.C.'s record in current affairs. Back-benchers directly connected with radio and television manufacturing or with advertising linked with more theoretical advocates of free enterprise under the energetic leadership of John Profumo and Ian Orr-Ewing. From outside Parliament the campaign was led by a formidable trio: Norman Collins, once tipped as head of B.B.C. Television, who had now left their employ; Sir Robert Renwick, a stockbroker with considerable interest in the electrical industry; and C. O. Stanley, the creator of Pye. From within the Conservative Central Office, Mark Chapman Walker, an expert in advertising, co-ordinated their efforts.

Within months of the Conservatives' victory, a back-bench study group under Profumo reported in favour of breaking the B.B.C. monopoly, and the Government were pressurized into publishing a White Paper whose details were thrashed out between a small team of back-benchers and Lords Salisbury and Woolton for the Government. The compromise consisted of a deal to break the television monopoly only. Radio, still the most important broadcasting medium, was left to the B.B.C. The debates which followed revealed the doubts many Conservatives had about the direct sponsorship of programmes, and the Labour party declared itself against the proposal.

The B.B.C. mounted a counter-attack, canvassing as a last resort the possibility of two public service corporations. Christopher Mayhew, dubbed by his Conservative opponents, 'the honourable Member for Lime Grove' (where the B.B.C. TV studios were), formed an anti-commercial lobby, the National Television Council, to which he skilfully recruited influential non-party and Conservative figures. The commercial lobby countered with the Popular Television Association who adroitly deployed contemporary figures ranging from the Test cricketer Alec Bedser, to the historian, A.J.P. Taylor.

Woolton's decisive move was to get the matter on the agenda of the Conservative conference in October 1953, and, predictably, a large majority voted down monopoly. Churchill did not like the measure, and was appalled when Central Office brought out a pamphlet entitled 'There's Free Speech! Why not Free Switch?' But few in his Cabinet had strong feelings, and much of the force of the case against the proposal was destroyed by Norman Collins's suggestion that an Independent Television Authority should control and enfranchise the commercial companies. This compromise was piloted through the Lords by another staunch supporter, the Lord Chancellor Kilmuir (formerly Sir David Maxwell-Fyfe). The more paternalist and traditionally minded Tory peers, led by Halifax and Hailsham, fought a desperate rearguard action but the Tory party was no longer theirs. A group of younger men had pulled off a remarkable coup. The old Tory image of a paternalist squirearchy was never the same again.

At almost the same time, Conservative resentment at the apparatus of state control boiled over in a more traditional direction. Crichel Down is a

Independent or commercial?

When we first became a government in 1951 we were unable to move nearly as fast as we hoped. We had, after all, been elected on 'Set the People Free', and that first Christmas rationing was tighter than ever. We were on one egg a week, two ounces of meat every week, and even in the later fifties we still weren't able to move as fast and as far as we wanted to.

Here was a field in television where we could go and where we could introduce some competition. We were prepared to give up sound because we felt then that television was a really important medium of the future with a tremendous growth. Many of us felt that the BBC was going far too slowly in grasping the opportunities in television which existed. A staunch ally was Lord Woolton. Although in the debate in the House of Lords he had said he was speaking for himself personally, it was quite clear that he was in favour of breaking the BBC television monopoly. On the other side I think there was Lord Salisbury and Anthony Eden, both of whom I think had considerable reservations. They'd built up a great respect for the BBC during the war and they didn't wish to see it changed.

It became clear that we had very considerable opposition. We had to fight the BBC, we had to fight the newspapers, we had to fight the bishops, and last but not least we had to fight the films. Films mounted a very considerable operation because they thought that if television was more successful, with more choice of programmes, then people would stay away from the cinemas, and one company went so far as to lend their chief public relations officer to back up the National Television Council which was formed to prevent the breaking of the BBC monopoly.
LORD ORR-EWING

Our campaign was aimed not to preserve the BBC monopoly necessarily, but to prevent at all costs advertising and commercialism on our screens. Some of us thought the best plan, since there was a Tory government, would be to organize the traditional Tories into a campaign against commercial television, and I must say it went extremely well. I remember writing a letter for *The Times* and getting Lord Waverley and Lord Halifax, and so on, to sign it. I didn't even sign it myself. The idea being that the traditional side of the Conservative Party would prevent the cabinet from commercializing broadcasting; but the times were against us. The Tory Party was under pressure from its constituency associations for being too Labour 'me-too-ism', and this enabled the business-type Tory MP to attack the government that it was socialistic; they wanted a new break – private enterprise freedom and so on – and this just carried the day in cabinet and we lost, though I think probably our campaign helped to get safeguards into the Act that wouldn't have been there otherwise.
CHRISTOPHER MAYHEW

Crichel Down

I wrote to the Minister and asked for this land back. He called for a report. No doubt he asked his senior civil servant to have a report produced and the senior civil servant would have passed it on to another one. It went down to the regional level, from regional level it went to county level, and then the county office. I think the youngest member of the staff was asked to produce a report as quickly as possible and with complete secrecy, but he got his facts entirely wrong. The report went back up the chain being approved by each successive civil servant until it arrived on the Minister's desk with the stamp of considerable authority. The fact that it was completely and utterly wrong in practically every important detail he was, of course, unaware of. The Civil Service woke up to this situation. They were in some difficulty. This is the Commissioner of the Crown Lands writing to his opposite number in the Ministry, he says: 'You may then be able to judge whether any of them' – that's the prospective tenants who had applied – 'are likely to have been serious competitors and we can then decide, in conjunction with the Ministry of Agriculture, what if anything we need to do, at least to appear to implement the promises made to them'. The civil servant at the Ministry wrote back and said 'I'm very glad you have asked so-and-so' – that's their agent – 'to get hold of the list of names, so we can consider whether there is anything that can be done with the view, at any rate, to appear to be implementing any past promises'. Of course that was the source of some trouble when it came to light. I think it was probably a considerable influence on the Minister of Agriculture's mind, the fact that his department had made promises to a number of tenants in deciding to have the whole thing looked into. I wrote to the Minister. Through this correspondence it was quite clear that the case that had been put up to him was incorrect in many important matters of fact. I suggested I should go and see the Minister. He did see me and he told me he would agree to an enquiry being held. I think the enquiry did a lot of good on a fairly narrow front. It did make the government at the time agree to a principle that when land had been taken for one purpose, and was no longer required for that purpose, it should be offered back to the original owners. I think it did a broader good than that because it did, I think, make people realize that it was possible, even with, perhaps on my part, a good deal of luck, to get a Civil Service decision rescinded, or at least enquired into. It encouraged other people to fight where they might have felt hopeless and done nothing about it.

COMMANDER MARTEN

beautiful piece of countryside in Dorset. In 1940 it was compulsorily purchased by the Air Ministry from three different owners. In 1950 it was transferred to the Ministry of Agriculture and by them to the Crown Commissioners for development as a single farm. They spent £34,000 on equipping it and let it to a tenant who had no previous connection with the property. Several local farmers had wanted to buy or rent parts of it, among them Commander Marten, whose wife, but for the compulsory purchase order, would have inherited a large part of the land. Their applications, however, never got beyond the Ministry's local agents. Marten decided to play it rough. In this he was helped by his family and political connections. He saw the Minister, Sir Thomas Dugdale (later Lord Crathorne), on several occasions. Eventually the Minister was convinced that only a public enquiry would clear up the affair.

The chairman chosen for the enquiry in the spring of 1954 was a Q.C. noted for his championship of individual liberty. The enquiry showed that regional officials had blackguarded the reputation of some of the people involved, misrepresented their own actions, and adopted 'a most regrettable attitude of hostility' to Marten's representative, 'engendered solely by a feeling of irritation that any member of the public should have the temerity to offer criticism or even question the acts or decisions of officials'. There was widespread satisfaction that the overmighty state had been humbled, but to bring the dangers of bureaucratic insensitivity home to the Civil Service, Dugdale resigned in July 1954.

'Remember, I didn't ask you to resign', Churchill told him; but he cannot have found the resignation wholly inconvenient. He was about to amalgamate the Ministries of Agriculture and Food. Dugdale's resignation was the end of his ministerial career, but he had made Crichel Down part of the collective memory of every civil servant.

'Setting the People Free' was close to Churchill's heart, but to nothing like the same extent as foreign affairs. He was conscious of his unrivalled prestige throughout the world and was determined to bring about some degree of thaw in the Cold War now so delicately balanced in the thermonuclear age.

The man who shared Churchill's dominant concern was Anthony Eden. They had worked together for many years but the relationship was no longer always easy. In part this was Churchill's fault. He had nominated Eden as his successor as far back as 1942. Both knew the party would

I take entire responsibility for Crichel Down. It was a very busy period at that time and I was very preoccupied with the floods on the east coast. Quite frankly, I entirely overlooked what was going on in the west country at Crichel Down, and by the time I saw there was trouble there, it was too late. All sorts of rumours were being bandied about in the press and elsewhere about the evils of the civil servant. In fact it got to such a state that people were saying that there was corruption going on. Well now, directly that situation developed I saw the only thing to do was to set up a completely independent enquiry to look into the whole matter. The enquiry did report, very critically, certain actions taken by certain civil servants, but completely exonerated them from any vestige of dishonesty in any way. Silly things had been done, but silly things in the name of the Minister, and the only thing to do under our way of government was for the Minister to hand in his resignation, and that I did. I've never regretted it. I think a great deal of good has come out of it. I think it was quite good for them to have a jolt. It's the result of a war economy where the Civil Service was completely all-powerful.

LORD CRATHORNE

accept the transference of power. But Churchill was unwilling to go. He had come to power late in life and was certain that he still had a unique role to play.

Eden knew he had to wait, but he was never sure for how long. He was at the height of his powers and was confident of his ability to handle the world situation in his own way. The relationship between Eden and Churchill was that of an indulgent father and a wilful son. They could not help but frustrate one another on occasions. Churchill decided that to pursue his main goal of a settlement with Russia, he must sacrifice many of his other dreams to Eden's predilections.

Europe was the first casualty. Whatever Churchill had hoped for European Union, his administration was now subject to antagonistic Foreign Office and Treasury advice. Moreover, Eden at heart had always been an Atlantic animal. Right at the beginning of Churchill's administration, the Europeans in the Cabinet had a fleeting moment of hope. Maxwell-Fyfe, then Home Secretary, Macmillan, the Minister of Housing, and Sandys, the Minister of Supply, had had high hopes of Churchill giving a lead towards Europe. But the Anglo-Europeanists' Europe was not at that stage the Europe of Jean Monnet or Etienne Hirsch. The

community model, now being extended to the European Defence Community (E.D.C.), was too structured and organized for them. They saw the closer association between European states as their goal and they felt the revolutionary implications of the community model should grow from common interest and not be imposed from above.

The degree of the division between the 'Atlanticists' and the 'Anglo-Europeans' was shown up quickly. In November 1951, Maxwell-Fyfe in Strasbourg and Eden in Rome gave contradictory answers in respective statements on the degree to which Britain would participate in E.D.C. Eden's voice was to be decisive; he rejected the proposition that Britain would play an integral part in E.D.C. Maxwell-Fyfe seriously contemplated resignation, but on balance it seemed better to work on Churchill from within. But Churchill's approach to European security was to tackle Moscow first. The Cabinet fell into line and the Anglo-Europeans were left hoping that E.D.C. would fail and that Britain would have a second chance to give Europe a lead towards the type of confederation she could accept.

Eden was equally determined to make it succeed without full British participation, and he had the full backing of the American Secretary of State: both men knew that Western defence made no sense without German rearmament. Throughout the spring of 1952 he set himself to reassure French fears of resurgent German militarism, and to prevent Soviet diplomacy from wrecking his delicate negotiations. In May 1952, a complex series of interlocking agreements restored sovereignty to the West German Government, brought E.D.C. into being although it remained to be ratified, and provided for both an Anglo-American guarantee of the new community and an exchange of guarantees between it and NATO. The Western defence organization was complete but the whole house of cards could come tumbling down if either France or Germany refused to ratify E.D.C. It was, however, a tribute to Eden's skill that the edifice was there at all.

Churchill was content to let Eden work out the day-to-day diplomatic responses; his mind was fixed on the long-term objective. In June 1952 he was telling his private office of his ambition to talk personally with the Russians. In March 1953 Stalin died, and Churchill was left as the last of the wartime big three – an old man, but a man with a

L'Europe des Patries

Eden felt himself out of the European swim. He became, and the Foreign Office under him became, sincerely opposed but implacably opposed to the whole European concept, to Strasbourg and all it stood for. He once said to me, 'Association, not participation. Association is as far as I'm prepared to go in any European connection'. And rather quizzically he added, 'You see the difference between us is that you're a European animal and I'm basically an Atlantic animal'.

When the Conservative government got in, in the late autumn of 1951, hopes for the Council of Europe were raised very high. The first thing that was under consideration was the European Defence Community, and don't forget that the year before Churchill had demanded the European Army at the assembly of the Council of Europe. What happened was that David Maxwell-Fyfe, then Home Secretary, later Lord Kilmuir, came out to Strasbourg and, representing the British government, said that although we couldn't unconditionally join the proposed European Defence Community, it was a matter of negotiation between the governments concerned, and that every method would be attempted. At a press conference afterwards, at which I was present, he said 'There's no refusal on the part of Britain'. On the same night, at a press conference in Rome, Eden, as Foreign Secretary, announced that we would not join the European Defence Community on any terms whatsoever. The Conservatives at Strasbourg sent a desperate message to Churchill, after Eden had turned down EDC, saying that we must make our goodwill known, otherwise Europe would fall apart and form something without us. It was a really strongly worded letter of protest asking if we had gone back on everything that we said. We got no reply to it at all. Inside the cabinet I thought – we all thought at Strasbourg – that Churchill was fighting a lone and desperate battle against the hostile cabinet for Europe. Not at all, not at all. There was no battle, because nobody in the cabinet put in a word for Europe as far as I can make out. Not even Lord Kilmuir or Mr Macmillan, who had been ardent champions of Europe. The curious thing is that Churchill lost interest in Europe. I'm quite clear about that. Why? Because he'd become obsessed with the idea of going down in history in a final phase of his premiership as a great peace-maker. The man who would bring about an accord between the Soviet Union and the West unaided and by himself.

LORD BOOTHBY

Anthony Eden had never been caught up in this enthusiasm for Europe. Now we know, from his own memoirs and Macmillan's memoirs, he was speaking consistently against Britain's entry into Europe. My feeling is that although, of course, Suez dominates so largely Eden's later career, it will be seen retrospectively as a lunatic aberration. But the refusal to accept the leadership of Europe when it was offered to us on a plate is, in my opinion, his major mistake; because this was not an aberration. It was a prolonged, consistent act of policy, and it was wrong.

NIGEL NICOLSON

We never had any great drive towards Europe in the early 1950s, and it's rather an extraordinary thing that neither Macmillan, myself, nor Anthony Eden really pressed for entry into Europe in the 1950s. If we had, of course, we wouldn't have had the difficulties we later had with de Gaulle or with France, as we would have come in on the ground floor. I can't quite explain it, but all I know is that the whole of Whitehall – I mean the Treasury, and the Foreign Office – were not in favour of us pressing the matter at that time. I think it was due to jealousy of the idea that Europe might be a federal republic in which we had to sacrifice sovereignty, and that is, I know, what Eden felt himself at the Foreign Office.

LORD BUTLER

I think Churchill's idea of a united Europe was more akin to de Gaulle's Europe des Patries than to the ideas of a United Europe such as are current today. I don't somehow think that this would have been his conception of what was right or possible because it would have meant subordinating this country to a greater whole. We wanted to be part of Europe, but not in it, and of course he always had at the forefront of his mind the conception of the close relationship with the English-speaking peoples, and above all of England and the United States.

JOCK COLVILLE

The Summit: a personal approach

Eden, who was for a very much more cautious approach to the Russians, didn't like the idea of summitry, particularly with Winston at the summit. He didn't like the idea of Winston going to the summit conference, he thought he'd give away too much. Churchill said he thought he'd detected a new breeze blowing from the steppes of Russia and that he was going to cash in on this and he hoped to get a summit meeting between himself and Malenkov and, if possible, with the President of the United States. But if need be he would go alone, and he was determined to go alone. Eden had hoped that we would have a negotiation, first of all with the Russians at Foreign Secretary level, and if that revealed that there was any chance of reaching some agreement with the Russians, perhaps going to the top level. But Eden, when he went off to the clinic to have his further operation, said from his hospital bed – he rang me up at the Foreign Office – his last wish before he was carted off in the aeroplane was 'Don't let that old man appease the Bear too much in my absence'. Because he was afraid that without the restraining hand of himself and with just Selwyn Lloyd and myself at the Foreign Office, we would not be enough to hold the old man back and that he would be in, as Eden thought, too much of a hurry to get an agreement and would, perhaps, concede too much at the end and would get off-side of the Americans.
ANTHONY NUTTING

I remember going with Sir William Strang, who was head of the Foreign Office, to No. 10. Sir Winston was in bed, sitting there in his usual way, with a table in front of him and pads on his shoulders, the cigar in his mouth and a large bucket for the cigar ash, with whisky and soda on the side. We went through every word of that speech and all the time he was saying – 'Now are you quite sure that the Foreign Office will agree with this? Are you sure I'm being right?' That could have been politeness, but I think he was genuinely very cautious and he genuinely wanted to feel that the head of the Foreign Office, at least, did agree that he was not being rash, but he was making a wise step in making this gesture for a summit meeting. The speech was the Prime Minister's own wording, but he was very anxious to make certain that we thought it was right, and we did think it was right.
SELWYN LLOYD

Churchill felt that the future of the world depended on some sort of *détente* with the Russians, and so he set himself a task, I think, really, his own principal task, that he would try and use his undoubted influence and prestige to bring this about. He fought for three years to do so. He made a speech on 11 May 1953 in which he opened up this possibility of a great peace move in Russia. A speech which, I may say, caused great indignation, both in the State Department and in our own Foreign Office. It was coming back from the House of Commons after that speech had been made that Churchill said to me, 'You know, Russia fears our friendship much more than she fears our enmity'. I think what he felt was that the Russians were having their restrictive policy in not allowing people out of the country and generally disallowing freedom because they were terrified of the contamination from the West. The great improvement in the standard of living, he called it the marvels of science, would themselves so improve the lot of the ordinary Russian working man that detentions would decrease automatically and, perhaps, the illiberalism of Russia would slowly disappear and the Russian people themselves would ask and demand to have a more liberal government. So the idea of easement was the thing that he was really working for the whole time that he was Prime Minister.
JOCK COLVILLE

Churchill was getting old and didn't really recognize people very much. The younger members were told by the Whips from time to time to go up to him and talk to him, rather like a flock of debutantes being introduced to an ageing man. Of course it was a rather forbidding experience; he couldn't hear very well, he couldn't see very well and he wasn't really very interested in one. I remember that after one of these conversations, when one or two of us had been trying to put to him some of those new ideas that were emerging from Butler's back room about the Industrial Charter and so on, Churchill said to Malcolm Bullock, who was a middle-aged, middle-length Tory, 'Who are these new young men Malcolm? They're just a set of pink pansies.' He wasn't really much in sympathy with the younger ideas which were really the ideas associated with Macmillan and Butler.

NIGEL NICOLSON

Churchill was immensely skilful, immense fun still, and, of course, he used his own disabilities so well, like being deaf. He would either not hear or pretend not to hear some intervention, which would make people laugh, and then he'd insist on the unfortunate man who'd made it, repeating it. The sort of crack which goes down well first time is rather a bore second time over; the wretched man would repeat it and Winston would say 'That's too swift a thrust for me to parry', and the wretched fellow would sink through the floor. On the whole he held his mastery to the end, I would say.

LORD RHYL

mission. He saw a final chance to discover where Russian intentions lay.

In April 1953, Eden had to go into hospital to have an operation on his gall bladder and Churchill took over the Foreign Office. Eden's operation went wrong: during surgery, the bile duct was accidentally cut. Fortunately an American specialist was in London at the time and offered to operate on Eden in Boston. The Foreign Secretary spent some time trying to recuperate at Chequers, but he finally had to go to the United States for his operation in June.

Churchill knew that Eden had serious reservations about a direct personal approach to the new Soviet leaders, Malenkov and Molotov, but he resolved to make overtures. In a major speech (on 11 May 1953) which he only cleared with the Foreign Office at the last moment, Churchill proposed big-power talks. Ten days later he told the the Commons that he would discuss his proposals with Eisenhower in Bermuda at the end of June. Meanwhile highly unofficial secret soundings were taken in London at the Soviet Embassy by certain

Churchill was always very sensitive to anything he thought might affect the common man. It is a very mistaken impression that he was not interested in these subjects, he was extraordinarily sensitive to them. I can remember an occasion when some minister brought something to the cabinet which he thought would go through very easily but it involved something hurting the ordinary family – something like a rise in the price of tram fares. Winston at once rose to this and said that we couldn't do this in a hurry, it was going to upset a lot of people, couldn't we find some other way round it? Quite unlike what people imagined him, a rather autocratic type of politician, a statesman to the manner born and all that, who didn't care a bit for the common people. He was much more sensitive to their faults, their wishes, their needs than any minister whom I've ever seen.

Churchill always assumed, you know, that nobody knew him very well, that nobody recognized him. When you go through the division lobby, as you pass through the tellers, unknown members of Parliament always stop and tell the tellers who they are; well, Winston had a habit of always doing this, in spite of his great fame and renown. He would stop by the tellers and say 'Churchill, W. S.', and then pass on.

SIR GEORGE MALLABY

I remember once going to see Churchill in 1953. He offered me a junior job in the government. On that occasion he poured out two glasses of Scotch and pushed one over to me. He drank his own and then pulled mine back to him and consumed that as well, leaving me with my tongue hanging out. But at that time he was a very gentle and feeling man. I remember him saying to me 'Don't tell the press about this, please', about the appointment. 'There have been several today but we don't want the press to know about them'. But he said, 'Of course ring up your wife and tell her'. And then he said, 'There's a little old woman in the Toxteth division of Liverpool isn't there, named Proctor? Who is your chairman – that little frail woman?' I said 'Yes'. 'Ah . . .', he said, 'do tell her, she's a darling'. He had remembered her from the middle thirties.

REGINALD BEVINS

I remember one of Churchill's colleagues told me how he'd gone into the cabinet room – on the afternoon before Churchill was answering questions. One of the most difficult things is to be able to deal with the supplementary questions which come up. You've got to think about these sometimes and this man came into the room and Churchill turned round to him and said, 'Get out boy, can't you see I'm rehearsing a spontaneous answer to a question?'

ROBERT ALLAN

M.P.s and officials close to Churchill. To the Foreign Office, the old man seemed to be really on the move. Simultaneously, Eden travelled to Boston for his operation.

In the late afternoon of Tuesday 23 June 1953, Churchill and the Italian Prime Minister, de Gasperi, posed for newsreel cameras in the garden No. 10. They then retired inside for dinner. Churchill was in fine form. But an hour or so later he was suddenly taken ill. Only Churchill's private staff guessed what was wrong. He had had a stroke. Next morning he insisted on taking the Cabinet and was dissuaded with difficulty from going to the House of Commons for question time. He was steadily getting worse, and on the following day, Thursday, an observant passer-by would have seen at Downing Street's garden gate a small party climbing into a car. Churchill was being taken to Chartwell to avoid any publicity. He asked his staff to tell no one: Lord Moran, Churchill's doctor, warned that he probably would not last the weekend.

Eden, that day, was being operated on in Boston. Some of Churchill's friends and leading ministers were warned of the position, and arrangements were made that if Churchill died the Queen should be advised to appoint Lord Salisbury as a Caretaker Prime Minister. A highly respected and senior member of the Conservative Party, Salisbury could not, as a peer, retain the office long. There was at that time no possibility of renouncing his title: the Act allowing a peer to do so was not passed until 1962.

On Saturday 27 June, while Moran's fears for Churchill's life were at their strongest, the following public statement was issued: 'The Prime Minister has had no respite for a long time from his very arduous duties and is in need of a complete rest. We have advised him to abandon his journey to Bermuda [to see Eisenhower] and to lighten his duties for at least a month'. The statement had gone through several drafts and the final version had been amended by Butler and Salisbury who struck out the following phrase '...arduous duties, and a disturbance of the cerebral circulation has developed, resulting in attacks of giddiness...'

Sick-bed government

We were all going to set sail in the *Vanguard* the following week for Bermuda where there was going to be a meeting with Eisenhower and where Churchill was determined to have a showdown if necessary and try to persuade Eisenhower to go with him to see the Russians. But on the preceding Tuesday there was this dinner – a mixed dinner party, men and women – at 10 Downing Street in honour of the Italian Prime Minister, De Gasperi, and Churchill was at his sparkling best. He made a most scintillating, amusing after-dinner speech all about the Roman conquest of Britain and implying that De Gasperi was coming in the steps of Caesar. Afterwards I was talking to one of the leading trade unionists at that time – there were always quite a lot of those invited; Churchill had a real liking for trade union leaders – when suddenly Christopher Soames came up to me and said 'Something has happened to the Prime Minister, something pretty bad'. And so I left Sir Thomas Williamson, whom I was talking to, and there he was, slumped on a chair, and it was quite obvious that he was very ill. So the important thing was to try to get everyone out of the room, and we somehow achieved it without anybody noticing anything was wrong at all. Churchill couldn't even get up to say goodbye to Madame De Gasperi, but nobody noticed it as being odd, and we got him upstairs. We couldn't get hold of Lord Moran who was out, so we put him to bed, and the following morning when Lord Moran came it was quite clear that Churchill had had a bad stroke, his mouth was drooping right down and he wasn't at all well. However, as soon as Moran had gone away he got up and attended cabinet.

JOCK COLVILLE

It so happened that Normanbrook, who was the Secretary of the cabinet at the time, was ill, and so I had to go and be the Secretary of the cabinet for that occasion. As soon as I got into the cabinet room and sat down next to the Prime Minister, I realized he was very far from well. I didn't in the least know what had happened to him, of course, but he was rather numb, he couldn't articulate very clearly, his hands were not really under his control and there was obviously something pretty wrong. I had no idea what had happened. Nobody told me. I could say I guessed, but I didn't think at the time; I just thought he's old and he's ill today, and he doesn't feel very well. And so we stumbled through the agenda as far as we could get. He was able, I think, to say enough to catch exactly whether he meant yes or no, but not much more than that. He indicated that we ought to meet again the following day to finish the business, and with that we all got up and went out of the room. Several ministers came up to me and said 'What's the matter with him?' and I said 'Well, I don't know, I think he's just not feeling well today. I don't know what's the matter with him, but if he's all right we'll meet again tomorrow.' So I went back to the cabinet office then and did the minutes of the cabinet meeting and made all the arrangements for the meeting of the cabinet the next day. Then I went off in the evening to see Normanbrook who was ill in bed in his house in Chelsea, told him what had gone on, and the anxiety I felt about it. Then I went home to my flat and at about 11 o'clock in the evening the Private Secretaries from No. 10 rang me up and said would I please cancel the meeting tomorrow because Churchill wasn't very well and they'd had to take him down to Chartwell, and they'd tell me more about it later.

SIR GEORGE MALLABY

On the Thursday, Lady Churchill, he, and I motored down, the three of us together, to Chartwell. He went to bed and he told me that in no circumstances was I to tell anybody what had happened, that he'd had a stroke. Well, that was all very well, but the next day Lord Moran came to me and said he didn't expect the Prime Minister to live over the weekend. What is more, that very day Anthony Eden was having a serious operation in Boston and as he was the obvious successor if anything happened to Churchill, I really was in a rather difficult position. I felt I couldn't abide by Churchill's instructions not to tell anybody. I did in fact tell a few of his closest collaborators in the government. I told Butler, who was next in charge, and I told Salisbury. I told Beaverbrook and Bracken, who, although they'd played no part at all in political life, were still very close personal friends. I told Alexander, who was the Minister of Defence, and I told Lord Camrose. I rang up the Queen's Private Secretary to say that Her Majesty might have to contemplate forming a new government, or sending for a new Prime Minister on Monday. By Monday, Churchill was feeling much better. He was still paralysed down one side, but he was sitting up and taking notice. He wasn't reading official papers, but he was demanding a novel, and within ten days he was looking at official papers again. I think that Christopher Soames and I, and indeed everybody at No. 10, felt it our duty at this time to try and make sure the machinery of government went as smoothly as possible, and to make sure that decisions were obtained from the responsible ministers. Of course, Mr Butler was presiding at the cabinet. He was effectively the acting Prime Minister. Churchill was quite well enough to be consulted on matters of major importance, and by the grace of God it was a very peaceful summer when nothing very dramatic happened.

JOCK COLVILLE

Churchill leaves Chartwell for Chequers on 24 July 1953. This was the first time he was photographed after his stroke a month earlier

When I got down to Chartwell certain precautions had been taken. There were an extra couple of policemen, who were there specifically to patrol the front of the house, the road and the fields at the back. They had just been informed, I suppose, that we had received a threatening letter about Sir Winston, but they knew nothing about the stroke. We ourselves, of course, knew, but some of the staff and personnel didn't know. They knew that Sir Winston was in bed, but this could be a regular occurrence with a headache or something like that. Yet on the afternoon that I actually got down he was dictating letters to the secretaries.

We had binoculars because right opposite Chartwell there's an immense bank, hill, practically a forest, of rhododendrons – wonderful when they're blooming in June, but quite a nuisance as far as protection was concerned. What we were specifically looking for was not assailants, but photographers. The actual news of his having had a stroke didn't come out until many months later, so there was no actual danger from photographers, but we were not to know this. Three or four days after the stroke, after he'd started coming downstairs, he of course wanted to get out into the garden. Whether he had had a stroke or not, he was always one for his garden at Chartwell. So we had a wicker chair and we tied and fixed a couple of bamboos, one on either side, and my colleague and I carried him around the gardens on this. Of course we always had to be sure that when we put him down he was hidden from the road and windows, and the rest of it, by bushes or hedges.
EDMUND MURRAY

I think it was rather scandalous, when you contrast it with the way the American public was told every detail, perhaps almost too many details, of the illness of President Eisenhower; when you contrast the total secrecy which surrounded the paralytic stroke sustained by the British Prime Minister. Nobody knew this at all – they were merely told he was tired and wasn't able to go to Bermuda. When you think of the power that is vested in the Prime Minister, it really can't be right in a democratic country that the public should be completely ignorant when he is stricken down like that; it makes constitutional implications very serious.
JOHN GRIGG

Churchill made a phenomenal recovery; within three days he was asking for his red boxes. It has been alleged that his Parliamentary Private Secretary, Christopher Soames, ran the country, 'the best P.M. we never had'. However romantic, this is untrue. Churchill's Private Office kept the day-to-day wheels of central government turning, while Butler presided in Whitehall and Salisbury ran the Foreign Office. Churchill stayed quietly out of sight at Chartwell, visited by discreet friends.

By the end of July he was fit enough to be driven to Chequers. He took his first cabinet in mid-August. By the end of September, both he and Eden, returning from holidays abroad, looked fitter, but there were questions in many minds – how long could the situation go on?

A searching test of Churchill's powers was coming at the Conservatives' Margate conference in October where he would have to stand up and

deliver the Leader's speech. Butler suggested that he should have a high stool to prop himself up on, but Churchill decided to dispense with such advanced technology. Not only was there top level speculation on Churchill's coming performance, but debate was growing on the date of the next general election. It was expected that Churchill would not fight another general election, therefore any hint as to when it might be, would indicate how long Churchill wanted to stay on.

At Margate, Churchill ruled out an election in that year and in 1954. The conference was apparently delighted. And there was widespread consternation and subsequent relief when, after Churchill had read the same page of his notes twice, he paused and, tongue in cheek, said: 'I don't often do that, especially when I am making a speech.' The conference passed off well, and if Churchill wanted it, he had made himself more time. He did. There were two outstanding and related problems: Germany and the Soviet Union. On the first, he gave Eden his head; he had bigger hopes on the second.

The world had not stood still while Churchill and Eden recovered from their illnesses. International tension eased appreciably in 1953, while Malenkov and Molotov were establishing their position as Stalin's successors. The Korean war was ended. An equilibrium, a stalemate, it appeared, had been reached between the great powers. Indeed, the word 'thaw' was now becoming fashionable.

Churchill, fully convinced by Margate that he could carry on, was determined to exploit the new atmosphere. Eden was worried that personal approaches to the Russians might weaken defence. But Churchill's mind was obsessed by thought of a personal mission to Moscow, like some latter-day dove from the Ark, to explore the possibilities of *détente*.

Such a mission would have to be cleared with the United States' Administration, which had already shown itself to be intensely suspicious of the idea. In July, Churchill insisted on taking Eden to Washington to get Eisenhower's endorsement for a personal visit to Malenkov. Those around Churchill expected little to come of the trip, but to their surprise Eisenhower at first seemed keen on the idea. Later his enthusiasm cooled, but Churchill nevertheless felt that he had got his agreement to 'a reconnoitring patrol'.

A tiff and a telegram

When Churchill was in Washington that summer in 1954 with Soames and myself he did in fact get Eisenhower to agree to a meeting with the Russians. Eisenhower became temporarily quite enthusiastic at the thought, but once John Foster Dulles got at Eisenhower it was found that by the next day Eisenhower had changed his mind. However, Churchill did get him to agree that if he, Churchill, met Malenkov or Molotov, at least Eisenhower would maintain a benevolent neutrality. So on the way back to England on the *Queen Elizabeth*, Churchill drafted a telegram to Molotov suggesting a meeting. This was not at all well liked by Anthony Eden, the Foreign Secretary, who was with him on the ship, and there was a very grave disagreement on the subject. Eden felt quite sure that this initiative of Churchill's would not succeed and that it would lead to a terrible disappointment and disillusionment. However, Churchill was adamant, and when we got back to England the cabinet met and Churchill put his proposals to them. Whereupon Salisbury and Harry Crookshank, who was leader of the House of Commons, decided to resign. I think it did cross Churchill's mind that if his own government didn't like what he was doing, he would of course put the matter to the country, put it to the consciences of the country and of the Conservative Party. He felt very bellicose for a time, and there was a serious fear that weekend that Churchill might merely take the bull by the horns and say, well, if the cabinet don't like it perhaps the country will. However, wiser thoughts intervened during the weekend. He was very constitutionally minded, Churchill; the idea of going against the unanimous view of his cabinet was something he couldn't really seriously entertain. He was also tremendously helped by the Russians, who quite suddenly sent a telegram saying they would like to arrange a meeting to discuss a European security plan, inviting thirty-two Foreign Secretaries from thirty-two countries to attend. Churchill, I remember, flung his papers on the floor when he saw this and said 'Foreign Secretaries of the world unite, you've got nothing to lose but your jobs'.
JOCK COLVILLE

At that period – '54, '55, '56 – the British government were very keen on the concept of summit meetings with the Russians, and were very insistent that this was the way to proceed with international relations. The Americans were always much more hesitant. Eisenhower and Dulles were both very sceptical of the value of summitry and very reluctant to engage in it. One of the defects of the summit meeting is that if it doesn't come off, there's nowhere else to go. You've exhausted the position at the top. Whereas at a second level you can always refer up to the heads of government, and that, of course, gives a let-out.
LORD SHERFIELD

Eden was still doubtful and protested vigorously when Churchill proposed during their return voyage on the *Queen Elizabeth*, to send a telegram to Molotov without consulting the Cabinet. After a blazing row Churchill reluctantly agreed to forward the draft telegram to London, but in the event it was despatched before the Cabinet had seen it. The Russian reply was cordial but vague, while the Americans were alarmed at Churchill's precipitate action. There was trouble in the Cabinet; Salisbury and Crookshank threatened resignation. After somewhat desultory talks between Molotov and Eden about a site for the meeting the matter came to a head on 23 July.

Churchill declared: 'Today's Cabinet will be decisive. They must support me or I shall go.' If they did not, he would tell the country why, perhaps even ask the electorate to decide. But within twenty-four hours a Russian proposal for a meeting of all the European powers, clearly designed to wreck E.D.C., killed Churchill's initiative.

Accentuating Churchill's disagreement with his colleagues, was the simultaneous row over the evacuation of the Suez base. Britain had made the first move towards Egyptian self-government in 1922, but it had been the task of a much younger Eden, as Foreign Secretary in 1936, to agree the most substantial step towards independence and to put Anglo-Egyptian relations on an alliance

Suez: Eden finds the exit

A real difference of opinion between the Prime Minister and his Foreign Secretary, going back certainly to 1952, was this question of the evacuation of British troops from Egypt. Churchill had convinced himself that the Russians had designs on Egypt, the Suez Canal and the Middle East. Eden took the view that to keep a few thousand troops in the Canal zone was something that this country could not afford. It was a great strain on our balance of payments and it was much more likely that we could turn the friendship of the Egyptians by removing our troops than by keeping them there. The cabinet on this mainly supported Eden. Churchill had two convinced followers on this, Sir David Maxwell Fyfe and Sir Walter Monckton. What solved the difference of opinion really was the letting off of a hydrogen bomb, because immediately that happened Churchill reached the conclusion that the whole strategic concept of the United Kingdom must be changed. What had been strategically sound before would now need to be revised entirely. He thought that in the new circumstances keeping a large force in the Canal zone was out of date and no longer effective.

JOCK COLVILLE

I was the first minister to meet Nasser in 1953 and I'd reported on a long talk with him to Eden. I think Eden was always looking to the future. He'd been a promoter of the Arab League, he believed in the conception of the Baghdad Pact. And I think he believed in friendship between Egypt and ourselves and he hoped that all these moves would be a contribution towards peace in the Middle East. And almost a condition preceding a settlement to a general alleviation of tension in the East was better relations between Egypt and ourselves.

SELWYN LLOYD

Eden undoubtedly did have a strong sympathy with the Arabs. In his earlier days he used to take great pride in the fact that he had done a great deal to create the Arab League towards the end of the Second World War. He had a strong sympathy for the Palestinians who had been evicted in order to make way for the Jewish settlers and, finally, for the Jewish state of Israel to be established. When Nasser first came to power, I remember on several occasions he expressed the view that the Egyptians had every right to maintain a blockade of the Suez Canal under Article 10 of the Constantinople Convention, under which they were entitled, if a state of war existed between them and any neighbouring state, to take steps to protect the Suez Canal. Eden maintained this against the Prime Minister of the day, Winston Churchill; he maintained it against his own Minister of State, Selwyn Lloyd, who took a different view. After the agreement was signed in 1954, when I came back and explained the upshot of my conversations, Eden seemed to want the opening of a new chapter, too.

ANTHONY NUTTING

basis. However, decisions on the continued British military presence in Egypt and the defence of the Suez canal had been postponed. When Eden returned to the Foreign Office in 1951, there was still no agreement. Within a few months Eden was dealing with a very different type of Egyptian. Young revolutionary officers had taken power.

Tortuous negotiations followed in which Eden worked his way towards an agreement which would allow the phased withdrawal of British troops, the maintenance of a British base which could be used in time of war, Egyptian participation in a Middle East defence organization and, in return, military and economic assistance to the regime. The Americans, although sympathetic to these aims, were, for anti-colonialist reasons, trying to push Eden towards a settlement – but they would not take part in the negotiations.

To both Churchill and Eden the Middle East was an area of great significance. As late as 1940, the defence of Egypt and its critical strategic position for access to India and the Far East ranked second only to the mother country. By the mid fifties oil had become the dominant consideration: more than half of Britain's oil supplies came through the Suez canal, and the demand was sure to grow. Almost all the oil coming through the canal was destined for NATO countries. Egypt's ally, Syria, controlled the only other major outlet for Middle East oil – the overland pipeline from the Gulf. Although India no longer played a dominant part in Britain's strategic conceptions, it was not only oil that made the Suez canal base vital. The loss of the Indian Army too meant that a fresh bastion had to be found to guard against Russian incursion into the Middle East.

Britain's traditional, perhaps somewhat romanticized, friendship with the Arabs was now reinforced by an obvious need to court them. Churchill personally felt a deep imperialist bond with Egypt: to leave it would be a 'scuttle' comparable only to Britain's 'senseless' departure from India. Indeed that earlier 'scuttle' made it imperative to retain Egypt. More realistically, Eden saw the necessity of working with Arab nationalism: even for something less than Egypt's full involvement in an alliance system linked to the West, he would be prepared to sacrifice the British presence in the canal zone. Friendly states like Iraq and Pakistan reinforced Eden's view. But the difficulties of negotiation were compounded by the uncertain political situation in Egypt and the reluctance of her rulers to allow Britain to reoccupy the base, Turkey or Iran being threatened with attack.

Early in 1954, promisingly, they conceded the case on Turkey, an important concession because of her membership of NATO and her geographical position. Eden was already working hard to bring Pakistan and Turkey closer together to help protect the vulnerable northern tier of the Middle East, the 'under-belly' of the Soviet Union. Eden, knowing the costs involved in tying down large numbers of troops in the canal zone and conscious of the need to reach a settlement, was determined to make an agreement with the new leader of Egypt, Colonel Nasser, to put the base in the hands of contractors in return for a promise that it could be reactivated in time of war.

Churchill hated the step, but, faced with close agreement between the Ministry of Defence and the Foreign Office, gave in. Privately, however, he still offered encouragement to members of the 'Suez Group'. This back-bench organization, some forty members strong, was determined to oppose the step and there seemed some prospect of a defeat in the House. The Suez Group's attitude to the Empire was to find growing resonance within the party. Twenty-five of them voted against the agreement when it was put to the Commons, but the debate was notable mainly for a dramatic intervention by Churchill in which he explained his 'conversion' to Eden's view on the grounds that in an age of nuclear warfare Suez-style bases were no longer essential.

The Government could now re-open talks with Nasser: a treaty was finally signed in October 1954 by which a phased withdrawal of British troops would be complete by 1956. The base would be put on a care and maintenance basis, and in the event of an attack on any member of the Arab League or on Turkey (unless the attacker were Israel) Britain would have the right to return to the base. Both parties would uphold the 1888 Convention guaranteeing free navigation of the canal. Although Eden had not created the Middle East defence organization that Britain and America had hoped would preface withdrawal, it was clearly implicit in the agreement that Eden hoped at worst for benevolent neutrality, at best for co-operation between Nasser and the nascent Baghdad Pact.

Britain's closest ally in the Middle East, Nuri-es-Said, friend of Lawrence of Arabia and Premier of Iraq, was already working for the inclusion of Turkey in the Arab League. Nasser was opposed to this step since Turkey was friendly towards Israel. Instead Turkey and Iraq signed a mutual defence agreement in February 1955 and Nuri pressed Britain to become a member. Eden discussed the question with Nasser in Cairo, but the Egyptian Prime Minister felt that the Pact, by its bad timing and unfortunate composition, had seriously set back collaboration with the West. Nasser further urged that security was not a matter of bases but sprang from economic and social advance. His interest and sympathies, he told Eden, were with the West, but it was not long before he was practising the diplomacy of 'non-alignment'.

Time-consuming as Middle Eastern diplomacy proved, it was not yet Eden's central concern. His attention was focused on Europe, where at the end of August 1954, France finally rejected E.D.C. Eden decided to undertake a diplomatic odyssey to tie German rearmament to NATO. In the course of six days intensive travel and brilliant diplomacy, Eden secured the consent first of the Benelux powers, then of Germany, and finally of Italy, before going to Paris where he reached deadlock with a determined Mendes-France.

When another conference met at the end of September, Eden had persuaded Dulles not to withdraw American forces from Europe unless some supranational force could be established. But the French still needed a harder guarantee against the possible imbalance that German rearmament might introduce. Eden offered to station four British divisions and the Tactical Air Force in Europe for as long as the European powers wished. Mendes-France agreed to sign. Ironically, Eden had in the end been forced to use an instrument and make a commitment to achieve German rearmament, that he had scorned to use in promoting French acceptance of E.D.C. By the spring of 1955, Western European Union was in being and German rearmament could begin.

Eden now began to consider a fresh approach to Russia. Part of his objection to Churchill's overtures had been the chance they offered Russia to prevent the completion of a Western defence framework, but he was equally worried about Churchill's age and his ability to see talks through without undue concessions. By the autumn of 1954 there were clear signs that Churchill, though

Eden the negotiator

When the French threw out the European Defence Community there was no institution available whereby the Germans could be brought into the Western community. Eden moved very, very quickly. The Germans, as he put it, must be taken by the hand and brought into the European family. So he set off on this remarkable pilgrimage around all the various capitals in the countries that had negotiated the European Army Treaty. He left the French till last because he knew that there lay the principal opposition. Using the West European Union in place of the European Army, he put it to the French that the Germans should be made members of the West European Union and admitted to NATO with the national army. The French didn't like this at all. I was present at the meeting with Mendes-France when Eden, Gladwyn Jebb and myself put this to the French. They put us literally in a corner, they sat us in a corner of a room and the French ranged themselves in front of us. Mendes-France and all his advisers, about six of them, ranged in front of us. There we were, cornered, and I could see Eden's back stiffening against the wall. He was determined not to give the one concession which he knew he had up his sleeve, which Mendes-France knew he had up his sleeve; namely, that we, the British, would guarantee to the French that we would be there in the West European Union with an army on the continent of Europe until the end of this century. This is what they hoped we would give for the EDC. We wouldn't give it to the European Army because this would mean putting our army into a European setting, but we would keep our army on the continent of Europe to hold the hand of the French. Eden had got cabinet authority to give it and was prepared to give it, but it was a question of when. Eden knew if he gave the concession at that particular meeting, then Mendes-France would pocket it and say 'thank you very much', and come back for more. So all through that meeting Gladwyn and I were sitting there itching, hoping he would make the concession there and then. Eden refused to give a single thing. He said, 'It is for you, the French; you rejected the only alternative, it's for you to bring the Germans in. Now you must agree to my proposal that they should be brought in to the West European Union and through that into NATO. You refused to make an army with them; all right, they will have to come in with a national army of their own'. It wasn't until one meeting later when he got Mendes-France to come to London that he finally made the concession. By this time Mendes-France was almost on his knees begging for this thing, and then it was all right. Eden was a brilliant negotiator.

ANTHONY NUTTING

far from senile, was no longer on top of his job. He read only the papers which interested him and was increasingly reluctant to make any decisions. As early as July 1954, Macmillan had told him frankly that he ought to go and it had been confidently expected that when his close friends Lords Alexander and Chandos retired from the Cabinet in October, he would go too.

But Churchill clung on, and despite Macmillan's promptings refused to make any clear or definite arrangement about the succession. Perhaps he would retire when the Commons celebrated his eightieth birthday in November. That date, too, passed with no announcement. Eden's frustration was clear. When would the next election be? Ought not Churchill to retire to give his successor time to play himself in before it?

Frequent promises to Eden had been made by Churchill about his date of departure and then broken. The elusive hope of talking to the Russians flitted on and off the international scene.

In the end it happened quite suddenly: Eden had to cut short a tour of the Far East and in the middle of a national newspaper strike – copies of the *Manchester Guardian* were fetching 4s. in London – Sir Winston Churchill resigned. Eden went to the Palace to kiss hands on 6 April 1955. The Crown Prince had come into his own.

Churchill's last period as Premier has been underwritten and underrated. The administration's tranquillity belied the fact that it was probably the most successful of post-war governments. Churchill had presided over the years when his party had come back from the wilderness; no one could seriously pretend that it was outside the mainstream of British politics in 1955. It was an extraordinary comeback and his administration marked the beginning of a period of consensus politics in Britain.

He handed over a more auspicious international situation to Eden than at any time since Hitler's rise to power. The economic situation was better than anybody could ever remember. To be sure, adjustments would be necessary, but the man who entered Parliament in the time of Queen Elizabeth's great-great-grandmother ushered in the age of affluence. Only one nagging question mark hung over the future – what frustrations would boil up once the dominant presence of Churchill disappeared?

The Old Master

One does feel that during Churchill's last year the whole spirit of British government was getting inward-looking just when we should have been more outward-looking. I think it was a real tragedy that Churchill's last year should have coincided with the movement in Europe, the movement towards the Messina talks and so on, because too many people were looking inward as to how soon a change of government was coming. In the end it was the imminence of the election that dictated the change of government and not the other way round. I think one of the finest moments of Mr Macmillan's career was the courage he showed both in confronting Churchill and in talking privately to members of the party about this. By the beginning of 1955 Macmillan, on quite rational grounds, felt the time had come for a change and he showed, I think, great courage in speaking about this and not concealing his views.

LORD BOYLE

Eden, I think, felt the succession ought to have come to him earlier and those in his entourage at the time, including myself, did get the feeling that Churchill was 'cat and mousing' a bit. One minute he was going to resign, he'd set the date and so on, and the next minute when the date came he said, no, I'm going on for a little longer. Subsequently I had come to the conclusion that this was not a kind of deliberate delay on Churchill's part. I think more likely he was determined that, when he left, Eden should succeed, because he was very fond of Eden, very, very fond of Eden. He wasn't absolutely certain, and particularly after Eden's illness (the succession of operations had obviously weakened him a lot), he wasn't convinced that Eden was physically strong enough or, perhaps, generally strong enough to take on the responsibilities of the premiership. I remember now, how the Prime Minister would buttonhole me in the lobby in the House in the division and say 'How do you think Anthony is – do you think he's all right? I didn't think he looked awfully well today', and that kind of thing. I often wondered at the time what the purpose of these questions was. I think it was that he couldn't quite make up his mind that Eden was strong enough to take on the job, and yet at the same time he was determined not to vacate the seat until he was strong enough because he didn't want anyone else to have the succession. I think this was the real reason behind Churchill's continuous changes of plan. But of course this did cause an understandable irritation on the part of Eden at the time, and he did show it from time to time to those who were fairly close to him.

ANTHONY NUTTING

Even then, right at the last moment after he'd told Eden that he was going, there was a message to say that Eisenhower was proposing to meet Adenauer and others and Churchill, he hoped, on the anniversary of V.E. Day, which was 8 May, in Paris. And Churchill said 'Well, I'm going to stay on as Prime Minister. We'll have a meeting which could lead on to the meeting with the Russians'. But by that time he really was getting too old; his own wife, his children and all his closest friends, we all felt that he must go, and this was felt, of course, even more strongly, I think, by a lot of his colleagues in his cabinet. So finally, he decided to resign.

JOCK COLVILLE

7 A political tragedy

Immediately on becoming Prime Minister in April 1955, Eden decided to call a general election. It was clear he should establish himself as successor in his own right and an election was fixed for the end of May 1955. He could have waited until October 1956, but the spring of 1955 was on the face of it propitious. Eden knew that Butler had an expansionist budget ready and both he and the party were keen to increase their Parliamentary majority from seventeen. He did not take the opportunity he had in forming his Government for a reshuffle. Macmillan became Foreign Secretary, but otherwise no major changes were made.

Eden's strongest electoral card was the economic record of the last Government. The 1955 Election was the first fought in what later became known as the affluent society. Eden wrote later: 'I knew that if we were to improve our position, I must in particular get my message to the better skilled industrial worker, who could be expected to benefit most from the kind of society we wanted to create.'

Butler's budget, six weeks before the election,

was much in the tradition of its predecessors. Sixpence off income-tax (Churchill had wanted him to take off a shilling) and two and a half million people freed from the burden altogether, made up an attractive package. But things were not as right as they seemed and Butler was almost certainly pushed further than he wanted to go in an expansionist direction. Import prices began to rise fast in the latter part of 1954, and this was causing anxiety over the balance of payments. Further, there was a strong current of wage-push inflation: wages were rising faster than productivity, thus pushing up costs.

Butler, sensing trouble, had in February raised bank rate and introduced purchase-tax increases to dampen home demand. A month later he was evidently satisfied enough with these measures to feel able to cut income-tax; this later laid him open to Opposition charges of an electioneering budget; but against a background of apparent industrial stagnation, Butler had in fact given away less than half his surplus. Eden would have liked to have

Heir apparent

done more. The popular belief was that Britain's economic position was buoyant and would go on steadily improving. This belief was especially strong among the middle and investing classes who had long railed against the constraints of the post-war years. To continue to satisfy them politically, when they felt their income differential was being eroded by the emergence of mass affluence, was important.

Throughout the election, Eden laid great stress on the economic record and emphasized that his aim was the creation of a property-owning democracy. The campaign passed off quietly and even politics seemed to take on some of the self-assured tranquillity of the early fifties. Eden was able to improve the overall majority of the Conservative Party to sixty: his own majority in Leamington and Warwick he increased by nearly 4,000 – a remarkable result for those days.

Eden was an intensely glamorous figure and his record was impeccable. He had entered Parliament in 1923; behind him was a Military Cross in the Great War and a first-class degree in Oriental Languages. He thought of himself, like others of his age, as one of the 'lost generation', a survivor from an *élite* decimated by the Great War. When he was publicised by the Conservative Party as a Man of Peace, they had in mind his life work. Picked out at an early age for office, he had specialized in League of Nations affairs. At the age of thirty-eight he was in the Cabinet and, within six months, became the youngest Foreign Secretary for 150 years.

'The policies which I upheld and pursued', he wrote of his career in the fifties, 'were based on my earlier experiences.' The thirties were years of growing international anarchy in which the twin dictators Mussolini and Hitler held the world to increasing ransom, finally precipitating it into war. Eden traced much of the trouble to the failure to uphold international agreements and enforce collective security. In particular he felt that the failure to halt Mussolini's Abyssinian venture in 1935 by the use of sanctions was a decisive step along the road to war. But Eden was still prepared to try appeasement, and resigned only in 1938 when it was apparent that the Prime Minister, Neville Chamberlain, would pursue the policy whatever the cost. His resignation made Eden's reputation and won Churchill's lasting admiration.

First of all, Eden had glamour, to the extent I've never known any other Tory leader have, or any other Labour leader either, in my lifetime. I can remember him coming to the constituency I was fighting in 1950. He had a style, a glamour, as an election speaker, which you couldn't help finding impressive. He really did make you feel when he arrived that this was the event he had been looking forward to more than any other in the whole election. The other thing words cannot express: what a fine and effective speaker he was, particularly in the House of Commons, when he was really on top form. I remember so well the speech he made winding up the debate on German rearmament at the end of the '51–'52 session. Now this was a subject he really understood deeply, through and through, and, my goodness, it was a persuasive speech; he knew he could really command the House of Commons.
LORD BOYLE

The older members of the House couldn't remember a Foreign Secretary who dominated the House of Commons as much as Eden did. In debate he would hold the House entranced. He wasn't a natural orator, he had no great gift for words but I remember very well sitting there, riveted in my admiration for his sheer performance. He immediately established in every speech a *rapport* with the House. He, you might say, almost courted it, the House of Commons. He was a very fine-looking man; he had immense elegance, but he wasn't in any sense offensive. I mean, he wasn't openly making use of his charm, it wasn't that at all; it was the combination of his good looks, his good manners and his enormous experience. When he came to speak on the platform at a party conference, I don't think he had quite the same effect because there the audience was less knowledgeable and much larger. It was the intimacy of the House of Commons chamber which was his real forte, and the fact that when he was speaking in the House he managed to adopt an almost conversational manner, an almost intimate manner, although of course he was always speaking in public.
NIGEL NICOLSON

When Eden became Prime Minister his whole experience before had been, of course, at the Foreign Office, which is very rare in Prime Ministers. It is, I think, a great loss for a Prime Minister in modern times, because the economy plays such a vital part in deciding the future of the government. He was very loyal to me in supporting me, but he was rather put off by the whole subject, especially by the reduction of expenditure which didn't necessarily appeal to his mind – which was one of social progress – even behind his knowledge of foreign affairs. So it wasn't easy because he was impatient about economics.
LORD BUTLER

For the greater part of the Second World War and throughout Churchill's peacetime administration Eden added to his reputation. He was reputedly more knowledgeable than the professionals and his intuitive feel for diplomacy was legendary. In the forties there was talk in influential circles of making him Secretary General of the United Nations. In the early fifties even his failures were transformed by diplomatic skill into great coups, and his touch seemed golden. He had put an end to the oil dispute with Persia, built a durable defence framework in Western Europe, and set relations with the Near East on a new and apparently stable footing. In 1954 he had extricated the French and the Americans from the morass of Indo-China, though in the process he and the American Secretary of State, John Foster Dulles, had almost come to blows and relations between them remained bad.

The frustrations of the last two years of Churchill's premiership had been hard to bear. Although Eden kept apart from the manoeuvring to expedite Churchill's departure, he occasionally let his notoriously sharp temper get the better of him in private. For a man of Eden's vanity – a quite open characteristic – Churchill's procrastinations were exasperating. He felt a strong desire to get on with the job, and when he finally became Prime Minister there was considerable psychological pressure to demonstrate quickly who was the boss. He could court audiences in the House; outside his charm, his looks, and his diffident, yet assured, bearing made him a first-rate electoral asset.

Eden's efforts in the spring of 1955, when he offered the Russians a package consisting of a demilitarized zone in Central Europe and a security pact brought a quick return. The Russians agreed to pull their forces out of Austria, in exchange for her neutralization. Eden hoped that this would be the prototype of a similar deal over Germany. In an altogether warmer atmosphere, plans were made for a summit meeting in Geneva in July 1955. The meeting, though genial, achieved nothing of substance except the recognition that major war had now become so terrifying a prospect that it was better to live with the *status quo*. Macmillan, in a characteristically raffish way, said, 'there ain't gonna be no war.'

One by-product of the Summit was the visit of the Russian leaders, Bulganin and Khrushchev, to Britain in April 1956. From this meeting, too, little

of substance emerged, but relations among the 'Big Three' were incomparably better than since the war, and, had all else been equal, the 'thaw' was accelerating.

Eden's first troubles came at home. The day after his election in May 1955, he had to face major strikes in the docks and on the railways. He was forced to declare a state of national emergency, and the dock strike added to a threatening balance of payments problem.

The pound was now particularly vulnerable because the Bank of England, with Butler's agreement, had chosen that spring to make it in practice convertible. Confidence factors therefore assumed new importance and forced the Treasury to take greater account of the balance of payments position.

But neither the balance of payments nor domestic inflation showed a satisfactory trend. Coal for example had an 18 per cent price rise in July, and the trade deficit for the past six months

The morning after

Everything had gone well in the '51 to '55 Parliament. At the end of that Parliament I think, precisely because freeing the economy, reducing taxation, all those things had been a success, we carried them just a bit too far. It's so easy to do this. There's always a tendency to think because you have found a winning line, you can't carry that winning line too far. I suspect that Mr Butler himself was never absolutely convinced of the overall reduction in income tax at the standard rate in 1955. I think that he, and perhaps some other people, would have preferred something more modest at that time. There was quite an argument inside the Treasury about this. If we were going to reduce taxation as we did in April 1955, the monetary measures in February 1955 should have been pressed rather harder.

LORD BOYLE

In the early spring of 1955 I imposed hire purchase controls and raised the bank rate. I thought by that time the inflation was under control. As we had an election coming up, I wanted a very short budget in the spring of '55, and therefore my Finance Bill had only one clause, which was to take sixpence off the income tax by which I took off about £154 million and gave it away. My gesture was not really all that expensive, but it did lead to criticisms later in the year because the economy then started to inflate to rather an alarming degree, and there became some doubt about the pound because there was a view that it might start to float. I had to go to Istanbul to attend a meeting of the International Monetary Fund and establish that the pound was fixed in a certain parity. That saved the pound; it didn't save the expenditure. I tried to get the government to reduce expenditure even more, and they were willing to do so under Eden's premiership. I had no alternative but to produce a second budget to reduce expenditure, and that I did by a mixture of purchase tax, which was extremely unpopular at the time, and a profits tax, which was also extremely unpopular.

LORD BUTLER

In 1951 the government began implementing its election pledge of 'setting the people free'. But those measures, and the result of them, had worn off by the time Eden became Prime Minister and then there was no very obvious action to be taken on the home front. Economists were giving, as was very often the case, conflicting advice, and the situation didn't offer, or demand, scope for dramatic action. Eden himself, by his training and by his inclination, was, of course, much more at home in foreign affairs than he was in home domestic affairs, economic affairs.

ROBERT ALLAN

We went on to a situation in the autumn where the economy appeared to be rather over-heated and certain action had to be taken. Eden was all for taking action. I think he felt at the time that to raise what was a comparatively small sum by infuriating every housewife was too little reward for too much unpopularity, and I think the Pots and Pans budget and the putting on of purchase tax made him lose confidence in the Treasury at the time. That meant, really, in fact, the judgement of the Chancellor of the Exchequer, and this is no real criticism of Mr Butler, who had very great personal difficulties and a long and very successful four years at the office of the Chancellor of the Exchequer. I think this was what made him feel it was time for a change.

SELWYN LLOYD

Eden inherited a much more difficult position than people appreciate. The other thing was, in certain ways, Eden saw rather clearly: for example, he was one of the few people in the government who did understand this point about the wages, about the 'cost-push' and the effect this was having on inflation. Looking back, I think it was a great pity that Eden didn't summon a meeting, that he didn't say, now let's have this out. I think the truth is, Eden, as Prime Minister, was too upset by day-to-day irritations, he didn't like reading particular aspects of criticism; these day-to-day annoyances psychologically knocked him off his perch a bit. I wish he had called a real discussion of Treasury ministers about economic policy, because in fact many of his ideas were more forward-looking than one realized at the time.

LORD BOYLE

Eden was a bad Prime Minister. For one thing, he could never leave his ministers alone. He was always fussing them, ringing them up in the middle of the night to ask them had they done this? Had they seen this in the newspapers? This showed a lack of confidence, and worry, in ministers – senior ministers, and then the junior ones, and from them it trickled down by the natural indiscretions you get in the lobbies and the smoking room in the House of Commons to the back-benchers. From there it slowly began to percolate throughout the country. There was a feeling that there had been a loss of grip, and this was publicly commented upon in the newspapers. Eden wanted to make some startling gesture in order to re-establish his position as a strong leader, as another Winston, and he was terribly conscious, I'm sure, psychologically, of being Churchill's successor. Was he going to match up to this strong man who had led the country throughout the war?

NIGEL NICOLSON

The smack of firm government

In January 1956 there wasn't much happening. I remember having talked with a number of young Tories, who felt that they couldn't get on with things on the home front. We'd had inflation. We'd had a railway crisis in the summer. We'd had quite a long period of Walter Monckton at the Ministry of Labour. Walter Monckton at the Ministry of Labour was something: I can't compare it to anything that goes on now, but I think it could fairly be called appeasement of the unions. So it wasn't surprising to find that there was a certain amount of discontent among the Tories, certain stagnation in government. Let me stress there was no question of revolt, there was no kind of plot, but just that people were rather fed up. I thought that this was a good subject for an article. I had noticed on one or two occasions at public lunches, and that sort of thing, that the Prime Minister had a curiously revealing gesture. He would say he was determined that so-and-so should be done. He would emphasize this point with the fist coming down towards the palm, but when you got to the climax, the fist did not hit the palm. It stopped short. This seemed to me worth recording. I said 'There's a favourite gesture with the Prime Minister. To emphasize a point, he will clench one fist to smack the open palm of the other hand, but the smack is seldom heard'.

You know from time to time newspapers perform acts of cannibalism. I think I'm right in saying that on this occasion the *Mirror* took half a page. The papers insisted there was a plot. A movement to get rid of Eden. By the Sunday, No. 10 felt moved to issue a denial that he was going to resign. To my mind, this reaction was really quite absurd, and my recollection is that it was done very much against the advice of the lobby correspondents.
DONALD McLACHLAN

I was in the room when he read the article and showed his irritation with it. He used to splutter and rage. I think if you want to understand my friend Anthony Eden you'll see that his father was a man of great independence of character and considerable ability to rouse his fury into a temper, and I think the occasion showed that he was the son of his father.
LORD BUTLER

The article really hurt him, it really hit him right between the eyes. I don't think I've ever seen him quite so stricken by a newspaper criticism as he was by that. He went off to Bradford; he insisted upon taking this up and replying to it. He happened to mention that he was going to reply to this attack on him, and I said for God's sake leave it alone. You'll be laughing at the end of the day if you show them that they are completely wrong. This you can only do by performance. You can't do it by replying to them, by demeaning yourself, by actually standing on a platform and replying to some journalist who produces criticisms of you; this is beneath you. And he said, 'Oh, you don't understand anything about politics, you're just a Foreign Office official'.
ANTHONY NUTTING

I used to go to Downing Street quite early in the morning, and I would sit in the bathroom while he had a bath and shaved and I'd be with him while he dressed, and we'd talk about what was in the papers and what idiotic speeches had been made by friends or enemies over the weekend or over the last day or two. He would, very often, have great outbursts about things that irritated him, editorial comments on this or the other. He had a feeling of frustration, you know, like 'I wish we could get this thing right', 'I wish we knew what to do', but it was a question that neither he nor anybody else had the solutions to, and they probably don't have them even today. When he was faced with a difficult situation he rather instinctively turned to an area where he was supreme, and in foreign affairs he was absolutely the master. He could deal with people he knew the background of, and he had great finesse. And, I suppose, if at any time any of us wants to restore our self-confidence, we move into areas where we know we are excellent, and he undoubtedly was in that field.
ROBERT ALLAN

was calculated to be £456 million. When first rumours of a floating pound were superimposed on these figures, the possibility of a panic flight from sterling was obvious. Butler was forced to deny that he would allow the exchange rate of the pound to find its own level and to take action on the home front. Late in July he imposed a small credit squeeze. The pressure on sterling increased and wages continued to soar. In October, Butler was pushed into introducing a second budget which took back most of the reliefs he had given in April. The imposition of purchase tax on certain kitchen utensils made it the 'pots and pans' budget. Butler's measures were the first 'Stop' in what was meant to be a major and continuing 'Go'.

Eden had refused to let Butler choose his own measures, but he bitterly resented the loss of popularity involved in those taken. It seemed a trivial sum to take out of the economy and he was both irritated and uncertain about an economic situation turned suddenly sour. Butler, plagued by faulty official advice, seemed tired and ill from the strain of watching his first wife die of cancer. Eden resolved on a reshuffle, making Butler Leader in the Commons and replacing him with Macmillan. Butler's appointment could be interpreted as either a rest-cure or demotion. Macmillan's was the result of his uneasy relationship with a prime minister active in foreign affairs.

Macmillan was careful to secure from Eden a promise that he would be supreme on the domestic front. The key appointment was Iain Macleod to the Ministry of Labour – a younger, tougher man than the pliable Monckton. As Eden said, 'The battle against inflation is on.' Eden urged his new Chancellor to think over some kind of deal with the unions based on profit sharing and price stability, and Macmillan curbed his expansionist instincts. In February he pushed the bank rate to $5\frac{1}{2}$ per cent and further restricted hire purchase; in what he soon saw to be a mistaken moment, he also suspended investment allowances. He even pondered over the introduction of a Capital Gains Tax. His budget proved neutral and was mainly notable for a vigorous moral debate over the introduction of a state lottery in the form of Premium Bonds. Nevertheless, the Butler economic miracle was clearly over; the Tory catch-phrase of the previous year – the free market – looked very tired.

In the long run toughness may have paid, but the electoral consequences could be gauged from Gallup poll findings. From the autumn of 1955 to the spring of 1956 the proportion of people approving of Eden's work fell from 70 per cent to 40 per cent. Hire purchase credit did not overtake the level of December 1955 until June 1958; by a remarkable parallel, the opinion polls showed that Labour would win a general election at any time during the same period.

Eden's fall from popularity was seized upon by the Press. On 3 January 1956, Donald McLachlan, then deputy editor of the *Daily Telegraph*, wrote an article with the theme: 'Most Conservatives, and almost certainly some of the wiser Trade Union leaders, are waiting to feel the smack of firm Government... In his new position (Lord Privy Seal), Mr Butler should have more time to help with the captaincy; but the spirit and the strategy can be created only by the Prime Minister himself.' The *Daily Mail* added: 'The Government's trouble seems to be not paralysis so much as a lack of will.'

Rumours grew of Eden's coming resignation; the Prime Minister was furious and his anger culminated in an unprecedented denial of any intention to resign. Eden replied to his critics at Bradford. 'This country', he said, 'is not on its way down, and this Government is not on its way out. As to the Government, we were elected not for six or eight months, but for five years. It is on our record at the end of those years that we are prepared to be judged, and I intend – if God wills – to be there on that day.'

Electorally, there was no response; the middle class wanted more than words. Heavy swings in by-elections showed themselves from the beginning of 1956, particularly in strong Conservative seats. Conservative abstentions were particularly obvious in Torquay, Gainsborough, and especially Tonbridge. The Conservative majority in the last dropped from 10,000 to just over 1,000 in June 1956. The swing away from the Conservatives was 8.4 per cent, a very high figure by contemporary standards. Tonbridge was a typical Conservative stronghold and reflected the growing disillusion with the apparent weakness of Conservative policy at home and abroad.

With things going badly at home, Eden instinctively turned to foreign affairs. He visited Washington in January 1956 to try to persuade the Americans to strengthen the Tripartite Declaration. This legacy of the first Arab-Israeli war was

The Middle East: the fuse is lit

I think the Glubb sacking was the starting-point of
the whole Suez episode. Up to that point the home
front had gone badly. At least the foreign front was
all right; at least our position in the world seemed
to be fairly strong, and at least the Suez Group
couldn't really get at him. The right wing in the
press and the party seemed to be, I don't say happy,
but reasonably devoid of arguments to deploy
against his handling of foreign policy. Suddenly, like
a bombshell, came the sacking of General Glubb.
After all those years of service to the King of Jordan.
This really undid Eden because it showed that
suddenly everything seemed to be going wrong, even
the foreign front seemed to be disintegrating, and on
this occasion, he, to quote a modern idiom, had lost
his cool – the first time I'd ever seen it happen. He
really lost his temper in the House of Commons and
made an appallingly bad speech. He allowed Dick
Crossman to get under his thermostat, and he really
blew it. I began to wonder very seriously whether he
wasn't a very sick man.
I spent practically the whole of that night after
Glubb was sacked in his room at No. 10 trying to
talk some sense. I was trying to get him to see this
thing in a rational light, trying to get him to see that
the King of Jordan had sacked General Glubb very
churlishly; maybe he'd behaved very badly, maybe,
but he had come to the conclusion that he couldn't
possibly grow in stature, the King of Jordan, so long
as this old oak in the shape of General Glubb still
spread its shadow over him. I tried to explain that
this was a very natural reaction. After all, the young
Kaiser had done it with Bismarck, history was
littered with examples of this kind, and there was
nothing more sinister in it than that. But, oh, no, I
didn't understand Nasser, I wouldn't accept any
criticism of Nasser, I was in love with Nasser, and so
on. He simply would not accept the truth about the
sacking of Glubb. From that moment on he said
'Nasser's got to go, it's either me or Nasser'.
ANTHONY NUTTING

designed to guarantee stable frontiers in the
Middle East. But the Americans brushed the
Prime Minister's proposals aside.

Eden's mission sprang from his worries about the
possibility of international anarchy in the Middle
East. Some stabilizing moves had already been
attempted. The Baghdad Pact, brainchild of Iraqi
Premier, Nuri-es-Said, was signed in April 1955.
Pakistan and Persia joined a few months later,
completing a northern bastion against possible
Soviet aggression. The initiation provoked denun-
ciation and counter-moves from Nasser. Baulked
of an arms supply from the West, Nasser turned to
Russia, and in September 1955 his arms deal with
Czechoslovakia was made public. The formation of
a joint high command with Syria followed a month
later. Although directed against Israel, it seemed a
veiled threat to Iraq. The Arab Middle East was
polarizing around Nuri and Nasser. Neither had
scruples about plotting against the other, and their
attention became increasingly focused on Jordan,
dynastically tied to Iraq but with popular feeling
leaning to Nasser.

Jordan was traditionally a British sphere of
interest and her army was British officered, British
trained, and commanded by a British General, Sir
John Glubb.

Cutting across these Arab rivalries was their
universal hostility to Israel. Refused arms by the
United States, and alarmed by Eden's public
advocacy of frontier revision to be followed by a
British and American guarantee as the road to an
Arab-Jewish settlement, Israel took fright at the
Egypt-Syria Pact and began to consider preventive
war. Ben Gurion, Israel's former saviour, returned
from his self-imposed exile to head the Israeli
Government.

Eden, as his frontier proposals showed, had not
ceased to hope for an easing of relations with
Nasser. To the Americans, the Egyptian President
was the authentic voice of Arab nationalism.
Britain and the United States therefore agreed to
help finance the high dam at Aswan, the key to
Nasser's ambitious projects for the economic and
social regeneration of Egypt. But the safeguards
built into the proposal inevitably meant that the
Egyptian economy would have been overseen from
Washington for the next five years, and not unnaturally Nasser began to stall.

The Baghdad powers were determined to persuade
Jordan to join them, but a mission to Amman in

January by the British Chief of General Staff proved counterproductive. Nasser's propaganda whipped up anti-British riots and three Jordanian Governments fell in quick succession. To restore order the new Jordanian Prime Minister promised to keep out of the Baghdad Pact. In response to a reassuring message from the new British Foreign Secretary, Selwyn Lloyd, who was to prove a more docile colleague than Macmillan, Nasser promised to stop Cairo radio from broadcasting propaganda against the Jordanian government and Britain.

He was not quite as good as his word: by February Cairo radio was again in full blast, this time against General Glubb. King Hussein abruptly dismissed him on 1 March 1956. His reasons were personal ones: resentment of Glubb's patronizing interference and the need to anchor the army firmly to his own person. Eden, deeply shocked, blamed Nasser. However wrong about Hussein's motives, Eden knew the damage to Britain's prestige. The Conservative Party, and especially the Suez Group, were outraged. But Eden, unwilling to attack Hussein publicly for fear of driving Jordan into Nasser's camp, made an appalling speech when the matter was debated in the Commons. As a political journalist wrote, the blow to Eden's prestige was 'reflected in the silent devastated ranks... behind him'.

Cyprus provided a check to the apparent slide. There Turkish and Greek Cypriots were not only at each others throats, but E.O.K.A terrorists were attempting to force the British to hand the island over to Greece. Talks with the Greek Cypriot leader, Archbishop Makarios, seemed to be bogged down. Two days after the Glubb debate, Eden, overruling his Colonial Secretary, deported Makarios to the Seychelles. The action met with a rapturous reception in Tory circles: the British would at last be master in their own house.

Eden's hypersensitive reaction was more than matched by men with tougher skins across the Channel. Guy Mollet, the French Premier, led an administration in which many were committed to Israel's survival. The French distrusted British attempts to build the Arabs into a Western alliance. and they were becoming increasingly mistrustful of Nasser, who had openly declared his support for Algerian rebels at war with France. By the end of June, after months of intensive Israeli lobbying, the French Government secretly promised Israel 'all she needed for her defence'.

Eden arrested Makarios and sent him off to exile in the Seychelles in the Indian Ocean. I remember very well the night when this was announced. I was going to address some small meeting in my constituency and I heard this news on the car radio as I was driving to the meeting. So I announced it to an audience who were mostly unaware of what had happened. There was an instantaneous reaction; they rose to their feet, they cheered themselves hoarse and this was, of course, exactly what Eden had wanted, and had prophesied by this action. I think it was really from that moment onwards that he felt his role to be that of the strong man who was going to speak up for England and for the empire, for this is what the Tory Party in the country really wanted, and in a sense he was perfectly right, they did want it.

NIGEL NICOLSON

I didn't of course attend the 1922 Committee meeting on the banishment of Makarios, but I can remember one of my closer friends in the House of Commons saying to me in the lobby that evening: 'I didn't like that stamping of feet when the Prime Minister came in'. He said Eden had unleashed certain emotions in the party which were dangerous, which could easily recoil on him in a few months' time.

LORD BOYLE

'I want Nasser destroyed'

I think all the time Eden had the feeling of the thirties; how, in 1936, Hitler had gone back to the Rhineland. This German leader, trying to revive his people after the depression and improve their standard of living, going into part of Germany through which a German river flowed – why not be nice to him? Why not let him do it? Result? World War II. Here was Colonel Nasser, the saviour of his people. Hitler had written *Mein Kampf*; Nasser had written the *Philosophy of the Revolution* – clear every Briton out of the Middle East, clear every white man out of Africa, have a pan-Islamic empire throughout the world in which, no doubt, Nasser had cast himself for the leadership. Here was the Canal running through Egyptian territory. Why not be nice to him, why not be reasonable to him? I think Eden felt the consequence of that would be one territorial demand after another, one Middle East country after another falling under Nasser's control. Although the Egyptians weren't Germans, nevertheless, given sufficient encouragement, the appetite grows with eating. This wasn't an ordinary act of nationalization, this was a military occupation of an international company, a force of arms, and if people got away with that, then there was no saying what they would get away with next. A time had come, Eden felt very much, when we had to take a stand.

SELWYN LLOYD

Eden's view of Nasser was exactly the same as his view of Hitler and Mussolini. That's what accounts for what you might describe as his personalization of Nasser, which I think on the whole was a pity, because I think we'd have got on better in the Middle East if we hadn't had such a strong personal bias.

LORD BUTLER

Eden rang up. I was giving a dinner for my disarmament conference colleagues. I had sent the Prime Minister a minute a little bit before this, suggesting one or two ways in which we might be able to improve our position in the Middle East; to re-establish our influence in the Persian Gulf and consolidate our position in Jordan and so on. The Prime Minister said, 'I don't understand all this poppy-cock you've sent me, I don't agree with a word of it'. I said, 'Well, it's only an attempt to try and think out a few positive lines of policy for the Middle East which you may or may not agree with; but these are a genuine effort to inject new thinking into it because all our thinking at the moment seems to me to be rather negative'. He said, 'Well, I suppose you think it's negative to want to get rid of Nasser'. So I said, 'Well, frankly, I do, because I think if you get rid of Nasser you'll just have chaos in Egypt'. He said, 'I don't care if there is chaos in Egypt, I don't care if there is anarchy in Egypt, I want Nasser destroyed'. All this over an open telephone line, too, at the Savoy Hotel. What the Savoy operators must have thought if they were listening in I simply don't know. This was again an indication that Eden was a very different man and I think a very sick man by comparison with anything I'd ever known before.

The nationalization of the Canal suddenly presented Eden with an opportunity and from then on he was hell bent for hostilities of some kind or another. Immediately, the reserves were called up, people were mobilized, and a great military operation was conceived, and planning was begun on it. The only problem was the pretext. How were we going to stage an invasion of Egypt simply in order to get back a piece of property? This presented a considerable difficulty for him.

ANTHONY NUTTING

Eden had been warned by British Intelligence that Israel was contemplating a preventive war but he knew nothing of this latest development which upset the balance of power in the Middle East. Growing suspicions of Nasser nevertheless brought the French and English Prime Ministers into much closer alignment.

Eden's suspicions of Nasser's pan-Arab policies were increasingly linked in his mind to memories of the leeway allowed to Hitler and the potential threat to Europe's oil supplies. Already in April 1956 he had warned the Russian leaders in London that oil was so vital that Britain would fight for it.

Eden's real fears of Nasser were compounded by Egypt's growing armed strength. He was further alarmed by rumours, which were believed by the Americans, that Nasser was shopping around for alternative means of financing the Aswan dam and the British were alarmed that the Aswan might prove too onerous a financial burden. Nasser's overtures to Moscow made Dulles in particular question the large slice of American help that had been offered. The British advice to Dulles, who was genuinely uncertain, was to play for time.

In the midst of this uncertainty Dulles was visited by the Egyptian Ambassador who told him that there had been consultation with Moscow. Dulles regarded this as blackmail and cancelled the loan. The British followed suit two days later.

It is unlikely that Nasser was unduly upset until 22 July when the Russian Foreign Minister Shepilov denied that any firm offer had been made to build the dam. Nasser was now on his own: on 26 July he announced his intention, for which plans

Together in 1954. Eden lectured Nasser on the virtues of a pro-western pact

had been prepared, to nationalize the Suez canal, partly in order to be able to pay for the dam.

To almost every British politician, Nasser's move was seen as the seizure of the canal. The *Daily Herald* commented, without arousing protest, 'No more Hitlers'. Gaitskell declared the situation to be deplorable. *The Times* pointed out smugly that the Egyptians would not be able to work the canal anyway. At least one member of the Suez Group argued that the head waters of the Nile should be cut off in Uganda.

A cabinet committee was set up to review the Suez emergency on the day following nationalization. It was dominated by Eden, Macmillan, Salisbury, and Kilmuir. Butler was deliberately excluded, but he edged his way into most meetings. Within forty-eight hours of Nasser's action, the

Cabinet had concluded that no immediate armed intervention was possible. Egyptian strength was over-estimated, and British forces were simply not geared or equipped for a quick seaborne operation. But something had to be done.

Murphy, the American Under Secretary of State, came to London at the end of July and was told that Britain was preparing to use force. Greatly alarmed, Dulles followed him to London, prepared to create a web of negotiation in which the British impetus to use force would be lost: 'A way had to be found to make Nasser disgorge', he said. It was an ambivalent phrase, but to Eden it seemed quite clear that, for all his qualifications, Dulles did not rule out force as a last resort. Both men hoped to internationalize the canal, but in practice only the British were prepared to use force. On 2 August, while Dulles was in London, the British Cabinet took a further decision: negotiations would be pursued, but force would be used if they had no result within a measurable time.

Eden's Cabinet had now set a course from which they would find it extremely difficult to deviate. But Dulles returned to the United States believing he had prevented war. Eden, meanwhile, ordered the mobilization of reservists. The British Chiefs of Staff reported that it would be at least six weeks before an Anglo-French force could seize the canal. The French, now that they had a pretext, were impatient to act; the desire to get moving independently of the Americans spread like a seismic movement through French political opinion.

Eden had completely recovered his old control over the House of Commons. There was a whiff of grape-shot in the air. Gaitskell was belligerent, although buried at the end of his speech were a few qualifications, quickly inserted into it by Kenneth Younger, about conforming to the U.N. Charter. Gaitskell clearly accepted Eden's view that this was Hitler and Mussolini all over again. Parliament went into recess, and a period of negotiation began.

The details matter little. The twenty-two major maritime powers met in conclave but their terms, put by the Australian Prime Minister, Menzies, to Nasser, were unacceptable. The Egyptians countered by suggesting a conference of all the canal users, deliberately trying to involve the Soviet satellites. Menzies had warned Nasser that Britain and France were ready to use force, but a public statement from Eisenhower that the United States

Dulles plays for time

Mr Dulles never gave us a good solid reason for the abruptness of his action over the Aswan Dam. Hussein, the Egyptian Ambassador, had been in Cairo for over two months and when he returned he asked for a meeting with Mr Dulles. Out of that meeting came the abrupt decision to cancel the Aswan co-operation. I'd say one thing, Dulles had emphasized a number of times the folly of the Egyptian plan to build a huge military establishment on this paper-thin Egyptian economy. They could not do both. And when the Gyppies planned to acquire all this expensive military equipment from the Soviet Union, it became obvious to Dulles that this would not work, and that, I think, was his principal reason.

Before my visit to London, I had no instructions. Eisenhower said, go over there and hold the fort and see what it's all about. That, really, was about the extent of my instructions. The President at that moment was not too alarmed at the situation and felt it could be ironed out.

In London, Macmillan was very practical and matter-of-fact about it. What I liked about Mr Macmillan in any critical situation was that he had tremendous calm and poise and avoided emotional outbursts. He had taken a very, very practical view. He told me, he was then the Chancellor of the Exchequer, that they had built up a reserve of about £500 million, that there was a military plan of operation under consideration. We talked very frankly about the practical aspects of the military operation which would, I think they said, be on a two-divisional basis and wouldn't last more than ten days. The objective was to chase Nasser out of Egypt. So I left that dinner with the distinct notion that this plan would be put into effect very shortly.

There was a mutual dislike, or distrust at any rate, between Eden and Dulles, which was unfortunate but very apparent. There was a personality conflict there obviously, but it was so obvious that there wasn't a harmonious relationship. I think Sir Anthony believed that Dulles just didn't understand the situation, and Dulles on his side, I think, believed that Eden didn't understand the American position.
ROBERT MURPHY

Unfortunately, Dulles was a very rigid man. He couldn't see, as Eden saw at Geneva in 1954, that his task was to get out in front. All he could think of was to hold on to Eden's coat-tail. This was psychologically the worst that he could have done. This only made Eden all the more anxious to go ahead.
ANTHONY NUTTING

Our interests were not parallel here. This represented for the British a problem which, for us, was of far less importance – I mean the oil supply. It did seem to me that Sir Anthony was committed to the use of force – that was the distinct impression I had. In his mind he thought that Dulles shared that view. When Mr Dulles used the words that Nasser should be 'forced to disgorge', I think that this undoubtedly, with the thoughts that Sir Anthony had in his mind, added up to a notion that Dulles was in harmony with the idea of the use of force. Dulles, I don't believe, ever had that notion at all. His thinking ran along the lines of pressures other than the use of military force; of an economic, financial and political nature. There was a failure, not a meeting of minds, on the subject, which led undoubtedly to further misunderstanding.
ROBERT MURPHY

I went down to Egypt feeling that I had complete American support, indeed American promotion, in what the Users Committee had to put to Nasser. I think that, as we left the matter in London, the British government were well entitled to believe that America was supporting the proposition and determined not to allow Nasser to get away with it. I've never been engaged in a more curious negotiation. When gentlemen meet, compliments are exchanged; so we all said hello to each other and got to know what the other man looked like, that sort of thing, and then an evening was appointed on which I was to put the case. I first of all asked Nasser if he would like to have an interpreter and he said oh, no. He thought that his English was in fact pretty good, so I put the case to a completely unresponsive audience. It was very queer, you know, it was like speaking to a brick wall. I resorted to all the old politician's tricks to introduce a bit of life into it, but no, it was a very dead reception. On the morning after I had put the case to Nasser I opened the papers, and read a report from Washington which contained the sad story that Eisenhower had said that under no conceivable circumstances could force be employed. When I say I was a bit rocked by this, it doesn't mean that I was all out for the use of force; I thought that was a circumstance which would depend on the course of events. But to abandon the one fear in the other man's mind that might have induced him to be a little careful was, I thought, throwing away the trump card. It was a shock, it defeated us. From that time on I thought we were bound to lose.

SIR ROBERT MENZIES

1956

After the failure of the Menzies mission through no fault of Menzies, the Americans came along with their idea of a Users Association. We thought that that was not a bad idea and then Dulles said, of course, it would have no teeth; it wouldn't, under any circumstances, exercise any physical pressure on the Egyptians of any sort or kind. Then I think we began to realize he was leading us up the garden path. In fact, I was not in favour of going into the 'Users' thing at all because I didn't see any future in it. Then I think the old relationship between Eden and Dulles began to resurrect itself. Dulles hadn't liked Eden because he thought of Eden's superior expertise and reputation as Foreign Secretary. Eden hadn't liked Dulles because he thought that Dulles was taking his allies much too much for granted all the time and was inclined to ride rough-shod over them.

SELWYN LLOYD

He was a strange chap, Dulles. His great defect was, unlike some of us, his love of having press conferences. He would look for a press conference as another man will look for a shop to buy a hat, but he didn't work out in advance what he was going to say. He would make one statement that satisfied the chronicler of one particular paper, who darted out of the room to get on the wire; but before his footsteps had died away Dulles would be saying but, on the other hand, then he had a second possibility, and a third possibility and a fourth possibility, and each of them got into a different newspaper. Strange defect, wasn't it, for a man of his ability?

SIR ROBERT MENZIES

One fundamental point, which it is always necessary to bear in mind when considering the events of that period, is that the American government was within a few weeks of a presidential election. Had they wanted to take military action, they would have had to recall Congress and get authorization to do it. This was obviously an impossible political operation for the American administration in those circumstances. Their attitude was, I think, in essence, we agree with you about Nasser, we agree he should be cut down to size, but as regards means, these are our proposals. The implication being, we can't take military action. If you wait until after the election, this is the implication, the situation might be different. Meanwhile, do work with us on the lines we propose.

LORD SHERFIELD

It was so easy for Sir Anthony to say – I'm not asking anything from the United States, just that you take care of the Bear (the Russians). Well that was a very nice easy formula, not knowing what the Bear might do, but I'm sure Mr Dulles did not want to be put in a position where we would take care of the Bear. Dulles's tactics were deliberate delay, in the hope that a peaceful solution could be worked out, that your public and world opinion would not countenance a military operation.

ROBERT MURPHY

What other means?

15 August 1956. Eden and Pineau, the French Foreign Minister

was 'committed to a peaceful settlement... nothing else', wholly undermined Menzies' position. Eisenhower was, of course, facing his second Presidential election within a matter of weeks.

Behind the feverish diplomatic activity, British and French military planners were making rapid progress with a seaborne invasion of Egypt. Cyprus, the major British base in the area, had no deep-water harbour. It could be used for air strikes, but the invasion fleet would have to sail from Malta, 1,000 miles and six days from Egypt.

In Britain, opposition to the Government's line hardened. Labour's leaders had begun to insist on the need for U.N. backing and the *Daily Mirror* drove home their line. Cecil King, its Chairman, finally convinced a reluctant Gaitskell that Eden was keeping him in the dark. He was; partly because he was convinced that Gaitskell was not master of the Labour Party. From the United States, Eisenhower wrote to warn Eden of the dangers of exalting Nasser to martyrdom. Eden was not deterred. The Anglo-French forces were ready and it remained only to put the case for intervention to the U.N., and to secure a Soviet veto, which would then justify the use of force by the French and British on their own account.

Dulles could only buy more time. Adapting Nasser's proposal to his own use, he proposed a Suez Canal Users Association (SCUA). The French were suspicious of this further delay, but Eden felt that, if it brought the Americans in, he could make use of the idea. Some of the Cabinet were dubious, Macmillan taking a particularly strong line while Selwyn Lloyd urged immediate recourse to the United Nations. But Eden had his way.

The decision for the first time during the crisis divided the House of Commons on a vote. When Eden read the three-power Agreement on S.C.U.A. there were angry questions about the 'further steps' mentioned as a consequence of any refusal of co-operation from Egypt. Nasser declared that the scheme meant war. Dulles did not agree, and in answering Press questions on 13 September, pulled every tooth out of the plan: it was not a concerted boycott; nor would the Americans use force to get through the canal, even if Nasser closed it.

Eden was dumbfounded and S.C.U.A. was dead even before the discussions on it got lost in procedural wrangling. A French delegate captured the feeling of Anglo-French exasperation: '*il faut coloniser le canal ou canaliser le colonel.*' Macmillan

The House of Commons was recalled in September 1956 for an emergency debate on the Middle East situation. In his speech Eden said that the government were determined to make Nasser give back the Canal and if he couldn't be forced to do so by diplomatic or economic means, then there would have to be 'other means'. The House leapt on those two words 'other means'. What 'other means', they all shouted? Eden shilly-shallied, but it was perfectly clear from that moment that the government were going to use force against Nasser in the last resort, and that the last resort was just around the corner.
NIGEL NICOLSON

'...coloniser le canal ou canaliser le colonel'

told Dulles bitterly that he would rather pawn the pictures in the National Gallery than accept humiliation from Nasser. When it finally became clear to Eden that S.C.U.A. was well on the way to becoming an organization to collect the canal tolls for Nasser, he and Mollet decided to put their case straight to the U.N. Security Council.

France now took the lead. From early August, the Israelis had been getting the arms they needed from the French. Dayan, Israeli Chief of Staff, had known from the beginning of September that the French and British would strike at Alexandria or

Port Said, if attempts at negotiation failed. Military men from France and Israel met frequently and the resolve to use force grew in Paris. Ben Gurion, the Israeli Premier, told Mollet that he was prepared to act against Nasser but only with French backing and, failing anything better, British neutrality. The key was France's policy – could they get the British committed to a firm date for an invasion.

Pineau, the French Foreign Minister, appears to have first suggested the idea of Israeli collaboration to Eden and Lloyd in London on 23 September, and Mollet to have raised the question again briefly when Eden and Lloyd flew to Paris on the 26th. But according to French sources, Lloyd was determined 'not to compromise Britain with regard to the Arab countries, and not to run the risk of involving Britain's treaty obligations with Jordan'. Eden is alleged to have said privately that Pineau was much too clever for his own good. He was to prove even cleverer.

The French were sceptical about the U.N. and even more so about S.C.U.A. They urged action at an early date, and drew from Eden the firm statement that if the U.N. could not maintain international agreements, Britain would be prepared to use force to re-establish respect for them. Mollet told the Israelis the British Prime Minister was prepared to see how the U.N. talks between Lloyd and the Egyptian Foreign Minister Fawzi progressed.

Meanwhile, Macmillan had returned from a two week visit to the United States. He had publicly and privately proclaimed Britain's determination to stop Nasser, and was convinced from his talks with Dulles and other members of the President's Cabinet that the United States would not interfere with Britain's plans. Back in London he threatened to resign unless the Government played out the hand to the end. Waverers in the Cabinet found Dulles' triumphant proclamation on 2 October that there were 'no teeth' in S.C.U.A. too much to take. The arena of action narrowed.

In New York, Pineau warned Dulles, with Lloyd present, 'that they did not believe any peaceful way existed'. But there was cautious optimism when Fawzi proved co-operative and six principles were agreed for the future of the canal. But no one could be sure whether Nasser would stick to them – particularly the clause about the canal's 'insulation from Egyptian politics'. Eden thought the principles weak and was probably not too regretful that an Anglo-American attempt to put an enforcement

'La mise en scène est prête'

Just before Sunday 14 October, when the French came to Chequers and saw Eden and myself there and put the plan for Anglo-French-Israeli collusion, Selwyn Lloyd and Fawzi, the Egyptian Foreign Minister, and Pineau, the French Foreign Minister, had in private serious meetings in New York under the Chairmanship of Hammarskjold, the Secretary General of the United Nations. They got an agreement, what's more, which gave us all that we needed in the way of guarantees for the future of the Canal.

ANTHONY NUTTING

Fawzi said that agreement was reached in New York. It isn't true. It's quite true that the six principles I enunciated myself, Mr Hammarskjold wrote them down, were incorporated in a resolution which was ultimately unanimously accepted by the Security Council; but the implementation part of the resolution was vetoed by the Russians. It was possibly a rather flimsy basis for a negotiation and, from what one's heard since, Nasser had not the slightest intention of reaching an agreement on those principles. The most disturbing fact, apart from the Russian veto which we had expected, was the fact that Mr Dulles had told me, the evening of the end of the Security Council debate, that the Americans were not prepared to bring any further pressure to bear on the Egyptians to make a settlement. They were actually suggesting that the Egyptians should get 90 per cent of the Canal dues instead of 50 per cent; it's quite clear that they weren't prepared to bring pressure to bear. That made me very dubious about the success of any negotiations which might take place, supposing the Egyptians did in fact bring forth proposals for carrying out the six principles. I thought it was possible for us to go on with negotiations. I could give my colleagues no promise at all of a successful conclusion.

SELWYN LLOYD

The French had already been in touch with the Israelis, quite clearly. The two French representatives, the acting Foreign Minister, Monsier Gazier, and General Challe, who was then a kind of military adviser to the Prime Minister, Guy Mollet, came over to Chequers. They asked us what would be our reaction if the Israelis were to attack across the Sinai peninsula and go for the Suez Canal. Eden was a little taken aback to begin with to know quite what the purpose of this question was, but it gradually began to dawn on him that there might be some conspiracy concocted by the French, who themselves had been as eager as we were to find a pretext, to have a bash against Nasser. After a little further explanation on the side of the French it dawned on him this was exactly what they were proposing: the Israelis should go for the Canal and that we and the French should intervene to separate the combatants, put out the fire. We were going to be the policemen, the fire brigade. As General Challe said, very graphically referring to the paratroopers

who were going to be involved in this exercise, '*et puis les paras vont tomber sur le canal*'. This was exactly what the object of the exercise was. Eden, of course, was simply delighted. This was the pretext he'd been searching for, which the French had been searching for, and the French had now come up with it.

Selwyn Lloyd came back to this country on Tuesday 16 October not knowing anything about what the French had been saying at Chequers and the new plan that Eden had suddenly taken up. Selwyn came back to London thinking, or generally saying to me, that he'd clinched it, he'd got what he'd thought was a reasonable deal. It wasn't everything that we would have wanted but it was a reasonable compromise and he seemed satisfied enough on his return. I had to go out of the meeting at Downing Street, which was taking place to decide how we would respond to this French proposal, and I had to tell Selwyn exactly what was afoot. Selwyn said to me in so many words – you're absolutely right, we must have nothing to do with this, we must go on as we are, further meetings with Fawzi to tie up the details, and so on. I tried to get Selwyn to come to lunch with me that day so I could still further fortify him with the Foreign Office point of view. Those advisers whom I'd been able to consult about the French plan were absolutely horrified by it, and they begged me to do everything I could to prevent the Prime Minister from going ahead.

I tried to get hold of Selwyn, but no, the Prime Minister had got him and took him off. Took him to Paris that afternoon and gave the answer to the French. From that moment on, of course, we were embarked. The only thing which seemed to stand in the way was, curiously enough, the unwillingness of the Israelis to be our stalking horse. Ben Gurion, I think very naturally, said, look, if you expect me to go and take my soldiers into the Sinai Desert and get them stuck and bombed to blazes by the Egyptian Air Force, you've got to give me some protection. The Suez operation could not be mounted as Ben Gurion saw it, as Ben Gurion planned it, without the help of the British, because we were the only people who had the necessary bomber force to what was called 'take out' Nasser's Air Force. It wasn't until we were prepared to give an absolute guarantee to Ben Gurion that he would go ahead.

ANTHONY NUTTING

General Challe said, 'Look, the Israelis are going to attack Egypt. The Israelis will be . . .' He showed a big map of the Middle East showing Egypt and the Sinai Peninsula. He said, 'The Israelis are going to be here, the Egyptians here, where is our place? Here', and he put his hand on the middle where the Suez Canal is silently flowing. Eden was very interested by the idea. He didn't give his approval at the moment but said, 'That's a good idea', because the Israeli intervention turned out to be an ideal pretext for Britain and for France.

BAR ZOHAR

'Our relations with Israel were not close or intimate . . . Therefore at this meeting in Paris, we asked the French ministers to do everything they could to make clear to Israel that an attack on Jordan would have to be resisted by us. This they undertook to do . . . To fail to carry out our engagement would be the end of our position in the Middle East; to have to carry it out would be disastrous to Western unity. No dilemma could be more difficult. If Israel were to break out against Egypt and not against Jordan, this dilemma would not arise. For this reason, if there were to be a break-out, it was better from our point of view that it should be against Egypt. On the other hand, if the break-out were against Egypt, then there would be other worries, for example the safety of the Canal. We discussed these matters in all their political and military aspects . . .

During recent months we had been mounting our military preparations to deal with any interference or other act by Nasser against our ships or our people. Now Nasser's policies were provoking Israel beyond endurance, and this also we had to prepare for.'

ANTHONY EDEN *Full Circle* p. 512-3

Guy Mollet wanted to try and convince Ben Gurion on the spot. On 21 October, Ben Gurion came to Paris in the plane which was the private plane of General de Gaulle. It was given to him by President Truman after the war. He arrived at this famous, mysterious, secret villa in Sèvres where the conference was to take place. He came with Dayan, the Chief of Staff, Peres his Head of Intelligence, and several officers. He met there Mollet, Pineau the Foreign Minister, Bourges-Maunory the French Defence Minister, General Challe, and other French officers. They talked about this project; Ben Gurion was against it. On the evening of 22 October, Selwyn Lloyd arrived with his Secretary, Mr Logan. Selwyn Lloyd was very much embarrassed and, let's say, upset, by the fact that he had to meet Ben Gurion and to talk to him. This was the awful, horrible, collusion with the Israelis which the British had worked so hard to avoid. They say when Selwyn Lloyd entered the room there was quite a cold wind blowing inside and the handshake was very formal. Ben Gurion explained that he didn't agree at all to the project; he didn't want to make a full-scale war, he didn't want the seventy-two hours to elapse before the Anglo-French attack. He wanted a protection of the Israeli skies by French fighters, and he wanted to be sure that the British would bomb the airfields of Egypt. He also wanted to be sure that if Jordan attacked Israel, Britain would not intervene on the side of Jordan. Because Britain had an alliance with Jordan at this time, there were not very many chances in the evening of this first day that an agreement would be reached. The only thing which Selwyn Lloyd agreed to was that this seventy-two hours would be reduced to thirty-six. Lloyd flew back to London with the impression that nothing would come out of the Sèvres conference.

BAR ZOHAR

authority behind them was vetoed in the U.N. Security Council by Russia.

Eden's attention was presently fixed on the Israeli-Jordanian frontier, where for several weeks Israel had deliberately provoked acute tension. Britain was forced to remind Israel of her obligations under the Anglo-Jordanian defence treaty and there was nearly a serious incident. To forestall Nasser's intervention, Eden persuaded Iraq to send a division into Jordan. The French begged Eden to call off the Iraqis; surely he could not want to provoke a situation in which he would be fighting Israel.

Eden's dilemma was clear, and the French, who had been planning a possible joint operation against Egypt with the Israelis and without the British since 8 October, now decided to offer a way off the hook.

General Challe and M. Gazier, acting French Foreign Minister and a confidant of Mollet's, flew to see Eden at Chequers on 14 October. Gazier asked what the British reaction would be if Israel attacked Egypt, and when Eden replied that he hardly saw himself fighting for Nasser, Challe sketched a possible 'scenario'. If Israel were to attack Egypt, France and Britain would intervene to protect the canal from the fighting, ordering both sides to withdraw from it. Eden was noncommittal but saw the attraction of the scheme: he would discuss it with Mollet.

The hook was baited, and Eden disposed to take it. On 16 October a small group of senior ministers met, with the Chiefs of Staff present. Rejecting any further negotiations as valueless, they discussed the French plan. Macmillan and Kilmuir supported it; Monckton, always an opponent of the use of force, argued against, with support from the Foreign Secretary's stand-in, Anthony Nutting. Lloyd, arriving in the middle of the meeting, at first wavered over the plan and was then persuaded by Eden during lunch. The certainly of France and Israel using force seems to have been decisive in his mind.

That afternoon Eden and Lloyd went to Paris. The meeting was not very satisfactory. The French were waiting to see how far Eden would commit himself to their scheme and the British were determined not to be drawn into a direct alliance with Israel. The talks, ambiguously and necessarily, revolved around certain possibilities. Despite Mollet's warning that the last chance of an amphibious

Doubts in the Cabinet

When Selwyn Lloyd came back from Sèvres, he was, I think, a little taken aback by Ben Gurion's absolute insistence on this guarantee. He seemed to think that the operation probably would not get off the ground. This was certainly what he said to me. He said 'I don't think you need worry so much about it because I think it's all going to fizzle out and I don't think the Israelis are all that keen on it'. So I said, 'Well, that lets us out'; and he said, 'Well, not entirely, because', he said, 'we've now got to decide how to deal with this thing. I mean if we don't deal with it by means of the Challe Plan, we've got to deal with it some other way, and the cabinet have got to decide how to deal with it'. I said, 'What about your agreement with Fawzi, this is the answer, surely?' He said, 'Well, the cabinet have got to decide whether it's peace or war'. I said, 'Which way are you going to advise it?' It was then that I realized how absolutely exhausted Selwyn was at this time. He said, 'Quite honestly, I don't know, I'm too exhausted to make up my mind'.
ANTHONY NUTTING

The French people, on the other hand, were very keen to find a solution. They pressed the Israelis very hard to find a new formula. This formula was suggested by General Dayan on the second day. He said that we were not ready to make a full-scale war on Egypt but if we just parachuted the troops about thirty miles from the canal and published it, it would be quite a threat on the Suez Canal. And it would furnish the British and the French with a pretext in order to issue their ultimatum.

Now the French were very happy about that. Pineau flew immediately to London with this proposal and succeeded in getting the approval of Eden. After he got this agreement he went back to Paris and they worked out the new formula, and finally, on 24 October, the English representatives arrived in Paris. They were Patrick Dean and, again, Logan. They brought the agreement of Eden, which was about six paragraphs, and which agreed to this new formula: just a small attack on Israel which could also be interpreted by the Israelis, in case something went wrong, as just a larger raid of retaliation on Egypt, but not a war. They also agreed to give the ultimatum to Israel and Egypt. This agreement was signed by Ben Gurion for Israel, Christian Pineau for France, and Patrick Dean for Britain. Ben Gurion flew back to Israel on the 25th. On the 26th in the afternoon, there arrived from Paris the official letters of agreement, the ratification of these agreements in Sèvres. One was signed by Guy Mollet, who approved of these agreements. The second was signed by Eden. Now Sir Anthony Eden didn't want to sign anything connecting him with Israel, so his letter was addressed to Guy Mollet saying that he ratified this treaty which was signed at Sèvres between France and Britain. Guy Mollet was very, very much interested to preserve the connection with Israel. Mollet made a photo-copy of Eden's letter and sent it to Ben Gurion with his signature, in order for Ben Gurion to sign it too.
BAR ZOHAR

I think the military situation was building up. Over 120 people had been killed on the borders of Jordan alone, I think, in September '56. The Egyptians and Syrians had the arrangements for a joint Arab military command. On 25 October, I think it was, the anti-Western parties won the General Election in Jordan. All the time there was the feeling of tension that the Israelis – or perhaps the Israelis and French together – would take military action. There was the feeling there was no certainty of success or of any progress in the negotiations and there was a situation, of course, building up all the time. I think it was certainly the feeling of impending crisis: the idea that you could let the whole thing run into the sand with the winter of fruitless negotiations, that option wasn't all that attractive.

Q. Could you tell us precisely when opinion crystallized on the inevitability of joint action by the three governments?

A. The Israelis took action on Monday 29 October. My recollection is that opinion began to crystallize during the previous week.
SELWYN LLOYD

When it actually got to the crunch, at the very end of the month, obviously several members of the cabinet did have acute worries about it then. I know from letters I received just how deeply worried certain members of the cabinet were.
LORD BOYLE

I think there was a difference in degree between some members in the cabinet who were keen on force. Of course, if you take the case of the Foreign Secretary himself, Selwyn Lloyd, he worked very hard at the United Nations, and with Fawzi, to try and get a settlement. Selwyn Lloyd worked away as hard as anyone else to try and avoid the use of force, if it had been possible.
LORD BUTLER

There was opposition in the cabinet to the final decision to go ahead. But most of those who opposed it were fairly convinced that the opposition was too late, that the decision had, in fact, been taken and that if they objected, they would object to what was already a *fait accompli*. I think in that they were right because the French had been given the go-ahead by Eden before the cabinet actually came to a conclusion about it.

ANTHONY NUTTING

assault before winter was slipping away, nothing conclusive emerged.

Eden's account is none the less revealing. On 18 October, the Cabinet was told of 'the growing danger that Israel, under provocation from Egypt, would make some military move'. A day earlier Ben Gurion had told the Israeli Parliament that the gravest danger facing Israel was from the 'Egyptian Fascist dictator'. At the same time Eden had labelled Nasser a Communist dupe and was watching Soviet arms accumulate in Egypt. But Ben Gurion was doubtful of Britain's precise intentions and of the dangers of an Israeli attack without sufficient air cover. On 22 October he and Dayan flew to Paris for secret discussions with the French. Without a written agreement and without a meeting with a key British minister, he would not go ahead. So on the evening of 22 October Selwyn Lloyd darted over to Paris. Like some disapproving 'family lawyer' he made clear his distaste for the project, agreed that British and French troops should be committed thirty-six hours after the initial Israeli action (and not seventy-six hours as had previously been agreed), and left, leaving behind a civil servant. At this stage Lloyd doubted if these discussions would come to anything.

But it was not a civil servant's signature that Ben Gurion wanted. Pineau went to London to persuade Eden, but it was not until the 26th that the 'declaration of intent' was handed to Mollet, apparently with an appropriately august signature. On the 24th the Cabinet was given a glimpse of the scenario, but only a few knew the script. Israel was going to attack. Britain and France's long delayed invasion could at last be launched. Monckton opposed the plan, but Butler, Heathcoat Amory, and perhaps Macleod, had growing doubts about it. Whether the exact nature of the concert with Israel ever became plain to every member of the Cabinet is open to doubt. But the Cabinet was agreed to the Anglo-French response to an Israeli attack.

Events now helped the plot along. The victory of pro-Nasser elements in the Jordan elections and the creation on 23 October of a joint military command between Egypt, Syria and Jordan steeled the 'weak sisters' in the British Cabinet. The insurrection in Hungary tied the Soviet Union down in Europe and distracted America's attention from the Middle East. In past years Eden's own attention would have been fixed on Hungary, but now his obsession with the Middle East led him to

135

The thing became quite ridiculous, because when we issued our ultimatum to both sides to withdraw ten miles each side of the Suez Canal, the Israelis still had another forty or fifty miles to go to get to the Canal, and the Egyptians were still in contact with the Israelis on the eastern side of the Canal. So, in effect, an order to both sides to withdraw ten miles was an order for the Egyptians to withdraw something like seventy to eighty miles to get to the other side of the Canal, and an order for the Israelis to advance forty or fifty miles to get up to the Canal.
ANTHONY NUTTING

take advantage of the great powers' preoccupation to launch the Egyptian adventure.

On Sunday 28 October the Israeli Cabinet approved the plan to attack Egypt. At dawn the previous day English and French aircraft carriers had sailed eastwards from Malta. The Israeli forces advanced more than forty-eight hours later, at 4 p.m. on 29 October. The British Cabinet met next morning and 'decided' to deliver an ultimatum to both Egypt and Israel that both should withdraw their forces ten miles from either side of the canal. In effect, Egypt was ordered to withdraw her troops and Israel to advance. Not unnaturally, when the ultimatum was presented that afternoon, Nasser refused. By 5 a.m. on 31 October, the Anglo-French operation was under way. The aerial attack on Egypt was delayed until dusk. The Americans were evacuating their civilians from the main Ilyushin base in Egypt, and Eden ordered the bombers to wait. The Egyptians were completely unable to take advantage of this sudden, short-lived reprieve. They could not fly Russian bombers.

The Anglo-French plan was to have an initial bombing offensive from Cyprus to 'soften up' the Egyptians while the invasion fleet, without a deepwater port in Cyprus, had a six-day voyage from Malta, 1,000 miles from Suez. A selective and largely accurate attack began at dusk on 31 October. Nasser realized that at last this was not a bluff. He ordered his troops out of Sinai and prepared for guerilla war. Within forty-eight hours he had sunk forty-seven blockships in the canal. The justification of the Anglo-French action, to keep the canal open, was gone.

At the United Nations, Britain twice used her veto, the first time she had done so, to stop United States' ceasefire resolutions. Eisenhower called off his election campaign, and abused Eden over the telephone.

Meanwhile, the Anglo-French fleet was at sea; Israel had gained her immediate military objectives and was waiting for a ceasefire. Everything happened too quickly for the French and British: there was a queasy lull before the invasion could begin. Restiveness grew and it was decided that paratroopers should go in before the invasion fleet arrived. The French had wanted this earlier, but the British had consistently over-estimated Egyptian strength.

Opposition at home grew; in the Conservative Party about a dozen members signed a protest letter to Eden. Gaitskell felt he had been personally deceived. Much to the fury of the troops, about to go into action, Gaitskell broadcast a demand that the Prime Minister should resign, and an appeal that dissident Conservatives should defect. Anthony Nutting, Eden's protégé, and Edward Boyle, Macmillan's Junior at the Treasury, resigned. Gaitskell, having been told of the growing doubts among Conservative back-benchers, hoped that Butler might consolidate an incipient Conservative revolt.

His broadcast says much of himself, but showed how little he understood the party opposite and their powerful bond of personal loyalty to their leader. Less noticed among those resigning was Eden's Press Secretary, appalled at the lies he would have to tell, whom the Prime Minister speeded on his way by a flying ink pot. In the House of Commons there were riotous scenes: the violence of the attack on Eden was unprecedented and for the first time since 1924 a sitting had to be suspended.

At dawn on 5 November the airborne landings at last began and twenty-four hours later troops arrived from the armada. Their advance was rapid, well directed, but curtailed. At midnight on 6 November, with British forces about twenty-five miles beyond Port Said and fast proceeding down the canal, the Cabinet announced a ceasefire.

This was an extraordinary reversal, but not altogether as remarkable as it appeared at the time. There were certainly doubters in the Cabinet, but they were too late, too timid, and insufficient in number to stop Eden before the operation began. But the great awkwardness was that Egypt and Israel were no longer fighting. Israeli forces were not on the canal. The combatants simply did not have to be separated and the Anglo-French invasion involved fighting Egyptians only. It is clear, however, that Anglo-French troops could have occupied the canal zone without great difficulty; the Russian threat to rain missiles on London was never taken seriously.

It had often been said that the man responsible for halting the operation was the Chancellor of the Exchequer, Harold Macmillan. British reserves were ebbing away, although hardly at crisis level. Macmillan reclaimed Britain's quota payment to the International Monetary Fund, but the American Treasury, which dominated this international

This far and no further. British troops stopped in their tracks

I was unhappy about certain aspects of the Suez Affair. I was notably unhappy about the long time the convoy took to reach the coast of Port Said, and that led to an immense mounting of world opinion. It took six days and, after all, if a convoy takes six days and there is bombing meanwhile – that did raise world opinion to a fever pitch and did make many of us feel very uncomfortable about the whole thing. I would have worried about it less if it had all been simpler. It was an extremely complicated operation, both in politics and military-wise. I think that led to a good deal of anxiety among some of us, about how it was going to work out.

I supported Eden in that we should try to settle the Canal issue and, if possible, internationalize the Canal, if possible without the use of force. That is to say, by means of the United Nations, and by means of the many other devices we adopted: the Canal Users Association, the intervention of Sir Robert Menzies, and in a variety of other ways. It went on for the best part of two months and I agreed that if we couldn't settle it that way we might have to use force, so I was behind Eden, and I admired his gallantry in trying to settle this matter. What I rather regretted was that we had to stop the hostilities when the Israelis stopped, and that we had to leave the Canal and leave the matter undecided. But I do believe that he did stabilize Middle East policy for some time, although it was not regarded by popular criticism as being a successful operation.
LORD BUTLER

organization, refused to release the money until the fighting stopped.

This 'ultimatum' was reported to the Cabinet by a 'white-faced' Macmillan. About his role, there will always be controversy and legitimate doubt. First in, first out, critics observed, but Macmillan has argued that it was his duty to bring the deterioration of the financial position forcibly to the Cabinet's notice. However, his assurances to senior American officials earlier that Britain was financially strong enough to stand the strain of the operation do perhaps indicate more than just an error of judgement. Macmillan had no suspicions that the Americans would block an I.M.F. advance, but his seemingly abrupt change from hawk to dove is open to speculation. He had been overheard telling his son-in-law much earlier in the crisis that 'Anthony's going to have a rough ride... I shouldn't be surprised if he lost his seat.' There were – and still are – friends of Eden, who saw Macmillan's conversion as a move which deprived Eden of his staunchest ally at the time of his greatest need.

In political terms Macmillan's change of tune represented a threat to Eden's leadership. It is of course true that Macmillan had always seen the

140

The hounds get the scent

The members of the party to which I belonged seemed to have gone mad. Gesticulating, yelling, shouting all over the place. I was appalled by it. Why should our members have gone almost insane because the Eden government decided to prevent Nasser from exploiting the opportunity he had in connection with the Suez Canal? I couldn't understand it – in my opinion Eden was right – I've said this on many occasions; I said it at the time – indeed there was a suggestion that I should be expelled from the party because of my attitude – but I believed I was right. The mistake that Eden made, and he wasn't altogether responsible for the mistake, was that he didn't go far enough.

LORD SHINWELL

Macmillan was detailed to invite me to submit to him the text of the resignation statement that I intended to make. All ministers when they resign are supposed by custom or tradition to make a statement in the House of Commons. I took my statement along. It was very anodyne and said nothing at all; it couldn't have suggested that there had been any collusion or any of the dark things that were being hinted at. Harold Macmillan shook his head and said in a sort of funereal tone, this was the most damaging statement you could possibly make, this will bring down the government, and so on and so forth. I said I thought that was ridiculous. He said, 'Look, I don't understand why you have got to say anything at all, you've been proved right'. This, from the Chancellor of the Exchequer.

ANTHONY NUTTING

My guess would be that there were between thirty and forty Conservatives in Parliament who opposed the Suez operation. Of course, in fact, only eight of them came out into the open. In the constituencies, the reaction was hostile to the rebels. We couldn't explain at the time why we were taking this particular line since we couldn't disclose what we knew. They saw it simply as a case of a subaltern shooting the Colonel in the back as they were leading us into action. There were a couple of other reasons for their strong support of Anthony Eden. One was the natural dislike, among middle-class Englishmen, of the Egyptians. I think it stemmed largely from people who'd been serving in the 8th Army during the war; secondly, from their antipathy to John Foster Dulles, the prime mover in the anti-British move at Suez. Anything which simultaneously – to use Monty's phrase – hit Nasser for six, and John Foster Dulles for six, must be good. They couldn't understand the people whom they'd voted into Parliament as good Conservatives opposing Eden in the crisis of his whole political career.

NIGEL NICOLSON

What struck me was the combination of sheer animal fury on both sides. Fury of attacking, fury of being attacked, plus moral indignation. The two together were really frightening. I remember Aneurin Bevan attacking Selwyn Lloyd; it was quite the cruellest and most effective thing that I've ever heard. I think he said the Foreign Secretary and his colleagues were not villains but cardboard villains. When he said this a howl went up from the Labour benches, which was really like the last moments of a fox or a hare.

DONALD McLACHLAN

Eisenhower was very angry at the invasion. I think more angry about the failure to consult him and the timing of the operation, perhaps. I think he was also convinced that it was the wrong thing to do. He didn't break it down into a line of reasoning, but he felt this was a seventeenth-century approach to a problem, and that we were now in another era and that the public wouldn't support this kind of a deal, and that it was just basically wrong.

ROBERT MURPHY

'With a heavy heart', Dulles at the U.N. provokes the first British veto

God on our side?

I was on HMS *Forth* sailing from Malta into Port
Said to the Suez invasion, when the Gaitskell speech
came over the Tannoy and all the troops aboard
heard it. I would say the reaction was one of anger.
After all, the import of his speech said that we were
indulging in an immoral and dishonourable
operation. We had no idea what we were going into
but we knew we would be in action the following day,
and if you are going into this sort of action you feel
you need the country behind you. You need the
major figures of the country behind you and that if
you are going to die, then you need God on your side.
The idea that you were sailing into something
unknown and difficult with a background so dissident
as this was very worrying. I think the majority of
the officers in that wardroom felt that this would
have a very bad effect on the morale of the troops
that they were commanding and that this indeed
might cause higher casualties than were necessary.
That was the main attitude. I think a lot of people
secretly perhaps felt much of what Gaitskell was
saying was true, or at least there was something
to be said for it, but they felt that at that moment
they were required to have everyone behind them
when they were going into war.
ROBIN ESSER

Hugh Gaitskell had a very difficult time over Suez,
because his immediate and first reaction, and one
that was made known in public, was that he was in
support of the action, because he felt that something
had to be done to prevent the building up of the
Egyptian forces, preparatory to what was thought by
all to be an attack. This did not last long. Once
Gaitskell had recognized that the party was united
under this general approach in defence of the
sanctity of agreements, then he had an even greater
problem to face. That was his broadcast. Should he,
when British soldiers are involved in action, try and
rally the nation against that action? Was this the
right thing to do? This was a moral issue with
Gaitskell and I know that this tore him very much.
Nevertheless, he finally came to the conclusion that it
was right, that the real issue should be put. He
should firmly make it clear that the United
Kingdom, as far as the Labour Party was concerned,
stood by the agreements that she had entered into. I
don't think he liked having to do it, because all the
time he couldn't help but feel these personal issues,
that men were going into battle and that he was
having to say it's the wrong thing to do.
LORD ROBENS

*A Labour Party sponsored rally in Trafalgar Square.
Much to the administration's surprise, the nation
showed itself divided*

I think people will always say that the threat of the
economic ultimatum from the United States
caused us to cease fire more than anything else. I
find that very hard to believe – I mean I just don't
think the cabinet was in the mood to be dictated to in
that sort of way, however much certain members
may have felt concerned about the economic
position. I would guess two factors played the
biggest part. The first was that our own allies in
the Middle East, that is to say Nuri (of Iraq),
wanted us to stop. After all, we had world opinion
overwhelmingly against us, Commonwealth opinion,
American opinion – our own allies wanted us to stop.
I think this did have an effect on the Foreign Office,
very understandably. But even more simply, the
cabinet felt that they had gone into this operation in
order to separate the combatants. Once the
combatants had been separated, once they'd ceased
fire, I think it would have been terribly difficult to
have got cabinet unity on continuing with the
military operation. I really think it was as simple as
that. All the doubts that members of the cabinet had
about the whole thing as individuals would have
come to a head when confronted with the
proposition: 'Are we to go on even when the
ostensible purpose of our intervention has been
achieved?'
LORD BOYLE

There was in the party a great deal of doubt about
our stopping hostilities. You remember the formula
had been that we would go in to stop hostilities, so
under the direction of the Prime Minister we stopped
the hostilities when the Israelis stopped fighting. The
French and ourselves had no alternative but to
withdraw. Of course I was left with the very difficult
job, first of all, of helping stop the run on the pound
which became very severe at that time. That I did
with the aid of long-distance calls to Mr Humphrey,
my friend and the Secretary of the American
Treasury. He told me he'd locked himself in a meat
safe in order to keep his family from interrupting his
conversations with me and he said that unless we
obeyed the United Nations resolution to withdraw
our troops from Suez, the Americans couldn't really
help us to save the pound. I rather took exception to
this as being a sort of blackmail but I rapidly saw,
with the aid of Macmillan, who by that time had
decided that it was better not to go on, to save the
pound, which we did. What really excited the
hostility of the Conservative Party was the
withdrawal. Many of them were quite ready to see
the United Nations forces come into Suez, but that,
after all, was a very reasonable conclusion of the
whole business. The difficulty was that the force
wasn't strong and it wasn't ready; it wasn't really
competent and it came in very slowly, and
therefore I got, during the period I was acting Head
of Government, a lot of resentment from the
Conservative back-benchers at that time.
LORD BUTLER

143

A man of honour

Looking over the boss's shoulder was not enough. Eden returns from Jamaica; Butler (behind), his deputy, thought he had recovered

operation as a gamble, and with characteristic realism saw the need to beat a graceful retreat. But Eden wrote less than one suspects he would have wished: 'There are always weak sisters in any crisis and sometimes they will be found among those who were toughest at the outset of the journey.' Nevertheless the fundamental truth remains: the operation had lost its justification. The arguments for going on to clear the canal before handing it over to the United Nations were simply not powerful enough to convince even those who took the plot seriously.

At all events, the United States was allowed to hold Britain to ransom. How far this was really the main consideration in Eden's or Macmillan's mind is a fascinating but unanswered question. Neither will say.

Eden telephoned Mollet at lunchtime on 6 November to announce the Cabinet's decision that there would be a ceasefire at midnight. Mollet was furious but he knew he could not go on without Britain. This unilateral decision had a profound effect on French political opinion and made French trust of Britain's motives exceedingly hard to win in the ensuing years. Dayan's offer to capture Ismailia and Suez in French uniforms underlined the problem: the French had been fools to allow the British to take the key command.

As American pressure grew, including threats to Britain's future oil supply, so did Eden's popularity. Anglo-French forces handed over to a hastily contrived U.N. force, which the Egyptians welcomed as liberators. Eden himself used a phrase for the whole affair – Full Circle. But the latter-day dictator – Nasser – was still in the saddle. British power, as Dayan not without pleasure was to remark, could no longer bring a war to an end at a place and time of her own choosing. Eden, a senior officer remarked, had 'obstinately decided, like a girl, to scratch out the eyes of his opponent but hadn't quite thought of what would happen afterwards'.

Despite a genuine and deep divide in the country, Eden's popularity was greater than for many months past. The extent of his prevarication and his hesitation did not become clear for a few weeks. His health was causing considerable concern to his doctors: it seemed that his bile duct was again giving trouble and a three-week rest was ordered. He returned from Jamaica on 14 December.

On his return the mood of the party had some-what changed. The British withdrawal had angered many Conservatives. Doubts about the conduct of the operation were widespread and in particular there was one unanswered question – why had the operation been called off? The whole thing seemed at half-cock and there was a strong suspicion of American pressure. Butler deputized while Eden was away and this feeling of unease reflected on him. His ambivalence towards the crisis did not help at a time when a strong lead was needed to mend morale. At a series of post-mortem meetings called by the Conservative back-benchers in their 1922 committee, it was Macmillan and not Butler who managed to suggest a sense of purpose.

Shortly after his return Eden also confronted the 1922 Committee. He said that if he had had to go through the autumn again, he would have acted in the same way. This was exactly what most Conservatives could no longer accept. They were overwhelmingly in favour of military intervention, but doubts on its handling prevailed. Many felt that Eden's judgement had gone.

Eden was, however, to be forced from office by ill health. Fever had returned over Christmas and it became clear that he could not go on without endangering his life. On 9 January, he tendered his resignation to the Queen.

Whatever the moral rights or wrongs of Suez, one thing remains quite inexplicable: no one had thought through the implications of the Suez operation, even if it had been a success. It remains a colossal gamble without a certain gain.

When Suez first commenced there was no doubt at all that Macmillan was the prime supporter of Eden in favour of going in. Had Macmillan been Prime Minister at the time, instead of Chancellor of the Exchequer, I'm quite sure that within two or three weeks we should not only have gone in but we'd have stayed in too, and the operation would have been successful in a military sense at any rate. But Eden dillied and dallied for so long that at the end of the day the campaign could never have succeeded. When it came to the crunch, of course, the Americans were threatening to let the pound go, and the Russians on the same day threatened to rain rocket-bombs over London. I'm afraid that Macmillan modified his attitude. I don't think he was viewing it from the personal point of view at all. I think he, like many of us, thought that the thing had dragged on for so long and the operation itself had been mounted so badly that he probably thought in his own mind – to hell with the thing.

REGINALD BEVINS

I don't believe Suez was a watershed, that it started a decline of our influence in the Middle East. We had world opinion against us, at least, publicly against us; therefore in that sense it was a diplomatic defeat. I think on the other hand it produced ten years of uneasy peace in the Middle East. There isn't all that much, even uneasy peace, at the present time. It produced a situation in which Nasser was shown to have military feet of clay. The other Arab states realised that he was not so militarily dangerous as they thought he was, and I believe it gave a period of comparative peace.

The tragedy was, the operation wasn't used when we had some control over part of the Suez Canal to get a peace settlement – it could have been used for that purpose. I think it was a piece of short-sightedness on the part of the Americans that it wasn't used for that purpose. In fact, later on Mr Dulles admitted to me that it had been a great mistake on their part that it wasn't used to get a permanent peace between Israel and the Arab states.

SELWYN LLOYD

During the whole of the period, from the first nationalization of the Canal by Nasser onwards, Eden was anxious and worried. As the situation unfolded, and as decisions had to be made, then I think probably his anxiety became less. Eden's courage at that time was absolutely phenomenal, because the House of Commons was violent and vicious in the extreme, and he went down there day after day to face this, becoming more and more imperturbable as decisions were made and policies carried out.

There was some advice contrary to his policy which he honestly paid attention to – coming in many cases from people who had been close to him and were friends. But there was absolutely massive support in the country for his policies. This could be seen by

incoming mail. The Conservative Party in the House of Commons, with very few exceptions, was enthusiastically behind him. Indeed quite a few members of the Labour Party offered him personal support, which also gave him some solace and comfort at a very difficult time.

Eden believed, and in my view with complete justification, that the Americans, even if they weren't going to actively support his policy in the Middle East, would at least be benevolent neutrals. When an indication came that they were actually going to take active steps which were hostile, I think he was shattered. I think he felt enormously let down. He was already under very great strain and this undoubtedly added very considerably to it.

ROBERT ALLAN

Eden came back from Jamaica in surprisingly ebullient form. I don't think he immediately had any idea of what was coming to him until he went to meet the Conservative back-bench committee and held a sort of post-mortem on the Suez operation. He shocked everyone there very much by saying if he had to make the same decisions all over again, even knowing what happened as a consequence, he would have made those same decisions. This remark was greeted in almost complete silence. People felt, I think, that the man must have lost his power of reason if he could say that, knowing what happened. It's from that moment, I think, that he himself began to realize that the sympathy of the party was draining away.

NIGEL NICOLSON

I seem to remember that we had a cabinet in the morning and towards the end of that Eden said he had to go to Sandringham in the afternoon to see the Queen. The cabinet continued without him. Then next morning he sent for me to say the reason he'd gone to Sandringham was that the doctors had said he mustn't go on. I was surprised and horrified and I really think that was the position of my colleagues.

SELWYN LLOYD

I thought like everyone else that it was one of the greatest tragedies in recent political history. I mean, here was Anthony Eden who all his life had dominated the House of Commons and his party by his knowledge of foreign affairs, and ultimately it was on an issue of foreign affairs that he fell, that his judgement went astray. I felt it also called in question his other great quality, his integrity, which had never been questioned before. He was a man of honour, and then suddenly he did something that drove you to doubt even that basic quality and so he resigned. It was on a January day, a very cold foggy day, that he set off from the Port of London in a ship to go to New Zealand having resigned as Prime Minister. The ship, of course, had to go round by the Panama Canal because the Suez Canal was closed for reasons that he knew all too well.

NIGEL NICOLSON

8 Where is the new Jerusalem?

Birmingham slum, 1951

Bevan was a man of immense vitality and charm. He was so charming and so funny, so amusing and so moving, that for somebody like me he was a miracle, and everybody felt this about him. All of us intellectuals, so called, we knew we would have an idea and would start telling an idea, and first of all he would say 'balls – absolute nonsense'; and then you knew it was a good sign, you knew you were on to something good. He said nonsense, it's outrageous, and then the thing would get fast and furious and you would watch your idea taken by this man – a man who wasn't educated in the normal sense, though he was deeply read. He would transmogrify your idea and make it into an infinitely better idea. This was a charm and a delight, this was what civil servants liked about him. He was a brilliant man, who learnt by talk.

Nye was flawed, though, because at that critical moment he just wasn't there. Bevan would have a bad cold on a critical problem. He hated fighting, quite honestly, he hated it. He kept saying 'Why should I submit myself to this kind of ignominy of fighting people like Gaitskell? Gaitskell will fight; I don't want to fight. I would like to lead this party, I don't want to fight it in this ignominious way'. He hated the in-fighting which you have to do in politics. He wanted victory given to him on a plate. Now that's a great weakness in a leader. You see, Gaitskell was a resolute man, he was nothing like as great a man as Nye Bevan, or as gifted or as imaginative. But he was pertinacious and so is Harold Wilson. They're fighters and they fight every inch of the way. They never give up, they're resilient, and Nye was constantly giving up, constantly depressed, lying down in his tent like Achilles. He was that kind of a moody creature; he was brilliant and deeply moody. I never thought he could have led the Labour Party and the more I saw of him the less I thought so. I thought he was the most wonderful inspiration a man could have in the party, without whom one wouldn't have had any ideas. A leader isn't necessarily the biggest man in the party. Clement Attlee wasn't the biggest man in the party but he was a far better leader than Ernie Bevin would have been because he was a tight little calculating, resilient, resourceful politician. You need to be that to be a leader. Nye wasn't cut out to be a leader, he was cut out to be a prophet. It's no joke being leader of the Labour Party, and Nye didn't want the bother, he just wanted to have it all led for him. I had every sympathy with him.
RICHARD CROSSMAN

The Achilles of the Left

The Left in full cry. A party of protest or a party of power? Nye Bevan wanted both; the electorate didn't

I thought that Bevan was the chief driving radical spirit, in the best sense of the word radical, during the '45–'51 government. During the period of that government we did have in the Labour Party, in the House of Commons, a group called the 'Keep Left' group, which was a left-wing group, but that group was not deliberately, or specifically, associated with Bevan in any way. But when he resigned from the government in 1951, immediately he became the obvious centre and focus of all left-wing feeling in the parliamentary party and even more in the Labour Party up and down the country. It was from that moment that some of us were described by the newspapers as Bevanites; that's how the term came into general currency. We had a number of informal meetings before the 1951 election when the Labour government was defeated, and then after the 1951 election we started to meet regularly in the House of Commons. I suppose there were about 30 or 40 of us and we used to discuss the business of the House of Commons and the relationship between the parliamentary Labour Party and the party conference. We went on for about a year or so with that operation, a perfectly legitimate parliamentary operation in my opinion. But the parliamentary party under Attlee took the most illiberal step of seeking to ban meetings of any groups in the House of Commons, except those that were officially approved by the Whips. We were bitterly hostile to this resolution, we opposed it very strongly in the parliamentary party. There have always been different branches and groups and organizations inside the Labour Party and the attempt to suppress it was a shocking act. This suppression worked to some extent; we weren't able to meet officially in the House of Commons. But we did thereafter meet, a much smaller number of us met, to discuss politics in our various homes, which we were entitled to do.

Our opponents, headed by Herbert Morrison at Transport House, thought we had a huge massive organization which was sending brains trusts all over the country and which was organizing in detail the election of people for the National Executive and the non-election of others, including Herbert Morrison himself. In fact we didn't have any huge organization, and we had very few resources; but we had *Tribune*, and we had Ian Mikardo, who is an extremely good organizer, and we did organize brains trusts that went into pretty well every constituency in the country. Local parties used to write in and ask us when they wanted a brains trust and we sent them. We had packed meetings all over the country. The very success of our brains trusts did add to the animosities in the party because the MPs who were opposed to us naturally didn't find it entirely to their delight that their local parties, or people in their local parties, were being stirred up by visiting brains trusts.

MICHAEL FOOT

When Nye Bevan and Harold Wilson and John Freeman resigned, we had the 'Keep Left' group as a going, highly organized, concern. We simply put the 'Keep Left' group at the disposal of the three great cuckoos that had arrived in our nest. It was a rather cosy little nest before, now there were the great big cuckoos in it. So we became Bevanites overnight, having been 'Keep Lefters' before. We had meetings; they were lunches. My fortunate, or unfortunate, wife provided every Tuesday for a large number of eager men who ate and drank well. I can even tell you where Harold Wilson sat or Nye Bevan sat. They were good meetings. We had meetings because we were forbidden. Some people would have classified us as conspirators. We weren't very good at conspiracy because throughout we had Desmond Donnelly as one of our members.

There were two sorts of Bevanites. There were personal Bevanites who really saw Nye as the man who had to become the leader of the Labour Party. I'm never absolutely sure whether Nye was one of them, because I wasn't. I think it's fair to say that neither Harold Wilson, Barbara Castle nor I thought it really likely that Nye Bevan could become the leader of the Labour Party. We were there concerned to have a strong vigorous Left in the party to make sure the Right didn't dominate the policy. So there were two kinds of people. There were people who were always thinking of manoeuvres and intrigues under which Nye could become leader, and there were those who were saying you must strengthen the Left in this way without having a split; there was a great difference therefore between what I call the personal Bevanites and the ideological Bevanites.

RICHARD CROSSMAN

LABOUR LOST –
1 Because its leaders were TOO OLD, TOO
  TIRED, TOO WEAK.
2 Because the Labour movement has been
  BAFFLED, BEWILDERED and BETRAYED
  by internal feuds.

The *Daily Mirror* summed up the result of the 1955
election with characteristic bluntness. But the
Labour Party found itself in a genuine dilemma in
the early fifties. Their narrow defeat in 1951 freed
them from the necessity to come to grips with
affluence, its problems and priorities, but whether
victory would have accelerated or foreclosed the
debate on the future direction of the party is an
open question.

Bevan's resignation from the government in
April 1951 presented the Left with a standard-
bearer. Many in the party were worried that the
momentum of 1945-50 was lost; those already in
the Keep Left group became Bevanites. That the
election programme of 1951 contained no firm
commitments to extend nationalization was seen
as a litmus paper test of the party's drift to the
Right.

The Bevanite response was to campaign up and
down the country through the pages of *Tribune*.
Travelling 'Brains Trusts' were organized to
mobilize local Labour supporters who feared that
the party had lost its soul. Further nationalization
– the famous 'shopping list' of industries – was in
the forefront of their campaign, and they aroused
the support of many constituencies.

In October 1952 the Bevanites almost made a
clean sweep of the constituency delegates on the
National Executive Committee (N.E.C.), the governing body of the Labour Party. The service of
Dalton and Morrison on the N.E.C. was abruptly
terminated: Morrison thus lost his chairmanship
of the policy planning committee, a position which
had given him overriding control of the party's
electoral programme.

Morrison's defeat was resounding. A dominant
figure in the Labour party for more than twenty
years, a crucial figure in the war Coalition and the
1945 Government, Foreign Secretary less than a
year before and Attlee's most obvious successor,
he had been thrown off the N.E.C. Attlee did not
lift a finger to help him. Deakin, the right-wing
chairman of the T.U.C., was appalled.

For twenty years a close alliance between the
parliamentary leadership and the trade unions had
dominated the party. The key element was the
right-wing leadership of the three major unions.
Deakin of the Transport and General Workers
Union was the heir to Bevin's position, and he was
usually supported by Will Lawther of the National
Union of Mineworkers and Tom Williamson of
the General and Municipal Workers. This trium-
virate, as the threat from the Left grew, would
concert their line. Their real forum was at the
Labour Party's annual conference where their
combined block vote made them almost impossible
to beat. Deakin loathed Bevan – he thought him a
wrecker of party unity, which as Ernie Bevin's true
successor he regarded as a crime and an affront.
'I'll have a talk with him' was Deakin's sinister
indication that he was about to pull someone into
line.

Deakin's traditional ally was the Deputy Leader
of the Labour Party, Herbert Morrison, and
Deakin began to cast around for a way of getting
him back on to the N.E.C. But already a counter-
attack on the Bevanites had begun. At Stalybridge
a few days after the party conference, Gaitskell
attacked 'fellow travellers' in the party and paid
fulsome tribute to Morrison's record. 'It is time to
end the attempt at mob rule by a group of frustrated
journalists and restore the authority and leadership
of the solid, sound, sensible majority of the
movement'. This was music to Arthur Deakin's tone
deaf ears. That was not all. Gaitskell went on: 'I
was told by some observers that about one-sixth of
the constituency party delegates appeared to be
Communists or Communist-inspired. This figure
may well be too high. But if it should be one-tenth
or one-twentieth, it is a shocking state of affairs to
which the National Executive should give immediate attention.'

Bevan was determined to hunt down Morrison,
whom he knew had far from unanimous support
in the parliamentary party. He stood as deputy
leader – a direct challenge to Morrison's one
remaining position. He was defeated by 194 votes
to 82, but a fortnight later he was elected to the
Shadow Cabinet. Many members, particularly
Attlee, wanted to keep Bevan in the Shadow
Cabinet so that he was under some form of
self-imposed control.

By the beginning of 1953, Bevanism had been
contained. But many Bevanites were in powerful
positions. On the N.E.C. seven out of eight

The Old Guard ousted

Gaitskell, like many of the party leaders at that time, was shattered by the 1952 Morecambe conference at which many of the famous old leaders were thrown off the National Executive by the constituency parties. Gaitskell, very unwisely in my opinion, accepted as gospel a statement by the *News Chronicle* political correspondent that a very large percentage of the constituency party delegates were secret members of the Communist Party. I think this was utter nonsense. But it was the only explanation which many people could find for the treatment of some of the party leaders at the Morecambe conference. By giving currency to this view I think Gaitskell won the support of some of the union leaders like Deakin, who were looking for a man who would fight.
DENIS HEALEY

The Stalybridge speech was a scandalous one. It was almost McCarthyite in tone – I mean the earlier Senator McCarthy not the recent one – because it made wide allegations of communism against sections of the party, without any possibility of proof whatsoever. It made particular allegations against journalists in the party who seemed to attract Hugh Gaitskell's hostility the most. It was the speech of a loser who'd been beaten by the votes of the conference and who tried to pretend that the votes had in some way been improperly weighted, which was not the case at all. I think it was an outrageous speech.
MICHAEL FOOT

Attlee, who was a very shrewd constitutional man, realized that a Leader of the Opposition is a very different person from a Prime Minister. The Leader of the Opposition has no patronage and therefore he just decided not to allow issues to come to a pitch. Gaitskell and people like myself who supported him were rather in despair at this time. The *Tribune* group and the Bevanites had got organized, they were holding these meetings all over the country, these brains trusts, in constituency after constituency, working extremely hard and winning a lot of support. There was also, of course, a certain built-in leftward trend amongst the representatives of constituency parties. Representatives of constituency parties in every party tend to be more doctrinal – I mean the Conservatives are more to the Right, Labour more to the Left, so there was a built-in leftward tendency which they were able to exploit. But we, Gaitskell and the rest of us, simply weren't organizing. We didn't quite know how to do it and we felt rather in despair. I think that was one thing that inspired Gaitskell's very bitter speech at Stalybridge.
PATRICK GORDON WALKER

High tide of the Left

constituency places were held by Bevanites, and in the Commons Harold Wilson missed election to the Shadow Cabinet by a hairsbreadth.

Pressure from the Left drove the N.E.C. to adopt selective nationalization which would extend the area of public ownership. A resolution advocating outright nationalization was turned down by the 1953 conference, but the revised party programme, *Challenge to Britain*, published in December 1953, contained pledges to acquire sections of the very broadly-defined engineering industry and key firms, as well as the more traditional proposals to take over iron and steel, road haulage, water, sugar, and to municipalize all rented housing. This was the high-water mark of the Left's influence on domestic issues.

Early in 1954 the Left was presented with an issue which had a deep hold on Labour Party and indeed national emotions – the rearmament of Germany. This was not an issue that split Labour on traditional Left/Right lines, although Morrison was a staunch advocate of a German contribution to Western defence. Most members of the party were only prepared to see German rearmament after a persistent and exhaustive effort to relax East-West tension. The breakdown of the four-power conference in February 1954 exposed the leadership. The Shadow Cabinet was divided. Dalton, Chuter Ede, Callaghan, and Bevan himself were totally opposed to 'guns for the Huns', although Western governments were going ahead with support from most European socialists.

Within the parliamentary party the rearmers won the day, Morrison's motion being carried by nine votes with four members of the Shadow Cabinet abstaining; an amendment from Wilson arguing that German rearmament should wait on further talks with the Russians was lost by only two votes. The N.E.C. accepted the change of line, which was thus official policy until conference ruled that autumn. Bevan waited a couple of months and then resigned from the Shadow Cabinet, ostensibly because he had been rebuked by Attlee for his criticisms of SEATO as a colonialist organization, accepted by Eden under American pressure. Responding to the wholesale frustration which he felt at being consistently baulked in the Shadow Cabinet, he was acutely aware of the political milage in the issue of German rearmament. His successor in the Shadow Cabinet was his former lieutenant, Harold Wilson.

We were in favour of extending and specifying the areas of the economy which should be taken into one form of public ownership or another. On the whole, the Gaitskellites argued that ownership was irrelevant to the whole question of how the economy was to be controlled. Then, superimposing itself on these quarrels in 1953 and '54, came the whole question of German rearmament where we opposed the proposals that were put forward by the Tory government of that time, with the tacit approval of Labour leadership, for the rearmament of Western Germany; the incorporation of Western Germany on a rearmament basis in the NATO alliance. We wanted to see a fresh attempt made at a settlement with the Soviet Union before Western Germany was given, in effect, a veto power of what was to happen in Europe. Although we believed that the Russians had presented many obstacles to this situation, and difficulties had arisen from their attitudes, we did believe the West, if it wanted, could reach a settlement with the Soviet Union. We believed that it was of paramount importance for the future of Europe that the settlement should be reached before Germany should have such a powerful voice in how the future of Europe was to be settled.

All through the middle fifties, Bevan was becoming more and more concerned and alarmed about the whole international situation and how he and the Labour Party could make a contribution towards preventing disaster. That was shown in his attempt to secure from Attlee, as leader of the party, an undertaking that the British government would never be the first to use the H-bomb. He demanded that the British government should make such a declaration, but he also demanded that Attlee should make a declaration of such a nature on behalf of the Labour Party. That led to an attempt to expel him from the party because they said he should never have put these questions in such a direct and brusque manner in the House of Commons. He also believed it was necessary for the West to make a different and more imaginative approach towards the Russians. He believed it was necessary for the Russian leaders, who were grappling with their own difficulties, to have some victories which they could bring home to their people from international diplomacy, and so Bevan was bitterly hostile to the rigid Cold War attitudes of the Western statesmen, in particular of Dulles.

MICHAEL FOOT

Attacked by the other Bevanites, he found a
solitary defender in Crossman, who tried to reconcile leader and lieutenant. But Bevan regarded
Wilson as disloyal. 'Do you mean you regard
Wilson as expendable?', Crossman asked. 'Of
course,' came the angry reply, 'You're all expendable.'

German rearmament dominated the party conference in October 1954, but an even more crucial
personal struggle for Bevan was provoked by the
death of the Party Treasurer in June. Williamson
suggested to Deakin that the unions' candidate
should be Hugh Gaitskell, who had never been a
member of the N.E.C. Bevan was determined to
oppose him. The campaign to secure votes revolved
as much around German rearmament as around
the candidates; the Left found it far easier to win
votes on anti-Germanism than Bevanism. On
German rearmament, last-minute changes of mind
gave the platform victory by the very small margin
of 48,000 votes. For the Treasurership, Gaitskell
defeated Bevan by more than two million votes.
It showed that the Left needed a cross-party issue
to make a decisive impression. To fight the election
Bevan had to give up his place on the N.E.C., and

he now resolved to capture the unions as an
essential preliminary to defeating what he described
as the 'desiccated calculating machine'. Wilson, by
contrast, did not speak on German rearmament
again.

Deakin, delighted at Bevan's public threat to
interfere in the unions, privately claimed, 'We'll
have him out within a year.' But the combination
of German rearmament and the announcement in
the early spring of 1955 that Britain would develop
the hydrogen bomb, nearly drove Bevan out much
sooner.

Bevan, by broadening the issue, took up the
Russian proposal for summit talks. The Shadow
Cabinet agreed with the Conservative Government
that this proposal was a ruse to prevent German
rearmament and refused to adopt Bevan's line.
Adroitly, Bevan coupled his proposal with a new
issue, the hydrogen bomb, in order to evade the
precise terms of Attlee's ruling, and tabled an
unofficial motion in the Commons. This was a
snub to Attlee. But then in the face of an official
rebuke, Bevan publicly demanded during the
defence debate that Attlee should clarify Labour's
approach to the Bomb. Would they use it, even if

The gulf widens

it were not used against Britain? Attlee evaded the point. Bevan and sixty-two followers abstained. Twice in one week Bevan had defied the leadership and there were pressures from the Right to put him on trial. They scented that their prey had moved into open country and was theirs.

The parliamentary party decided in March 1955, to withdraw the whip from Bevan, but by only 141 to 122 votes. 'If thy Nye offend thee, pluck it out', Attlee said, but he resolutely opposed any further action by the N.E.C. Deakin had no doubt that complete expulsion from the party would follow automatically. He went so far as to publicly instruct Attlee where his duty lay. Bevan then had his biggest stroke of luck: Churchill announced his intention to retire. An election could not be far away. Bevan was restored to the fold a month later.

Labour went into the election uneasily united. They were defeated; it was a sign of things to come that the first manual worker to be a Tory M.P. was returned. Deakin's death, ironically on May Day, had removed the Left's toughest critic. However, observers and an emerging group of young men on the Right were to point out that while the party had been wrangling over Bevan they had given too little attention to a more fundamental difficulty: in what direction did the party wish to go? The routine of opposition was not enough for a party with a strong doctrinal commitment, but the electorate's verdict gave no hint of the direction which would bring most return to Labour.

A more immediate problem than that of policy was, however, Attlee. Under his leadership the party had, since 1951, adopted an essentially defensive posture, waiting for the Tories to undermine the Welfare State. Nothing had happened. Worse, the age of affluence had begun. The thirties seemed a long way off, and Attlee had neither the inclination nor capacity to break out of Labour's traditional cast of thought.

Dalton offered his own resignation from the Shadow Cabinet, observing that it was time for the older men to make way. Four of the old guard resigned; 'Not a bad bag with one barrel', observed Dalton, never loathe to claim credit. Attlee added fuel to the flames with a rare public interview in which he deliberately spoke of handing over 'to a younger man'. Morrison was sixty-seven.

Dalton was campaigning vigorously for Gaitskell, whose months on the N.E.C. had made him as well known to the whole movement as he was

By 1951, the Labour Party didn't know where it was going and the Left were quite determined to get control of the party. During those years in opposition this conflict was continued and it personalized itself eventually as the Gaitskellites versus the Bevanites. This was a great pity that it got personalized, because it prevented any real *rapprochement* between the Right and the Left of the party.

Aneurin Bevan was a brilliant man. I probably disagreed fundamentally with three-quarters of his views, but there were occasions when I could have grasped the other quarter with both hands.

That it was bitter there is no doubt, and the bitterness was not just in terms, in my personal experience, not just in terms of the difference on principles or the way one should do things; it was a personal deep bitterness in which the personalities were being discussed in a manner which I would never believe it would be possible to describe one's fellow human beings, one to another. It was deep and bitter and the longer the differences went on, the more bitter things became. It came to the stage when people refused to talk to one another, they would pass one another in the corridors, they would listen to speeches in the House, looking for ways in which they could criticize; not for ways in which they could give praise or appreciation for what was being done.

Week after week in that shadow cabinet one could see the conflict growing up; even the very voting for the shadow cabinet was not based on the merit of the people. It was whether you were a Gaitskellite or you were a Bevanite, and the votes were totted up to see how one could keep either the Gaitskellites off or the Bevanites off.

Secret meetings were taking place on both sides all over the place – in rooms in the House of Commons, in restaurants and private dining clubs, and so on. Instead of the party putting its best brains together for the future of the party's policies, it was engaged in internecine warfare of the very worst kind and type. I tried hard to act as a sort of mediator. I don't think that this was highly successful, and I wasn't the only one, if I might say so, who resented this rift. I think a number of us my own age in those days were also anxious to see the end of this awful bitterness in the party, because it was not of our own making – we were the youngsters really, and we were looking to the future. But it was based upon this whole problem of the leadership question, the problem of Herbert Morrison and Attlee, who were not on the best of terms, and all this spread. The reason we didn't win in 1959 was because we dissipated our energies and forces in trying to destroy one another, instead of concentrating our whole energies on building up good political programmes that would be found to be acceptable to the people of this country.

LORD ROBENS

already to the parliamentary party. But Gaitskell was not yet, even in his own mind, a candidate for the leadership. The right-wing union leaders, still determined on a show-down with Bevan, looked to Morrison to wield the axe, and were thoroughly dissatisfied that Attlee had not taken the initiative in forcing Bevan out the previous spring. Nevertheless, Attlee's clear hint that Morrison might not expect the succession, was enough to provoke serious discussion of Gaitskell's claims.

Attlee was determined not to hand over to Morrison. He detested, as had Bevin earlier, his 'disloyalty' and thought his 'heavy-handedness' would lead to damaging splits in the party. Attlee thought that although Bevan could not become leader, he was important to the movement and must be handled with care. Events now played into Attlee's hand – and none too soon: that August he had a slight stroke. Morrison, taking an increasing share of the parliamentary burden, was not coming across well in the Commons. At Margate the right-wing unions used the pre-conference rally to urge, in scarcely veiled terms, that Attlee should step down and make way for Morrison.

But it was Gaitskell, fresh from another, more crushing victory over Bevan for the Treasurership, who made the most impact. Displaying widely unsuspected emotion and humour, he convinced most delegates that he not only knew the plumbing of government but had a genuine socialist vision. The conference was moved to prolonged applause and Bevan stalked out angrily: 'Sheer demagogy', he muttered.

When Parliament reassembled in the autumn of 1955 many pressed Morrison to make a dash for the leadership. Attlee's silence was deafening: Dalton clamoured for a young man – he talked of the unsuitability of 'a caretaker who is approaching seventy' – a clear reference to Morrison. The longer Morrison waited, the more his stock fell. Meanwhile, Gaitskell, presented with Butler's 'pots and pans' budget, seemed to be getting the Government on the run.

Dalton exerted all his persuasive skill on M.P.s: so impressive were these efforts that Gaitskell began to be canvassed and he told Morrison he was going to stand. Gaitskell's band wagon steadily accelerated with help from well-founded leaks in the *Daily Herald* that Attlee was about to retire. Attlee was aware of the trend and wanted to catch it on the upswing. He timed his retirement

perfectly; on 14 December, the vote for the leadership was announced: Gaitskell 157, Bevan 70, and Morrison 40. Morrison never forgave Attlee for this final demonstration that when tactical skill was required Attlee could leave the most prestigious and expert operator in the party out in the cold.

The election of Gaitskell was more than a change of leader. It installed 'revisionism' at the very top of the party. Gaitskell and younger men around him, particularly Anthony Crosland, offered much more than the traditional Right. Morrison had argued for a period of consolidation but this implied a basic reversion to old orthodoxies. The Morrisonian wing had fought off the Left in the early fifties, but their function was limited; they offered no way forward. Their attitude of consolidation implied a forthcoming reversion to the doctrines of an older generation, and had the 'age of affluence' gone sour they would have been in business with a return to traditionalist fervour.

The Gaitskellites or revisionists were asking more fundamental questions and their answers were expressed by the most talented of the group, Crosland, in his book *The Future of Socialism* (1956). The revisionists queried one of the fundamental assumptions of Labour thinking – that it was necessary to proceed to a fully collectivised economy. Crosland argued this by an analysis of the change in society since earlier socialists had defined their aim. Britain, he argued, was no longer a classically capitalist society. There was full employment, little poverty, and a welfare state: these standards had been maintained by Conservative governments since 1951. Crosland implied that socialist aims need not be achieved by further nationalization and he stressed the ethical ends of socialism, particularly equality by the promotion of welfare, redistributive taxes, and an education which did not depend on the financial position of the parents. The revisionist case rested far more on social considerations than on those of economy. But in the economic sphere Crosland argued that the power of the proprietor class had been eroded by the appearance of a managerial class, which foreshadowed the separation of ownership from control in business. The implication was enormous: the further expropriation of firms was beside the point. Socialist ideals could be realized by comprehensive education, and by manipulating taxes and reshaping the economy, with emphasis on its structure.

Gaitskell emerges

The absence of a class and economic diagnosis of Labour's purpose was anathema to the Left, but the level of debate remained largely theoretical until after the 1959 election. The period from 1955 to 1959 was a quiet one in terms of internal party squabbles. This was due, in no small part, to external events and an alliance between Gaitskell and Bevan. Internal party manoeuvring of some complexity allowed Bevan to succeed to the party Treasurership, although not without strong opposition from George Brown. In a way the most interesting thing about this election was that it marked the end of right-wing hegemony over the block vote. Jock Tiffin of the T.G.W.U. followed Deakin to the grave in 1956. The T.G.W.U. succession fell to the left winger, Frank Cousins. Ernest Jones, Will Lawther's successor at the N.U.M., proved less adroit at controlling the extremely democratic constitution of the Miners Union.

But what really brought the Right and Left of the party together, however uneasy an alliance, was the Suez Affair. The moral indignation of Gaitskell and the passionate advocacy of Bevan complemented each other well. It was above all an offensive alliance with a common enemy clearly in view. Bevan's anti-Americanism was never more in vogue. By the end of 1956, Bevan was made Shadow Foreign Secretary and this meant that he was close enough to the top not to insist on tying the leadership's hands by open challenges at conference. Pressure from Bevan, at least for binding commitments, ceased. There was widespread expectation that the Conservatives were on the run, and in that mood the annual party conference met at Brighton in 1957.

Gaitskell saw it as a major opportunity to move the party forward. A 'rethink' on the future of public ownership, 'Industry and Society' was presented to the 1957 conference by Harold Wilson, its part-author. Apart from steel and road haulage, nationalization was seriously demoted in the party programme. Nationalization was reserved for any part of industry that was found to be seriously failing the nation after thorough enquiry. Instead, the Government would buy shares but strictly on business grounds. Opposition came not only from Frank Cousins on the Left; it also came from the 'old' Right.

'Industry and Society' was attacked by Morrison and Shinwell, the latter claiming that nationaliza-

Attlee held on long enough to make it impossible – well, very difficult – for Morrison to succeed. One of the cruel things in politics in opposition is that you've always got to add three years or four years, or whatever the rest of a parliament's life is, to any man's age, because that's the time he would have to form, if he won, the government for five years. You've then got to add nine years to his age. If you're going to judge people by that standard, then Gaitskell was the only possible one, or at any rate the only possible one to beat Nye Bevan. It was that that got Gaitskell the votes. Lots of people wanted to beat Nye Bevan, but weren't quite sure between Gaitskell and Morrison. The age factor was the determining thing.

PATRICK GORDON WALKER

Bevan had to settle for the fact that Gaitskell had been elected leader of the party. He did not like it, and to the day of his death he did not believe Gaitskell was the right leader of the party. He thought that Gaitskell had led the party wrongly in his attempt to depart from the commitment to extended public ownership. Bevan was perpetually faced with the problem of how he was to assist in keeping the Labour Party as an instrument which could become an effective government, and how he was to keep an element of socialism to combine. The idea that Bevan ever made a deal with Gaitskell about it and said, well, that's that and if you sign I'll do this – nothing of the sort. He thought that the way in which the party had been led in the 1959 election was one of the causes why we lost, and after the election was over he said he prophesied that Gaitskell would never be a Labour Prime Minister of this country. Of course, he didn't foresee the tragic development which was to cause that prophecy to come true. But he felt in his bones, that Gaitskell was leading the party away from its proper course.

MICHAEL FOOT

Party of government or party of protest?

The position was that by 1951 we had carried out more or less the whole of the 1945 manifesto, and we had to decide where we went from there. We obviously had to come up with some new and general programme and approach. There were three alternatives. First was the traditional left-wing one, that we should go back to all the old orthodoxies and classical text and somehow repeat them. The second was equally dangerous in my view, what one might call the Morrisonian approach of this sort of sterile moderation, a moderation with practically no content to it; and there was a third one, to which I was very strongly committed: to try to produce a new, fresh, what came to be called revisionist, policy which would be relevant to conditions of the fifties and sixties, not to the conditions of the 1930s. There was a real, major decision to be argued out and taken.

ANTHONY CROSLAND

In 1956 there was Anthony Crosland's *The Future of Socialism*, which really did mean a very great deal to a younger generation. It was the first systematic attempt to restate democratic socialism for over twenty years. Instead of looking back to the Labour government of '45 to '51, it was seeking to indicate the direction in which the Labour Party might move. The emphasis was on social reform, on spending more money on social serices, on efficiency; much less on the ownership of industry and nationalization which was the classic centrepiece, if you like, of the Labour Party. The late '50s were a much better period, we knew the direction in which we wished to move, and the Labour Party adopted, in a series of booklets, very much the view which the more thoughtful elements in the Labour Party were proposing.

WILLIAM RODGERS

The whole revisionist movement was, I think, an attempt to do two things. First of all a negative thing: to shift the Labour Party away from its traditional semi-Marxist base, which tended to make the party think that ownership was all that mattered, and therefore that nationalization was the essential feature of any Labour programme – socialism being defined as nationalization. I think that was the negative task. The positive task was to get the party committed to a series of radical issues which seemed relevant to that moment of time, and not twenty years earlier. They weren't all totally new issues, but even when they were old they had to be cast in a more relevant form. For example, the traditional welfare objective; a belief in a greater equality of wealth; and then some rather newer things on the wider belief of social equality which concentrated its attention on the crucial equality sector of education. A belief in higher public spending generally, not only to relieve poverty, but for much wider reasons as well. Belief that in an increasingly important field in what was then called town and country planning – and now has the wider name of

environmental planning – that this must come up to a much more central part of Labour policy. There was a real interest in the consumer, as opposed to the producer in materials. Lastly, a belief in the crucial importance of economic growth, and in getting the economy right. I wouldn't say we succeeded in actually producing the method of doing so very easily. I know that I was personally wrong on one major thing: I thought we'd broadly settled the problem of economic growth by the middle 1950s, but that turned out to be incorrect. For myself, I wouldn't alter any other of the basic themes or arguments of *The Future of Socialism*. The assumption of economic growth was the foundation for these plans.

These ideas certainly didn't go down with all sections of the party at the time. There was a lot of very strong vocal and emotional opposition to them. People very much disliked having a challenge to the creeds that they had believed all their lives, had been brought up on, it's perfectly natural. So there was a great deal of very resentful hostility to this attempt to pull the party into a very different stance. On the other hand, I think, on the moderate wing of the party, there was a certain sense of relief; I'm not just talking about my book now, but about the whole revisionist movement. A sense of relief that it was possible to articulate in language that seemed genuinely socialist, a policy for the Labour Party that was relevant and had every chance of being acceptable to the electorate.

ANTHONY CROSLAND

Why I objected to the Gaitskellites, I mean to Tony Crosland, whom I argued with at length, was that I knew what they were trying to do. They were trying to take the Labour Party, the old-fashioned Labour Party, and turn it into a modern party, like the modern Social Democrats in Germany or like the American Democratic Party, a party of government, as they put it, not a party of protest. Now I passionately believed then, and I believe now, that the Labour Party can only survive if it still remains a party of protest, a party of crusades, a party of causes. A party which isn't just solid responsible politicians who will run the Treasury well, but a party which will shock, which will come in with momentum, which will change things. Change can't come just by setting up solid alternative government; change comes if you shake things up. You can only shake things up if you're committed to shake things up, as I well know in Whitehall. So there was this conflict. Gaitskell said you can't win unless you seem to be a responsible party of government. I would have said you can't hold the movement together unless we remain a traditional party of protest. Now of course both sides were right and both sides were wrong. This is because this is a matter of attitude, of posture.

RICHARD CROSSMAN

tion was 'the vital principle on which this party was founded'. The way was at least open for a major row on Clause 4 of the party's constitution which stated: 'To secure for the workers the full fruits of their industry and the most equitable distribution thereof that may be possible upon the basis of the common ownership of the means of production, distribution and exchange.' But, scenting power, the revisionists were unwilling to force the pace.

In terms of Labour's history as a political party, 1957 was a considerable turning point. The leadership were more or less united. The opinion polls showed a steady Labour lead and the Suez operation was a good stick with which to beat the Government. In 1957 the whole issue of Britain and the Bomb became clear. In May, Britain exploded her first hydrogen bomb. The power of the H-bomb and its massive emission of radioactive fallout exposed Britain's total vulnerability in any thermo-nuclear war. The 1957 Defence White Paper admitted that 'there is at present no means of providing adequate protection for the people of this country against the consequences of an attack with nuclear weapons.' To many, this sounded like an admission of madness.

Many members of the Left, Michael Foot for example, were expecting Bevan to come out in favour of their resolution calling for unilateral renunciation of nuclear weapons. Bevan had never stated this as his policy, but the Left was appalled when he condemned unilateral renunciation of nuclear weapons as 'an emotional spasm' and said, 'If you carry this resolution and carry out all its implications... you will send a British Foreign Secretary, whoever he may be, naked into the conference chamber... able to preach sermons of course...' By staking out his position so clearly on the *multilateral* side of the disarmament issue, Bevan excluded himself from the leadership of the Left. Unilateralism became a latter-day German rearmament issue within the party but with an even wider moral appeal. Bevan and Gaitskell were to grow closer together as pressure from the unilateralist Left increased. With the powerful endorsement by the party of 'Industry and Society' and the equally powerful rejection of unilateralism, the Right seemed entirely in control with a leader of their own mind in unchallenged command of the movement. It only remained for the Labour Party to seize the initiative from a rocky Conservative administration.

We were deeply disappointed by his speech at the conference of 1957, but the speech, in my opinion, was greatly misinterpreted at the time and has been greatly misinterpreted since. He was not saying that he must have nuclear weapons to go and bargain with the Russians. He was saying that if we were going to have a chance of getting the Americans to come to a negotiation, it was better that a British government didn't have all its attitudes about weapons tied in advance. He was appealing for a free hand as a negotiator. Don't forget that at that conference many people thought that within a few months it would be possible that a Labour government would be in power and that Aneurin Bevan would either be Foreign Secretary or, at any rate, the second most powerful person in the government. So what he was really pleading for at that conference was for a free hand as a negotiator.
MICHAEL FOOT

I was greatly shocked by the speech Bevan made at the Labour Party conference in 1957, because to me it did seem that Britain's possession of nuclear weapons was building up into a major issue in British politics, and that young people in particular were very concerned, and that the Labour Party ought to have had a clear policy on this. This would not only have dissociated the Labour Party from Britain's continuance of nuclear tests and from having American bombers stationed in these islands carrying these nuclear weapons, but would have been against Britain herself manufacturing these weapons and relying on them as part of a defence policy. Aneurin Bevan, in my opinion, should have come out clearly on this issue.
COUNCILLOR HUZZARD

FIRST

BRITISH RAILWAYS (SOUTHERN REGION)

B.R. 31777/6

RESERVED

FOR

MR

DOWNS

B1

1-3

PARTY

Mate to Macmillan

When Eden came back from Jamaica it wasn't clear that he wasn't going to continue as Prime Minister at all. I thought he was going on and, to be frank, in the particular competition for being Prime Minister, I had made very few arrangements or dispositions, as they say in the military way, and I was totally surprised after Christmas when Eden informed me he was going to Sandringham to tender his resignation.
LORD BUTLER

Butler threw away his chance, I think, of becoming Prime Minister by his extraordinary ambivalent attitude to the Suez crisis. One didn't know from day to day whether he was in favour or not. In all his public speeches he supported the Prime Minister up to the hilt. But one heard that behind the scenes he was taking his own different attitude; that he hadn't known until it was too late what was going to happen, and that he thought the whole thing had been grossly mismanaged. This point of view percolated down to the back-bench members and he gave the impression that he was presented with a poisoned chalice. He could either throw it away, spurn it, or else he could drain it to the dregs – he chose to swallow it. But everybody thought, and some perhaps even knew, that his whole instinct was to oppose Sir Anthony Eden on this. Of course, it was a strange thing that Macmillan was the man who was the first to say – let's go in; and the first to say – let's get out. So you can say Macmillan was the arch-criminal in the whole Suez operation. And yet, somehow or other, he managed to give the impression that he was the only man in Eden's absence, in Eden's illness, who could handle this ghastly situation. And so he became Prime Minister, and I thought quite rightly.
NIGEL NICOLSON

The meetings of the Private Members Committee, the 1922 Committee, at that time were a great strain. To do Macmillan justice and to give a proper historical account, there is no doubt that if Macmillan and I hadn't worked together then we might have had real party trouble. This basis of collaboration went on, of course, after he became Prime Minister and I became his principal lieutenant; we were able as a result of working together at the end of the Suez period to produce harmony in the party and a forgetting of Suez was really quite remarkable.
LORD BUTLER

In the case of Suez, Rab had appeared to be devious, even in the House of Commons itself. Macmillan had tried and failed, but Butler hadn't even tried. Secondly, those who knew Butler well knew that it was almost impossible to get a decision out of Rab on anything, however important. It was like getting blood out of a stone and there is one quality a Prime Minister mustn't have and that is the inability to make quick decisions.
REGINALD BEVINS

Macmillan established himself as easily the strongest member of Eden's Cabinet during Suez and its aftermath. He had stood firm behind Eden in believing that it was probably necessary to use force, and had consistently pressed his case from the time force was ready in mid-September until a satisfactory *mise en scène* had been found for the Israeli attack on Egypt. The intense diplomatic activity from the end of July had worn Eden down. By the time of the invasion, Eden had suffered at least one bout of fever and probably needed to have another operation to clear the bile duct, but there was no evidence in the autumn of 1956 that he would have to retire.

Unlike Macmillan, Butler as Lord President and Leader of the House of Commons no longer had the departmental base from which to speak with an authoritative voice over the whole range of economic policy. Also Butler had been the most senior minister with doubts over Suez: his ambivalence was clear in Cabinet and in private talks with Tory members in the House. Butler's position as chief doubter put him at the head of any anti-Eden group that might develop, but traditions of loyalty to the leader in the Conservative Party are very strong. Moreover, in the aftermath of Suez, the party was in no mood for 'palace revolutions'. There was suspicion about reasons for the ceasefire and anti-Americanism was rife. The party's overwhelming need was for someone to lead them out of the mess in which they found themselves. Too many untied ends had been left by Suez, too many suspicions, too many rumours. When Eden was out of the country party morale slipped lower. On his return, his appearance at the 1922 Committee – when he admitted ignorance of the exact terms of the Tripartite Agreement – did not inspire confidence.

Whether Eden could have led the party out of its difficulties remains an open question. A fresh bout of illness made him retire and ended speculation on his political future. In the then traditional soundings for a new leader, Butler was on the face of it the natural favourite. But his position, particularly in the Cabinet, but also in the party, had become less strong. In speeches to the 1922 Committee, Macmillan had performed better than Butler. He gave the impression that he knew where he was going and that Suez had taught Nasser a lesson he would not forget. Butler, more honestly perhaps, was more circumspect. But the party was in no mood to appreciate the realities of Britain's

I can recall one of those meetings attended by Butler and Macmillan. I suppose it was one of those ghastly memories that I've got from twenty years in politics. What was ghastly? In the absence of the Prime Minister, ill, perhaps fatally ill, two potential successors looking for the position that would enable them each to down the other, and doing it with a complete show of bonhomie, unity and goodwill. That was one of the occasions when Harold Macmillan, I don't know whether it was his third or fourth rehearsal, used his famous simile of the Greeks and the Romans. One saw the difference in style, in character, of the two men, the different pose, if you like, of the two poseurs. But Rab lost the chess game, in that by the end of the year the people in the party on the whole believed that it was he and not Harold Macmillan who had counselled withdrawal, who had held his hand in the crucial hours. This wasn't so and was, to the best of my knowledge, rather the reverse; but Rab ended up on just the wrong spot on the chess board.
ENOCH POWELL

The room was absolutely crowded, every single back-bench Conservative MP was there. We'd been told that we were going to be addressed for ten minutes, first by Rab Butler who would then answer one or two questions, and secondly by Mr Harold Macmillan who would also answer one or two questions. Both had taken a good deal of trouble with their speech. Harold Macmillan was the master of a short speech, both in timing and in every way, and in ten minutes he produced a very good atmosphere and a very confident result. I think a great number, I should think 90 per cent of the people as they went out of that room, would have supported Harold Macmillan.
LORD ORR-EWING

It is, however, quite untrue to say there was a small cabal of senior ministers who manoeuvred Macmillan into the leadership of the party. The party was consulted extensively, and at every stage. I was abroad at the time, and they even took the trouble to ring me up to find out who I wanted. There was no doubt the overwhelming majority of the party preferred Macmillan to Butler. If there'd been a vote it would have been exactly the same.
LORD BOOTHBY

position in the world. Cabinet soundings showed an overwhelming preference for Macmillan. More selective soundings of the parliamentary party by the Chief Whip Edward Heath showed a preference for Macmillan and a strong stop-Butler minority. The Queen was advised to send for Macmillan. Eden was not consulted. Later that evening, 10 January 1957, Macmillan was seen feasting off game pie and champagne at the Turf Club with Heath.

Macmillan's inheritance was a difficult one. Relations with the United States were worse than ever; Nasser had not been toppled; the French, baulked by British insistence on climbing down at Suez, were confirmed in their traditional suspicion of 'Albion Perfide', and were also confirmed in their determination to find a new political base in the Common Market which was in process of formation. In Cyprus, the fall-back position from the old Suez base, rioting and arson were commonplace. Britain's position in the world was shown up for what it was; it would be Macmillan's job to find her a role. At home, Labour had a 5 per cent lead in the opinion polls and the Conservatives' stock was falling. The party itself was badly shaken and divided, and there was a general acceptance of the fact that the Government could not go on. Macmillan himself admitted to the Queen that he did not expect his administration to last six weeks.

Macmillan set out to defuse Suez and develop a style of government greatly different from that of his predecessors. Gone were the incessant telephoning of ministers, the fussing over minor matters of administration. Macmillan's studied calm gave an impression of strength. In selecting his Government he neither apologized for the past nor gave hostages to the future. Selwyn Lloyd, who as far as the public was concerned would have provided a scapegoat for Suez, was retained as Foreign Secretary. To take over at the Treasury, he appointed Peter Thorneycroft, an unrepentant member of Eden's inner group on Suez and a man with strong European leanings.

One member of Eden's Cabinet did not survive. Anthony Head, who succeeded Monckton as Minister of Defence in mid-October, was sacked. Not only had he said enough to a Conservative back-bench committee to suggest some Anglo-Israeli connivance at Nasser's downfall but he refused to agree to Macmillan's proposals for a large cut in conventional forces. Butler, whom Macmillan had to secure, was given a choice of what office he would like. Macmillan was relieved when he choose the Home Office; there was no need to move Selwyn Lloyd. Lower down the scale, Macmillan skilfully balanced the obvious champions of Left and Right. Julian Amery, aggressively pro-Suez, came into the War Office as number two and Edward Boyle, who had resigned over Suez, did likewise at Education. It was some measure of the range of Macmillan's appeal within the Tory party that both men were his devoted protégés.

The weakness of Macmillan's inheritance was its strength. If Macmillan could lower the temperature, the party would rally to him, but the post-Suez adjustments had to be made with the minimum of confrontation. It was in recognition of what had gone before that Macmillan wrote out a notice: 'Quiet, calm deliberation disentangles every knot.' An assiduous private secretary stuck it up on the wall of the Private Office. From 10 Downing Street a new confidence began to ripple out to the highest circles of government: it was a slow process, nor was it enough to ensure the party stayed in power. But if this self-confidence could be deepened and widened, Macmillan could be assured of an exceptionally authoritative personal position. He established very early a clear ascendancy over his rattled Cabinet.

But there were other, equally important fences to be mended elsewhere. Macmillan set off first to Paris and then on to Bermuda, where Eisenhower suggested they meet. In Paris, Macmillan did not find himself welcome: the bitterness and suspicion about Britain and her connection with the United States were intense. But in Bermuda, Macmillan found Eisenhower willing to close the gap between them, partly because he was genuinely anxious to heal the rupture and partly because he wanted missile bases on British soil. Though Eisenhower still found his British friends obsessed with Nasser, the conference was a success. Eisenhower, an old friend from the war, now willingly agreed to make up their differences. It was a step quite central to Macmillan's policy. Just before Macmillan left Bermuda, Eisenhower gave him a piece of good anti-colonialist advice – to release Makarios and negotiate with him.

Cyprus, despite Macmillan's breezy remark to Selwyn Lloyd at the press conference after Ber-

Eden would ring up, sometimes as often as a dozen times a day, to ask why there had been a certain speech made in the provinces by a member of the Opposition, why an answer hadn't been given, and that sort of thing. When I came to Macmillan, it was with the greatest difficulty that I telephoned him at all. Because when you raised the telephone to your lips, ears, or wherever you put your telephone, he showed great irritation and pretended not to hear you, so that it made you immediately think that you'd been unwise to telephone at all. That rather put one in one's place, and I'd been trained in the Eden school of ringing up half a dozen times a day, so I found it at first rather difficult to get used to the Macmillan school which was completely different.

Macmillan has told people in my hearing that he didn't expect his government to last three months, and I don't honestly think he did expect, after he received the commission from the Crown to form a government, that it would last. I think Conservative MPs were so shattered by the difficulties which arose at the time of Suez, and the difficulties in which our armed forces had been placed so that they themselves had consolidated their ranks, and finding Macmillan an able Prime Minister, which, you will remember, he was through all his initial period, I think they decided to consolidate behind him.

LORD BUTLER

Macmillan called together the party at a luncheon in the Savoy Hotel. I shall never forget his speech, it was a brilliant piece of political manipulation. His theme was that Britain had always been at her greatest when she had led, and not when she had conquered. That was an extraordinarily subtle approach after what had just happened. After that meeting I walked out with Ted Heath, and I said to him, 'That was a marvellous performance', and he said 'Yes, I agree. The trouble is, you see, that Macmillan cannot really put himself over to the public in that sort of way. He's not a flagon of beer, he's a glass of very fine wine, and it's only on such occasions as this when he is among his intimates, you might say, that the bouquet of the wine comes out.'

I remember him saying to me once, you must realize in this day and age the Americans are the Romans and we are the Greeks; they have the power, we must have the ideas. Then on another occasion he came to a meeting of Conservative candidates with a rubber ball in one hand and a match box in the other and he rolled the rubber ball over the table, and with the other hand he slapped the match box on its different sides and said, 'Now, the art of politics is to make a match box into a ball, you mustn't have firm edges and straight edges. It must all be very smooth, and if you can make match boxes into balls, then you're beginning to understand what politics is about.'

NIGEL NICOLSON

I think it was very unfortunate that Macmillan became Prime Minister at the time he did, and particularly under the circumstances that he did, because it was widely thought by Tory MPs, and particularly by the general public, that he had got the job because he was the hard-liner over Suez, and more generally because he was a hard-liner on Britain's position in the world. He was a tough imperialist figure and in general a man of the Right. This was very much the general feeling about Macmillan when he became Prime Minister. It was generally assumed that this was the reason that he'd got the job, that he was well to the Right of his rival, Rab Butler. The opposite was true – if anything he was significantly to the Left of Butler, and I think this misunderstanding about his position dogged him throughout his premiership, and to some extent determined his way of running the country. There was a fatal contradiction between what people thought he was and what, to some extent, he felt he had to encourage them to think he was, and what he really was. And this produced a contradiction not only in people's minds, but also, to some extent, in his conduct of affairs.

JOHN GRIGG

I think Macmillan himself would deny the epithet of 'unflappable', because when he was deeply concerned with the success of some negotiations, he would become very nervously strained. I remember going to Bermuda, the first meeting with the Americans after Suez. He was desperately anxious, as we all were, that it should be successful. He worked himself up until he was really quite ill; a cold, a temperature and all those things. As soon as there was a successful communique and a good press conference he became himself again.

SELWYN LLOYD

Motto for Private Office
& Cabinet Room
———

"Quiet, calm deliberation
Disentangles every Knot"
———
H.M

muda – 'What's happening about Cyprus? Do you know anything about Cyprus?' – greatly worried the Prime Minister. Makarios was, for the Conservative party, political dynamite. By a fortunate coincidence, Macmillan had to hand a powerful political card to offset the repercussions of a realist approach both here and in the Middle East generally.

He had felt for some time that defence was taking too large a share of government expenditure and had appointed Duncan Sandys as his 'hatchet man' to get defence spending down. Conscription, a popular target of abuse, was to be abandoned and Britain's conventional forces almost halved in size. More important, the Defence White Paper published in March asserted Britain's complete dependence on the H-bomb, now at an advanced stage of testing, and gave the go-ahead to a strategy based on deterrence. In theory, Britain would return to the top table, on a par once more with Russia and the United States. Not only would the glories of Britain's new-found power be used to conceal concessions over Cyprus, but over Suez itself. The comment of one prominent officer that 'You couldn't have opened the canal with an H-bomb' went unheeded.

But as was to happen often in later years, the illusion of power could be played on by Macmillan to great political effect. In April, Makarios was released but not allowed to return to Cyprus; in May, Macmillan announced to the House that he could no longer advise shipowners not to use to canal; in the same months, the tests of the British hydrogen bomb were successfully completed. These three major steps were not achieved without some discontent. Lord Salisbury resigned over the release of Makarios. The doyen of the Tory Right and alleged king-maker in Macmillan's own appointment was allowed, despite alarmist newspaper reports, to sink from view. His colleagues were already restive with his tiresome insistence on how much Britain's place had changed in the months after Suez; they could see now – barely – some hope for the future. Salisbury was soon voicing, publicly, other more prescient worries over the rising numbers of immigrants into Britain; most Conservatives, imperialists and liberals alike, found this objectionable, even vulgar.

When Macmillan recognized Nasser's control of the canal by telling British shipowners to use it, fourteen Conservatives abstained and eight resigned the whip. But the Tories were in no mood to tolerate those who rocked the boat; some of those who put principle before expediency left the country. The remainder of the party put Suez behind them.

Macmillan's conclusion was simple: 'We are not foolish enough to think we can live in this world without partners'. A point of greater subtlety he argued in private: Britain, he would say, was at her greatest not when she conquered, but when she led. It was a point he loved to dwell upon when he characterized Britain as Greece where America was Rome. He would talk often of the innate capacity of the British to be a civilizing influence on the world, and on the survival of Graeco-Roman culture. In real politics, it was adapted in a sub-Churchillian way to a brokerage between the superpowers. It seems, in retrospect, that Macmillan had realized the dramatic fall in Britain's power since the war but had not appreciated just how far it had gone. He managed to seem for long a more important figure in world politics than in fact he was. He did not demur from capitalizing on an illusion which in part he shared.

Macmillan had a good opportunity to gauge the state of the party at the conference in the autumn of 1957. He had appointed Lord Hailsham as chairman of the party. In unparalleled scenes of jollity and absurdity, Hailsham snatched the president's bell from the good lady to whom it rightly belonged and rang it loudly declaring, 'Let not the Labour party ask for whom the bell tolls, it tolls for *them*.' The conference, although slow to warm to this magnificent show, cheered Hailsham to the echo as Macmillan, who did not look as pleased as he might, got up to deliver the leader's speech. He was further put out by shouts from Empire Loyalists, but was soon comfortably in his stride, and every sentence was punctuated by laughter and applause.

'I read, during the recess, that Mr Gaitskell was suffering from a crick in the neck. I was very sorry. But not at all surprised. It is the occupational disease of left-wing leaders.'

When, however, he asserted that unlike the Labour party, Conservative politicians did not stab one another in the back, some laughed more knowingly than others.

By autumn 1957, Macmillan had gained the confidence of the Cabinet, the parliamentary party, and the conference. But he was making little impression on the country as a whole and middle-class supporters of the Conservative Party were still grumbling. A by-election defeat, the first suffered by any government since the war, was the tip of a very nasty iceberg – a persistent Labour lead of anything up to 13 per cent during 1957. There was another worry too, the economy.

Peter Thorneycroft had been able to introduce a mildly optimistic budget in April 1957, despite the scares of the previous autumn that the fall in reserves would lead to a run on the pound. 'Expansion', he said, 'must be the theme.' But by the summer of 1957 Thorneycroft became worried about price rises and wage increases. Political pressure was mounting to control prices. Thorney-croft attempted to launch an incomes policy – 'a guiding light' – for pay increases, but the Cabinet would not have it. They rejected any interference with collective bargaining and shrewdly suspected that the 'guiding light' might become the minimum rise. Thorneycroft partially salvaged his position by appointing a three-man Council on Prices, Productivity and Incomes – soon dubbed the Three Wise Men. But without real powers, and

unwilling to announce 'guiding lights' which would have met with little response, the three 'wise' men fell back on advocating deflationary policies.

A devaluation of the French franc in August 1957, followed by rumours of a revaluation of the German mark, again exposed the weakness of sterling. This produced a widening vicious circle: as people worried more about the pound, the more they transferred funds out of sterling and the more sterling. This produced a widening vicious circle: as more reserves were brought into play to prop up sterling, the more financiers began to fear a devaluation. It was to be the same saddening and sickening story repeatedly over the next decade.

Thorneycroft, under the mistaken impression that the economy was overheating, responded with his deflationary September measures. The bank rate went up to 7 per cent, a rate unheard of in the halcyon days of the early fifties. Macmillan was far from keen on Thorneycroft the deflationist and asked for twenty-four hours to consider the proposed new bank rate. But caught unawares and lacking any alternative to hand, he sanctioned it.

Thorneycroft's measures worked with remark-able speed. No so much because of their severity, which appealed to the Chancellor and his formi-dable assistants, Financial Secretary Enoch Powell and the Economic Secretary Nigel Birch, but because the underlying trend in the balance of payments was good. By the end of 1957 Britain was heading for a large surplus. The Chancellor's assistants saw inflation as the main danger, and were increasingly determined that the Chancellor should cut public expenditure. When the trio began to talk of controlling the money supply and holding back public spending, which, in the face of rising costs, meant a real decline in welfare, Macmillan and some of the Cabinet began to part company with them. Macmillan's definition of what was politically acceptable was a good deal more accommodating than Thorneycroft's.

As the autumn drew on, Thorneycroft lost Macmillan's support. As the sums in dispute became smaller, Thorneycroft's insistence became sharper. Argument moved from the level of arithmetic to principle. Thorneycroft's stand was doubly dangerous and put Macmillan in a difficult position. The allocation of money, Thorneycroft's prime responsibility, involved many spending ministers. If Macmillan placated the Chancellor too far he ran the risk of resignations by ministers

The politics of inflation

In the previous seven years under the Conservatives, the balance of payments on the whole had been in our favour. There had been relative stability in prices, and taxation had been steadily and quite sharply falling. From that point onwards, all that was reversed. At that turning-point we saw the division between Harold Macmillan who saw still, as in the 1920s – which I believed so determined his outlook – unemployment, recession, deflation as the true enemy, always waiting round the corner and only with difficulty held at bay; and Thorneycroft, who, more correctly, it has proved, saw inflation as the post-war enemy and saw as the central issue the maintenance of a stable value for money: a purpose to which he was prepared to postpone other desirable objects of government. The battle was fought and the battle was won, if you like, for inflation, for public expenditure, for an increase in the share of the state. I think, like so many of these turning-points, it was already determined in the situation and in the character of the two men.

Nobody can stand against a Chancellor of the Exchequer as long as he is backed by the Prime Minister. The moment the Prime Minister moves to the other side, then you shouldn't insure the life of the Chancellor of the Exchequer for very much. Towards the end of 1957, Thorneycroft, who believed that his colleagues had deliberately committed themselves to what he saw as the priorities to his analysis of the problem, found the Prime Minister was slipping away from him and was reverting to his basic, I would say his pre-World War II, outlook upon economics and upon government and society. It would be a caricature; a complete falsification, to say that either Nigel Birch or I, or both of us, shoved Peter Thorneycroft into resignation. For one thing, nobody outside the cabinet can shove a cabinet minister into doing something that he isn't determined to do; above all resigning, above all a Chancellor of the Exchequer resigning. Moreover, throughout, and right up to the last minute, Thorneycroft consistently said both to Birch and myself, 'You know, you are in no way committed to resign with me, this is a decision for you, there is no question of your letting me down if you don't come with me'. So those who say that Peter Thorneycroft was in a sense a pawn in the game, but behind him were the figures of Nigel Birch and Enoch Powell, couldn't have been more wrong. We were, if you like, minor partners, and it was Thorneycroft's decision, and I'm prepared to say, in the light of the events of the last thirteen years, Thorneycroft's achievement.

ENOCH POWELL

There was a very heavy run on the pound in August '57 and we lost nearly a third of our reserves. Peter Thorneycroft did deal with it brilliantly. The acute stage of the crisis only lasted two and a quarter months and we got back on a level keel again. But it did show how weak our position could be if we allowed inflation to get ahead. Now clearly, economies are hell for politicians. It is always very difficult; inflation can be good for votes and I think there was a certain difference in opinion. My own feeling was that the real danger was getting a general expectation of perpetual inflation. If you didn't take a grip of the situation the disintegrating morale and the material effect of continual inflation on the people of this country would grow, and it would be much more difficult to deal with. The disagreement was nominally on the question of cuts and expenditure. Fifty million was given as the figure; the actual figure was considerably larger. To my mind it was simply, were you going to inflate for electoral reasons, or were you going to stick fast to try and stop it?

LORD RHYL

True, Chancellors of the Exchequer have mostly had their troubles with their colleagues a little later than Epiphany, the sixth of January, the day of the final breach; but in 1958, this was determined for purely mechanical reasons, namely that the Prime Minister was about to leave on his Commonwealth tour, and that therefore the crucial decisions on expenditure, since the estimates would appear long before the Prime Minister returned, had to be taken then. This necessity arose from the fact that Peter Thorneycroft was fighting, and rightly fighting, on government expenditure. If he'd been prepared to run along for two or three months and say, well, I'll crack on some more taxes when the budget comes along and even it up that way, then there would have been no need for a crisis over Christmas in 1957-8, but his thesis, being on the level of government expenditure, was the key to the whole situation. He had to fight on the estimates and, given the Prime Minister's programme, estimates in principle had to be determined right at the beginning of that year.

ENOCH POWELL

Thorneycroft was advised very much by two very independent people, namely Enoch Powell and Nigel Birch; he couldn't have found two more intransigent advisers than those two. They advised him to stick out and obtain his demands. I remember Peter Thorneycroft submitting a paper to the Prime Minister with the word 'required' written on the top, and underneath, certain cuts in the social services and defence services which would have, in the case of the social services, done, I think, considerable harm to the country. Then I myself ranged myself with Macmillan in saying that we couldn't stand for a paper which said 'required', which was, in fact, an ultimatum. I remember people saying that Peter Thorneycroft was more keen to take the advice of the junior members than he was to take the advice of the government. Macmillan therefore accepted his resignation, said it was a little local difficulty, left me in charge, and departed for the tour of the Commonwealth.

LORD BUTLER

Treasury team quits on eve of Premier's journey

CABINET SENSATION

Comment

TUESDAY, JAN. 7, 1958.

DOWNING-ST TORNADO

OUT of the blue, the Government is hit by a sudden, tremendous crisis. We cannot remember any parallel to this in modern times.

For a Chancellor to resign almost without warning is a heavy blow. But for his two junior colleagues on the Treasury bench to walk out with him—that is surely unprecedented.

What makes it worse is that this grave upset has happened on the eve of the PRIME MINISTER'S departure for his five-week Commonwealth tour.

Mr. MACMILLAN'S decision to make no change in his arrangements shows remarkable coolness and also a complete confidence in his deputy, MR. R. A. BUTLER, who will have to cope with a new Treasury team only a few weeks before the Budget.

The most extraordinary thing of all is that this unexpected Cabinet tornado has arisen o v e r a mere £50,000,000. Such a sum in the context of modern national finances is chickenfeed.

'rinciple

BUT it was at that point that Mr. THORNEYCROFT stuck and refused to budge. It was on that obstacle, apparently, that he resigned his great office and perhaps sacrificed his future career.

Why, why, why ? In an unusually sharp exchange of

THORNEYCROFT RESIGNS AFTER ROW OVER SPENDING

Thorneycroft

By T. F. THOMPSON, Daily Mail Political Correspondent

MR. PETER THORNEYCROFT has resigned as Chancellor of the Exchequer. He leaves the Government after a Cabinet crisis over spending. MR. DERICK HEATHCOAT AMORY, Minister of Agriculture, becomes the new Chancellor.

Mr. Thorneycroft's two chief lieutenants at the Treasury have also resigned—Mr. NIGEL BIRCH, Economic Secretary, and Mr. ENOCH POWELL, Financial Secretary.

This Cabinet crisis boiled up on the eve of Mr. Harold Macmillan's six - week Commonwealth tour. The Prime Minister flies to New Delhi today.

Mr. Thorneycroft, 48, resigned because his Cabinet colleagues would not chop the Financial Estimates for the coming year by £50,000,000 to keep Government spending down to this year's level.

The Prime Minister objected that this "would do more harm than good." Mr. Birch and Mr. Powell agreed with their chief. The rest of the Government stood by Mr. Macmillan.

FUCHS TELLS HILLARY
I go it alone

By Daily Mail Reporter

A PUBLIC row last night flared between Sir Edmund Hillary and

FIRST MAN SHOT INTO SPACE
186 miles up—parachuted back, say Russians

By Daily Mail Science Reporter

RUSSIA has shot a MAN into space AND brought him back again alive, according to reports from Moscow last night. Space Man No. 1 was fired in a rocket. He zoomed 186 miles up and then parachuted successfully to earth. The

Daily Mail artist's impression of the space man.

experiment took place a day or so after the New Year. There was no official Soviet announcement about it, but the reports spread rapidly in Moscow and the censors allowed the news to be flashed to the rest of the world.

Two Western correspondents said that "reliable sources" confirmed the news. According to early reports the man—undoubtedly a volunteer and probably a scientist—landed somewhere in Russia.

Some Western experts wondered if the man had perished on the way down and had not, as reports

TRAIN HITS BUFFERS

I walked into the office at 10 Downing Street, the most curious place to work in Europe: everything is always completely calm, like the centre of a hurricane. When I arrived my colleague came across and said 'We've got a little bit of trouble here, we've got the resignations of the whole of the Treasury ministers on our hands'. Then Harold Macmillan, who had seen three resignations, walked into my room and behaved as if nothing whatsoever had happened. 'Good morning, my dear boy, and how is your lovely wife, your children, are they all right?' and so forth, and he walked around the other Private Secretaries asked after them, and then he went into the cabinet room and deliberately dealt with other work. Then he left for his Commonwealth tour (he was to depart about dawn the next day). That is one of the beauties of Harold Macmillan; the Chancellor of the Exchequer and his two other ministers had resigned and Harold Macmillan gets into an aeroplane to go and fulfil an engagement in Australia the next morning. The press and television people come up and ask, 'What about these resignations?' He says 'It's just a little local difficulty', and goes off to Australia. A frightfully good way of running a government.
LORD EGREMONT

whose social programmes had been unacceptably cut. On the other hand, inflation and welfare spending were traditionally linked in the party's mind, and their sympathy and support might well go to Thorneycroft.

Macmillan let Thorneycroft have his head until the last moment, allowing opposition to build up against him. The clash came in early January, when the budget estimates were being considered earlier than usual before Macmillan set off on a Commonwealth tour. On the eve of Macmillan's departure the entire Treasury team resigned. Macmillan hurriedly replaced Thorneycroft with the well-liked Minister of Agriculture, Heathcoat Amory. Just before he boarded the aircraft for his tour, Macmillan dismissed the whole business as, 'these little local difficulties'. For the time being, as with Salisbury, Thorneycroft and his views sank without trace. What bubbles there were, were punctured deftly by the acting Prime Minister, Butler.

Although Macmillan's first Commonwealth visit to India, Pakistan, and Australia was not organized

Two things together quite suddenly launched the
super-Mac period: the Ed Murrow television
interview and the bus strike in 1958. It was one of
those things that couldn't have happened without
rather careful preparation beforehand, without
slogging work. But it was those two things together
that suddenly raised him to a new high level in
public opinion. I can remember him during the
summer of 1958. Very characteristically, he had sent
round a note that he would like to see all the
ministers who were looking after their departments.
As he expected, practically nothing but junior
ministers came round to Downing Street – all our
bosses were away. He looked at us round the table
and said 'Oh, I thought we seemed to be very well
governed just now', and welcomed us all.
LORD BOYLE

as a public relations tour, it certainly had that success. Macmillan was the first prime minister to tour the Commonwealth and by the time he reached Australia he was beginning to revel in the publicity. He grew appreciably in stature as a major international figure; he realized quickly that it was easier to appear as a statesman abroad than in his own country.

Macmillan was beginning to emerge from the shadow of Churchill and Eden. His Edwardian appearance and mannerisms became one of the favourite subjects for cartoonists, a sure sign of success, and his public stock went up markedly when he submitted himself to a lengthy television interview with two American commentators, Charles Collingwood and Ed Murrow, in May 1958. He showed historical breadth, a great sense of confidence, and a keen sense of humour. 'Unflappability' and 'SuperMac' were coined; first as terms of abuse, but as 1958 went on, increasingly as terms of admiration. The opinion polls reflected this trend.

The self-confidence Macmillan drew from these displays of popularity was matched in the initiatives he took within the Atlantic Alliance. The Defence White Paper of 1957 committed Britain to a nuclear strategy and the first sign of a retreat from the Far East into Europe was there for those with eyes to read. By the early summer of 1957, Britain had successfully tested the hydrogen bomb and to the Americans her surprising capacity to produce cheaper and more efficient bombs made a pooling of efforts attractive.

The launching of the Russian sputnik in October 1957 shook America. The missile that had put a satellite into space could as easily carry a nuclear warhead. For the first time 'Fortress America' was herself vulnerable. Macmillan was able to exploit the new climate. He successfully urged that the mutual exchange of nuclear information could only benefit the whole alliance, and Eisenhower promised to arrange the amendment of the McMahon Act which, contrary to wartime promises, prevented any release of American nuclear information to Britain. Macmillan also accepted the stationing of medium-range missiles – the Thor – on British soil, adding greatly to American missile preponderance over Russia, but giving Britain a nuclear shield while she equipped her own V-bombers with hydrogen bombs and developed her own missile, the Blue Streak. This was a significant

gain for Macmillan. Britain was in the nuclear stakes but her entrance fee was pooled. The special relationship had been paraded with a vengeance. For the first time since Suez it was becoming clear that British interests in the Middle East and elsewhere would not be thought redundant in Washington. The American military operations in the Lebanon and British help in Jordan, which saved an incipient crisis, were an outward sign of America's change of attitude to British policy in the Middle East. The eventual empowering in June 1958 of the President to allow the transfer of information, nuclear materials, and non-nuclear components of atomic weapons to Britain confirmed the new solidarity. Macmillan felt buoyed up by the new closeness of the United States and Britain. He now felt that the wounds of Suez were healed and it gave him a new confidence that he could negotiate from a position of strength in any peace initiative.

An almost Churchillian dream of a new summit conference began to visit Macmillan more frequently. He talked frequently to colleagues about the peace of the world and the terrible dangers threatening mankind. Macmillan approached the summit with a visionary zeal sharpened by a politician's sense of timing. Macmillan's preoccupation with the dangers of nuclear weapons, the pressure from C.N.D., and growing public anxiety about fallout led him by 1958 not only to put his whole weight behind the disarmament conference but also to attempt the more limited goal of a nuclear test ban. He persuaded the Americans at the end of 1958 to agree to a Soviet proposal that a test ban could be negotiated separately. Dulles was hesitant, and almost broke off talks in the spring of 1959.

Macmillan was determined to make progress through personal diplomacy. His repeated attempts to secure a summit meeting throughout 1958 were lent fresh urgency by Khrushchev's six months ultimatum in November 1958. Khrushchev threatened that unless the German situation could be resolved, he would unilaterally sign a peace treaty with East Germany and put an end to Allied rights in Berlin. While the Russians proposed a summit Eisenhower wanted a Foreign Ministers' conference first. The West Germans and De Gaulle pressed for a stiff negotiating position.

But Macmillan decided to gamble on personal diplomacy even at such an unpropitious moment.

Neither the Americans nor the British Ambassador in Moscow was that sure this was the best moment to choose, but Macmillan pressed on. 'I informed, though I cannot honestly say I consulted our allies', he wrote later. By 21 February 1959 he and Selwyn Lloyd were in Moscow: the first ever peacetime visit by a British prime minister. The visit defused the situation, despite rows with Khrushchev who complained of 'toothache' which he decided later had been cured by a 'British drill'. Although Macmillan's party had to keep the taps running in their hotel rooms for fear of bugging, the Berlin ultimatum was buried. A British suggestion about the on-site inspections necessary to a Test Ban Treaty was adopted by the Russians. But above all, Macmillan had been able to make personal contact with the Russian leaders. To English cartoonists, keen to identify any pre-election gimmick, he provided his white fur hat: they seized on it greedily.

When Macmillan returned from Moscow in March 1959 speculation was already rife on the date of the general election. Adenauer, not unnaturally worried by the fate of Berlin, wondered whether Macmillan's trip had had more to do with British politics than international diplomacy. For the first time since before Suez, the Conservatives by the summer of 1958 had moved ahead of Labour in the opinion polls. Some observers have put this down to Macleod, the Minister of Labour, and his stand against the London bus strike, which was thought to have punctured wage inflation. Possibly; but the economy was already being reflated. There were five reductions in the bank rate in 1958; bank credit restrictions were lifted and in October *all* hire purchase controls were ended.

Moreover there were profound changes more important than buoyancy in the economy. People were beginning to feel the expanding torrent of affluence on a scale quite unknown in British history. Butler's boom had set the tone; but Amory's had really begun to deliver the goods. Social changes in the late fifties influenced political behaviour; 'never had it so good' became the catch-phrase of 1959. Hire purchase debt from the beginning of 1958 began to increase rapidly; mass production and mass consumption ironed out some of the more obvious social differences of the past, particularly in clothes. By 1959 television sets and vacuum cleaners had reached the majority of working-class homes. By occupation, more of the population had become middle class and many more regarded themselves as such. Aspirations were on the way up; pride in class distinctions on the way down. On the Left, among those who had already detected these shifts, conscious counter-pressures developed to enhance working class origins. They were the conservationists of the late fifties.

'The voter', said Lord Woolton, no mean judge of the electorate, 'is also the consumer.' The Cabinet thought so too as they prepared to argue over the 1959 budget. Macmillan, worried by heavy seasonal unemployment (the acceptable limit for the fifties, 500,000, was exceeded that winter) pressed Amory hard to take the brake off. It had, after all, been Macmillan who as early as 1957 invented the phrase 'never had it so good'. All his expansionist fervour came to a head in early 1959; unlike more traditionalist Tories, he did not disdain mass affluence, but encouraged it. The brashness and vulgarity it brought did not worry him; he played piper as he led his way through the consumer society of his own creation – the flowering New Towns. His historical perspective of how much had changed overrode in his mind the possible dangers of materialism. Mass prosperity had arrived on a scale unprecedented for a man of sixty-five whose experience as a younger man had been of aristocratic houses and mass unemployment. The assumptions and expectations of affluence on this scale were genuinely a surprise; he revelled in them, delighted that his own hopes of general prosperity had been exceeded. His latent radicalism made him want to escape from the deep economic divide of the past; continuous references to his own heritage as a crofter's grandson seemed to be being re-enacted on a huge scale. The possible spiritual loss to the individual did not worry him: he was more concerned to extend this affluence to the public sector and reshape it to modern needs. As for a sense of purpose, 'people should get it from their archbishops'.

Amory, a naturally cautious Chancellor who had done little to exploit the fall in import prices during 1958, wanted to cut income tax by 6d. Macmillan wanted 1s and insisted on at least 9d. After a tussle, he got his way. With Britain having her biggest balance of payments surplus since 1951, Amory unsuspectingly gave a violent push to a boom that was already gathering speed. Within a year, industrial production leapt by 10 per cent. It was

Mirage of Summitry

almost a Japanese experience: there was nothing there to sustain it. But it was to last long enough.

In the long pre-election run up in 1959, Macmillan showed his skill and deficiencies as a statesman. A series of colonial problems came to a head. Over Cyprus, Macmillan secured an uneasy settlement between the Greeks and Turks with the help of his appointed Governor, Sir Hugh Foot. Foot's patient negotiation and his capacity to conciliate reversed the trend away from further military involvement in Cyprus. The Labour party were less than generous to Macmillan's achievement; they were in the process of trying to bring home to the British people what little vision the Government were showing in colonial affairs.

That lack of vision was demonstrated brutally in two areas, Kenya and Nyasaland. In Kenya, where British troops were suppressing the Mau Mau revolt, some detainees were beaten to death in Hola camp. In Nyasaland, where there appeared to be the threat of a rebellion from nationalist groups, the Governor had taken firm action and imprisoned Dr. Hastings Banda. The Devlin

When the Russians gave their six months' ultimatum about Berlin I felt it absolutely essential that Macmillan should go to Moscow. I think he had arrived at the same conclusion, and we went. We had certain things to discuss, especially the ultimatum over Berlin, which could have led to a very, very serious situation indeed in Europe at the end of six months. We also wanted to talk about disarmament. I think we haven't had quite the credit we should have had, for most of the significant initiatives over disarmament really came from the British since 1951. We'd first put forward the idea of the Test Ban Treaty, not only in the atmosphere but also underground. We produced a formula, and we wanted to go and discuss this with the Russians. We also wanted to introduce the idea of periodic summit meetings, on Churchill's idea that jaw-jaw is better than war-war. If you can have people talking, going on from meeting to meeting, it's bound to lead to a gradual reduction in tension, and I think we both felt desperately that it was essential to go to Moscow to put this point of view over to the Russians. We got reluctant agreement from the Americans for us to do it. Some other of our allies were rather angry that we went at all, but I was perfectly convinced in my own mind it was the right thing to do.
SELWYN LLOYD

Candy floss summer

I think the 1959 election was successful for the Conservatives because Macmillan was proving himself a very able and competent Prime Minister. He was very powerful in the House of Commons, he was able to control debates with very carefully prepared speeches, which were rather unlike Churchill's but nevertheless had a great effect on the Commons itself. And I think the economy was encouraged before the election to expand, and therefore was at its very best shape when the '59 election came along.

There was a certain amount of criticism of 'You never had it so good', even in the mind of Macmillan. At one stage he attempted to go back on it, and he didn't exactly say 'I didn't say it', because he couldn't say that, because he had said it; but he did feel in his own mind that it did perhaps present too materialistic a conception. There were certain efforts made by some of us to try and get back to the atmosphere of not only his own book, *The Middle Way*, which he wrote as a young man, but also the Industrial Charter which I'd brought in in 1947.

LORD BUTLER

Macmillan was very specially caught up in the feeling of guilt about the economic conditions of the 1930s, about the great depression and the great unemployment. The propaganda against the Tory Party in the 1950s towards the end of the Labour government's time was concentrated on two themes: that it was a warmongering party and that it was a party of mass unemployment. It was a trauma with Tories at that period that these two horrible things were being associated with their party in the public mind, and it was absolutely essential to get rid of these two ideas. The warmongering idea, was dispelled, perhaps not altogether successfully in view of Suez, but still it was, to a large degree, dispelled. The unemployment one, that lingered on; and I think with Macmillan really it was a particularly strong influence. As MP for Stockton-on-Tees in the 1920s and 30s he had seen unemployment at first hand; he was a sensitive man, it had a very deep impression on him, and I think it was impossible for him, for compassionate reasons, to do the things to the economy that needed to be done.

JOHN GRIGG

Commission, reporting on Nyasaland, declared that 'Nyasaland is, no doubt temporarily, a police state.' British policy, in both areas, was coming badly unstuck; the Labour party tried urgently to inject some element of morality into the situation. The Government behaved with less than complete honesty. Speculation that the Colonial Secretary's resignation was being held up for political reasons was later proved correct.

The Nyasaland disturbances were the harbinger of further troubles in the Federation of Rhodesia and Nyasaland. To buy time and kill the issue while he fought the general election, Macmillan advanced the date at which the Federation's future was to be reviewed and appointed a Royal Commission under Monckton to do the job. But it made no electoral difference. It was, indeed, an extraordinary summer: Barbara Castle accused Macmillan of going to the country 'in the sun tan election... designed to catch the heat wave vote'.

Macmillan, who had resisted pressure for a June election, waited till the last moment before he announced on 18 September 1959 that there would be an October election. Ten days or so before he had a visit in some pomp and circumstance from President Eisenhower. In a joint television appearance from 10 Downing Street, while Churchill and Eden had a quiet drink together in an anteroom, Macmillan lectured Eisenhower on the Western world. The superiority of the Prime Minister over the President was demonstrated as Macmillan led

Eisenhower through a series of historical hoops which made the American seem more colonial than the Highlander. Eisenhower was made to seem the errant son being told the facts of life by a kindly father. This public demonstration of the weaker half of an alliance gently riding roughshod over the stronger gave Macmillan encouragement that the summit was just around the corner, but an announcement to this effect had to be withdrawn by Downing Street a few days later. The President had, after all, seen Churchill with similar aspirations only five years earlier.

But the election campaign was on. Macmillan was not confident of victory until Gaitskell promised that Labour's welfare programmes would require no increases in taxation. It was so typical of Macmillan in a way; the groundwork had been done thoroughly, as little as possible had been left to chance, yet it was only an opponent's exploitable mistake that gave Macmillan confidence.

'The only thing that frightens me is that we all may feel – oh well, it's solid as a rock, everything's all right now, and now we can have a little tipple of socialism because we've done so well on this good position we now are in. It's safe to have socialism.

My friends, it's never safe to have socialism. We have given you a very good summer. And, since election promises are all the fashion, I challenge Mr Gaitskell to meet this one: I promise you it'll rain on October 9th (the day of the declaration).'

Summer on the grass at Canvey Island

'It will rain on October 9th'

The golden autumn

Macmillan had a profoundly cynical view of politics and he thought it was only worthwhile being there if you took epoch-making decisions: 'Right', he'd suddenly say 'get out of Africa' – you know, that's quite a thing to decide; and 'the wind of change', or 'get into Europe', or 'go to Suez' or, even more surprising after three days, 'get out of Suez'. He was a tremendous card in that way and I have a taste for that. A man of that kind is bound to catch himself sooner or later because one of these gambles won't come off, and an unsuccessful gamble is, of course, more devastating than four successes. Therefore a man of Macmillan's type was always bound . . . his luck would go one of those days and then the bottom would fall out. And also I think he was getting old, by the way. In politics you're very lucky if you have more than three or four years when the going's good.

RICHARD CROSSMAN

Macmillan was talking to us one day about the difference between Conservatives and Socialists and he said – 'Well, you see, the Conservatives know there are books to read, pictures to look at, music to listen to', and then he paused, 'and grouse to shoot'. This was very Macmillan. Of course, this comparison between the Conservatives and Socialists was absurd and he knew it very well, but he was mocking at himself, he was mocking at this Edwardian image. It's true he liked shooting grouse, but what he was really doing was showing us that politics is in part a game, in part a succession of highly distorted images, and his own image had been distorted, but he was amused by it.

NIGEL NICOLSON

Macmillan had great intellectual self-assurance and his intellect was of a very radical and progressive kind. But possibly, also, a certain emotional insecurity which had made him during his life crave to be accepted by, and to be able to accept, some great colourful hierarchy in which he could both lose himself and find himself. At the very beginning of his adult life he very nearly joined such a hierarchy, when Ronald Knox very nearly persuaded him to join the Roman Catholic Church. It was a very close run thing. I think it was probably the influence of his family, Macmillan's family, which prevented his going over to Rome at that time. I think throughout his life he had needed this kind of enveloping hierarchical establishment and he emotionally needed it. The army gave it to him. At the time he was Prime Minister, at that period of his life, I think he was increasingly finding it in the world of great houses in the patrician establishment of this country; and this again, I think, produced a contradiction, because intellectually his sympathies were very different, and yet, emotionally, he went that way, and this produced a contradiction.

JOHN GRIGG

It did not actually rain on 9 October, but Macmillan's soft mockery showed his sense of what would actually happen: the Conservatives won an overall majority of 100 seats, the only time since 1832 that a government has increased its majority three times in succession. As Macmillan said, with characteristic insouciance, 'I don't do anything – that's what's so splendid about it. I don't even have to shift my house.' More formally, he declared 'the class war is obsolete.'

The 1959 election left Macmillan at the height of his power: the Suez fiasco was forgotten and had had no electoral consequence. The wound has remained healed to this day and any attempt to reopen it has been met with a traditional British reluctance to face failure. The Conservative Party had recovered its shattered morale and was just beginning to feel its inherent strength as *the* governing party restored. Delighted by Labour admissions that the working class solidarity could no longer be counted upon, the Conservatives regarded their future as secure.

For a brief period, Macmillan set out to exploit his established lines of policy and then he sought to alter radically Britain's place and role in the world. Throughout the autumn of 1959 and the spring of 1960, Macmillan worked hard to prepare the ground for a summit. He overcame the traditional reluctance of the American State Department for personal diplomacy at the top by appealing to Eisenhower's vanity. Macmillan coaxed him forward by stressing the mark on history he could make before the end of his presidential term. Macmillan's blandishments might have been rebuffed had Dulles still been Secretary of State, but, near to death, Dulles had been replaced by his deputy Christian Herter, who had not the same authority over the President's views. After a triumphant visit to the United States by Khrushchev the summit was finally fixed in Paris for May 1960. For a brief moment Macmillan appeared the arbiter between East and West.

Shortly before the summit, Macmillan characteristically gambled with his prestige; he ran against the establishment candidate for the Chancellorship of Oxford University. He loved Oxford in a purely romantic way; the Oxford he revered was of Edwardian times, when all Lord Nuffield had was a bicycle shop. As the campaign hotted up, trains packed with voting M.A.s left Paddington. It was remarkable that passions ran so high

The broker goes bust

over a post of purely symbolic importance. Macmillan won and, as a final gesture, wore his ceremonial mortar board the wrong way round at his installation ceremony.

Ten days before the summit, the Russians shot down a high-flying American spy plane – the U2 – and forced a confession from the pilot. Months of patient work were upset and Khrushchev belaboured the West in Paris. Feverish attempts by Macmillan and de Gaulle to keep the conference going were met by Khrushchevian homilies. American imperialism, he said, was like a cat that got at the cream and had to be smacked. Although there was some suspicion that Khrushchev was being manipulated from behind, the meeting ended in farce.

Macmillan sank into profound gloom; all the Churchillian dreams of reconciling East and West were shattered. He even considered resignation. The failure of big-power brokerage brought into sharp relief serious questions over Britain's future role in the world. There were many in all parties who felt that a cross-roads had been reached. Was it now to be little England – an appendage to the United States with waning power – or, at the other extreme, some sort of Atlantic Sweden, neutralist, and dedicated to international organizations, leading by example? Not all saw the dilemma in quite these terms but some on the Left, at least, were well prepared to take the neutralist line.

Certain changes were already afoot. The Empire was slipping away: Ghana had received her independence in 1957 and by 1960 plans were far advanced to give other colonies their independence. Despite the shameless political manoeuvring over the Hola and Devlin reports in the summer of 1959, Tory policy towards black Africa was fairly clear. Independence, in the fullness of time, would be theirs.

By 1960 there were active discussions over the independence of Nigeria and Tanganyika, and Macleod at the Colonial Office was juggling with fancy franchises that indicated the road to power for black nationalism, while hoping to reassure European communities. Really serious problems emerged where black and white Africa met – in the Central African Federation.

Set up in 1953, it comprised Southern Rhodesia (now Rhodesia), Northern Rhodesia (now Zambia), and Nyasaland (now Malawi). Strong nation-

That Paris summit meeting, I think, happened largely because of Mr Macmillan. Eisenhower didn't have any faith in it, as far as I know. But I believe that Harold Macmillan did have, and he may have been quite right. I'm sure, from the standpoint of British domestic politics, that this did represent something of importance to Mr Macmillan's position. So I think Eisenhower was largely persuaded to go along on the notion of being helpful to Mr Macmillan as much as anything else; rather than a thought or a hope that we Americans could get any profit out of that Paris meeting.
ROBERT MURPHY

The summit failure revealed very starkly the clash between the two giants and the fact that the honest broker in the end, when the chips were down, if they were both stubborn, had very little except honeyed words to use. The other reason why he was upset was because he did genuinely believe in the desirability of a *détente*, and obviously this was a setback, at least to that. But the effect of the summit was to shut off one avenue of advance into a better world. I suppose it was natural that he should, and the government's attention should, turn more on to the other area which, at the time, was Europe.
SIR PHILIP DE ZULUETA

At the summit – the summit that never was in Paris in 1960 – Macmillan was deeply upset. This idea of someone who was always completely imperturbable is not true. When he was very much concerned with the success of particular negotiations he could be terribly emotional and very flappable.

Mr Macmillan was certainly devastated by the failure of something which he'd done so much to promote himself. The calmest person, I think, was General de Gaulle, who said to Mr Khrushchev, at about the only meeting we had, that he couldn't understand why he was so much upset at the U.2, when a sputnik was revolving around the earth all the time, taking photographs of France for all he knew. He thought he was being quite unrealistic by being so touchy about it. But I think we don't yet know, and I doubt if we ever will know, the truth about the Russian refusal to co-operate in that summit meeting. I don't think we know exactly what happened. I have a feeling that Mr Khrushchev was very disappointed indeed that progress couldn't be made.
SELWYN LLOYD

The wind of change

alist movements in Northern Rhodesia and Nyasaland underlined the dominance of white Southern
Rhodesia within the Federation to attract support:
by 1959 black nationalists, particularly Kaunda in
Northern Rhodesia and Banda in Nyasaland, saw
the Federation itself as the only obstacle to
independence. The Prime Minister of the Federation, Roy Welensky, had strongly objected to any
idea that the Monckton (Federal Review) Commission should consider breaking it up by allowing
any of the territories in the Federation to secede.
Macmillan had apparently agreed to leave any
discussion of secession out of the Commission's
terms of reference, but privately he had assured
one of its members, Lord Shawcross, an ex-
Labour minister, that they were not debarred from
considering it. The different interpretations put
on the terms by Welensky and the British Government sowed the seeds of mistrust.

But this was not the only difficulty. Responsibility for the countries in the Federation was split
between the Colonial Office and the Commonwealth Relations Office, and they had very different views about what should happen. By July 1960
Duncan Sandys was at the Commonwealth Relations Office and Iain Macleod at the Colonial
Office. Any debate over the future of the Federation would need the agreement of these two
disparate and tough men. Rows between them were
to become the subject of daily gossip in the
corridors of power.

Late in 1959, Macmillan decided to go and look
at Africa himself. It was the first visit by a British
prime minister. Denounced publicly by Nkrumah
as an imperialist and confronted by posters
in Nigeria welcoming 'Hail MacNATO', Macmillan saved himself for political confrontations
demanding more finesse. On arrival in Salisbury,
Rhodesia, Welensky demanded to know how
much truth there was in very high-level assertions
that Macleod wanted to release Banda, the Nyasaland nationalist leader, from detention. Macmillan
used adroit footwork to outpoint Welensky, a
former heavyweight champion of the Rhodesias

and retired early to bed. Banda *was* released, but only after Macmillan had left the Federation.

The Premier's last port of call was South Africa – scene of one of Macmillan's most masterly speeches – the 'Wind of Change' – where he argued that national policies must take account of the strength of African nationalism. Macmillan had mulled over this speech for a long time. Perhaps because of Macmillan's elliptic turn of phrase or their own stupidity, the South Africans did not realize the import of his words until after they had cheered him on his way.

The wind blew in South Africa, but nothing changed; two months after Macmillan left, sixty-three Africans were shot at Sharpeville, many of them in the back. Macmillan's theme had been given point and the fast-moving trend towards self-government accelerated outside South Africa.

Throughout 1960 Welensky emerged as the major problem. His telegrams showered into Whitehall with redoubled fervour when the Monckton Report was published in October. The

Report's main recommendation was that there should be a broader federal franchise. But it added that if after a trial period any territory wished to secede, it could do so. Welensky saw the slippery slope; the organization of which he was Premier was breaking up under him with British connivance. He started to fight a desperate rearguard action, but he could never pin down his target, nor was he accommodating enough to accept the elaborate constitutional schemes drafted by Macleod in an attempt to hold the Federation together. Of Macleod, who had devoted considerable effort and ingenuity to this task, he wrote later: 'He was subtle and secretive; but in face of rational firm opposition, he could not always control his own feelings.' Macleod's visionary zeal for a genuinely multi-racial democratic Federation met with fierce opposition from the old white trade union boss from the copperbelt. They represented two quite different ages.

The Federal Review Conference, in January 1961, deepened Welensky's suspicions that the

I think it was an absolute tragedy that Macmillan didn't come clean about the necessity for decolonization, not as a liberal thing, but as a great act of national self-interest – enlightened self-interest certainly, but nevertheless self-interest. He was inhibited from making a clear statement on this to the British public, particularly before the 1959 election, by the circumstances in which he had become Prime Minister. It was because of the false position which he was in – having become Prime Minister at the time he did and for the reasons that he did – that he was unable to come clean to the British public about his real motives and his real intentions over decolonization. This meant that a great many innocent people – silly people – felt after 1959: well, obviously he's won an election, he's a Tory Prime Minister, he's a hard-line Tory Prime Minister we believe, he's a good old right-wing traditional figure; now he'll move sharply to the Right. Instead of which, of course, to use this shorthand that one has to use, he went to the Left. A lot of people were disconcerted and bitterly disillusioned, indignant and resentful about his doing this, because he had never explained what his position really was and what his intentions really were. I think it's an absolute tragedy that much of the ill will which was generated during those years immediately after 1959, which affected not only Macmillan himself but perhaps even more Iain Macleod, who really bore the full brunt of that ill will, was caused by this false position which Macmillan was in, as a result of becoming Prime Minister after Suez.
JOHN GRIGG

Face to face with Welensky under the shadow of the Monckton Commission. Welensky tries to read the actor's eyes

Macmillan became increasingly tired of the niggling problems that were associated with the Central African Federation. So much of it was in so much little detail, the voting structure and so forth; I think he was tired of that. After all, Macmillan was a man who saw things very much with a broad view, and was not so much concerned with the finer details. I think he found it tedious as it went on. Without being disrespectful to Welensky, they were not in the same class of intellect. On the whole, Macmillan found the whole of that interchange rather boring.

LORD REDMAYNE

In 1961, when Harold Macmillan was presiding over the Commonwealth conference, I had a long talk with him at the weekend down at Chequers. Quite blandly we both assumed there wouldn't be a crisis over South Africa because we thought that Nehru was the man most likely to be emphatic about these matters, and he wouldn't want to split the Commonwealth on colour lines, you see. As long as we played it cool, there would be hard words spoken, but there wouldn't be any critical dénouement. In the result, just as Harold and I were sitting there quite early in the conference looking at each other, I think with what must be admitted a rather smug way, up popped the Prime Minister of Canada, Diefenbaker. When he had finished speaking the fat was in the fire, because he had made this a red-hot issue. He broke up all our ideas. He presented the non-white countries with a very vocal ally and supporter. Of course everybody came to the party and I found myself, as usual, pretty well isolated on this matter, because I do happen to believe that the Commonwealth doesn't exist to give orders to its individual members or to intervene in the domestic affairs of its members.

SIR ROBERT MENZIES

Macmillan regarded African problems rather in the light of the clan system of the Highlands before 1745. He regarded the tribes of Africa as being the equivalent of the Campbells and the MacIntoshes and the rest of it. He tended to argue from his idea of the history of Scotland at that period to the history of Africa in the twentieth century, and anyone who knows Africa knows that parallels simply don't exist. My own feeling was that some of his judgement went astray because of this false historical analogy which is typical of a Highlander. In the same way it may have applied to Macleod, because I've always felt that the Scotch, particularly the Highlanders, have a certain antipathy to English institutions, such as the federal idea which was primarily the outcome of an English constitutional colonial imperial conception. I think that one of the results of this was that Macleod and Macmillan were much more sympathetic to the aspirations of the African peoples for independence than perhaps the average English politician or statesman would have been. I think it did come in some degree partly from their attitude to history, and partly from their inborn feelings for subject people, to which they perhaps felt that they belonged.

Iain Macleod's attitude to Africa was a feeling that the wind of change was blowing very strongly through the continent, that out job was to try and ensure that we were able to give, with the least trouble and turmoil, effectiveness to the aspirations of African people. He was, and I think he regarded himself as, a reformist at the Colonial Office. As far as Duncan Sandys was concerned, he was a much more traditional Commonwealth Secretary; he was a tough negotiator. I have always felt that he tended to push these negotiations harder than was justified in the circumstances, because one can exhaust the other side and get agreement, perhaps in the early hours of the morning after a twenty-four-hour discussion, and then when they go to bed and wake up the next morning they feel perhaps what they'd agreed to wasn't as good after all. I think that was the reason why many of the solutions which Duncan Sandys produced during his period as Commonwealth Secretary haven't lasted.

I think that probably the mistake in handling Roy Welensky was that we were treating him too gently; we should have been more frank, more tough with him right from the beginning, then we might have made a greater success of the Federation of Rhodesia and Nyasaland. Welensky saw his allies to some extent with the right wing of the party, but he was himself a very reformist politician within the context of Africa. He had this background of trade unionism. He felt his allies were the group in the Conservative Party interested in maintaining an imperial British presence in central Africa, and of course he relied increasingly on advice he got from the right wing of the party, which wasn't always in fact very accurate or well-advised.

LORD ALPORT

Government was playing with constitutions. Quite how Welensky thought he could keep the Federation together without these sorts of electoral concessions is unclear.

The drift of events in Africa was further confirmed by the Commonwealth Conference in March 1961. South Africa had adopted Republican status, and therefore had to reapply for membership of the Commonwealth. This raised the question of whether she should be a member at all. Macmillan and Sir Robert Menzies, Prime Minister of Australia, were both sure that South Africa should remain in. But pressure from the new Commonwealth, unexpectedly led by Diefenbaker, Prime Minister of Canada, forced the issue into the open. South Africa withdrew.

During the Conference there was a memorable private confrontation between Welensky and Macmillan. A few weeks earlier Welensky had called up some Federal reservists. His reasons were far from clear, and the British Government had flown planes and troops to Nairobi. Welensky challenged Macmillan to explain their presence. 'But of course,' sighed Macmillan, according to Welensky's account, 'of course Roy, we all make mistakes. Those aircraft and those troops weren't to be used against you. We were collecting them in case you needed help...'

Despite these elaborate and painstaking attempts to bamboozle Welensky, by 1961 it was clear that the British wanted to wash their hands of the Federation. De Gaulle's experience in Algeria was very much on Macmillan's mind and he could see no future in tying British fortunes to those of the Federation. The Federation eventually broke up in 1963. Macmillan, tiring of Macleod's zeal and his constant rows with Sandys, put Maudling at the Colonial Office. But the final dissolution was presided over by the master of subterfuge, Butler. The Central African Federation was broken up into three constituent parts. The central core of the problem, the white settlers in Southern Rhodesia, remained to bedevil a future administration.

The deliberate sleight of hand with which Welensky was ditched prevented any really organized opposition growing in the Tory party. Welensky's attempts to incite the right wing were useless in the absence of any clear trend of government policy. The retreat from empire in Africa was a masterful reversion of traditional British policy, accomplished with hardly a murmur of dissent.

Had it been attempted by a Labour Prime Minister, it is hard to believe that the Conservative Party would have so easily aquiesced.

By mid 1960, therefore, Macmillan knew that Britain's fitful if somewhat fanciful role as mediator between the great powers was finished for some time; he also knew that any latter-day imperial role was incongruous, out of time, and likely to have no return. The deep-seated radical in Macmillan looked for a way forward, without the trappings of the past. There was one area, showing signs of abundant vitatity, which might revive the nation's purpose and sense of direction: the challenge was Europe. Almost miraculously Europe became identified with the future, Africa with the past.

There is a dream world of post-war development which runs something like this: if only the British Government had joined the movement for European integration on the ground floor in the early fifties Britain would have shared in the rapid growth rate of the E.E.C. countries, dominated any political arrangement between them, and would not have wasted large sums of money on maintaining sterling as an international currency and the external trappings of major power status like hydrogen bombs. But it is useless to project a world so unreal.

In the fifties, there were few British politicians who saw Europe as Britain's future. Those Conservatives who saw a united Europe as some sort of third force, Macmillan among them, did not on the whole share the enthusiasm of Monnet for a highly formalized structure. Macmillan had nearly resigned in 1952 out of frustration with Churchill's refusal to follow up his European initiatives, but he has never explained why, in the autumn of 1955, as Foreign Secretary, he did not press harder for more notice to be taken of the groundwork then being laid for the E.E.C. His rejection of the invitation to attend the Messina Conference was cold in tone, although it did not quite close the door on co-operation. Part of the reason may lie in Eden's bossy disapproval of the European idea and Macmillan's reluctance to resign for a project which the entire Foreign Office thought was doomed to failure. But Macmillan had never been an advocate of constitution building. Supranationalism must grow: it could not be imposed by vote. Whatever the reason, Britain by 1956 was counted out of the first steps towards the E.E.C.

Joining the club

'He says he wants to join – on his own terms.'

Macmillan did not intend Britain to remain isolated. He was a strong advocate in Cabinet of taking up the concept of an industrial free trade area from the original European proposal for a Common Market outlined in the Spaak Report. Once he became Prime Minister he lent his weight to a British effort to bring this into being. He appointed Maudling as minister responsible for developing this scheme, but it proved to be a mistake; without major departmental backing, the negotiations lacked impetus.

Macmillan's strategy was to encourage the Treaty of Rome, which set up the Common Market, to be signed – as it was on 25 March 1957 – and then to introduce an industrial free trade area. He made it clear to Selwyn Lloyd in a Minute in June 1957 that he was prepared to accept a

I think what mattered to Macmillan, he's often said it, was the way in which the old world, Europe, would adapt itself to the new conditions, and he used to compare it to the ancient world, with Rome as America, and Greece as Europe. You could have a whole series of nation states, if you like, the Greek city states in modern guise, or you could build the new Constantinople in Europe allied to the great empire of the United States. But at the same time with its own life, and its own power, and I think he certainly saw the EEC as a way towards something new of that kind. I don't think any political leader tries to see too far ahead – that's to say, he may have a vision beyond the mountains, but he pursues his way up to them according to the possibilities at the time. So I think he was fairly flexible in his methods, and perhaps the EFTA and the free trade area might, in his mind, have developed in a similar way to a similar goal.

SIR PHILIP DE ZULUETA

The trouble with the Free Trade Area was, I'm afraid, that there was no clear conception. That seems to me to have been at the root of the difficulty. Now later on it's quite possible that everyone had suspicions that there was an idea that this could be a kind of substitute for the Common Market and, on the French side, that's the reason why all of a sudden the negotiations were broken off. But at the very beginning there had only been a very short sketchy report, prepared in a matter of weeks, and it was a very different thing from what had been done for the Rome Treaty. That is to have an overall review of the problems, a kind of co-ordinated answer for several problems. If you approach a new negotiation without an overall plan then you start with a proposal by one delegation, a proposal by another one, and finally you get nowhere.

The day it started, some people who knew the work I had been doing in the Community told me 'Well, you should see Mr Maudling and talk with him', and so I did. I said 'You know you are not only the head of the British delegation, you are the Chairman of this conference. Now as the Chairman you absolutely need a small international staff, not a British staff around yourself. You need to have some people who have a different point of view, who can tell you what proposals would meet with difficulties in this or that country'. He said 'I know, I've heard about the Brussels Report', which meant he probably hadn't read it, and he said, 'So much work has already been done in our case, it's a very difficult matter. We just have to sit there with the chief of the delegation and take decisions.' I said 'I hope you're right, but I don't see what you're going to decide upon, because I don't think the issues are clear and I'm afraid the way this starts, you'll be in lots of difficulties pretty soon'. It never achieved any decision on any issue.

I must say most of the real Europeans weren't favourable to EFTA, to the large free trade area, at all. It was a dilution of the original concept and it led nowhere in political terms. So after the failure of the Free Trade Area negotiations, I'm sure that many people in Britain began to realize that the Community meant something, it had a future, it was there to stay.

PIERRE URI

I think that from the start the idea of the Free Trade Area was a device directed against the Common Market. It excluded agriculture, it included only industrial products, and it was directed towards providing a split between Germany and France. France was interested in agricultural problems; Germany didn't like it, especially Mr Erhardt who didn't like any commitment on agriculture. I think it was engineered to destroy the Common Market and replace it by something which would exclude agriculture, and which would not have had the institutional arrangements for which the EEC was the model. On the British side, there was the idea they they should build something which would be the Common Market without agriculture, without institutions; this was the aim of the Free Trade Agreement, which failed. They hoped probably that the Community would go in that direction. I think the participants on the Continental side recognized that it wouldn't have the power and efficiency which was expected from the Common Market.

Even in Continental Europe, it took time for people to understand the new structure because it was a complete innovation. There were no precedents. It is an organized dialogue between the Commission, which is responsible for the common interests of the participant countries as a whole, and the representatives of various governments in the Council of Ministers. So that you have to find an agreement between the common good and the day-to-day problems, often very difficult problems from the various countries. That is quite a new system where there is a kind of dialogue between common interest and the interests of individual countries.

ETIENNE HIRSCH

There had been a slight coldness between Britain and France towards the end of 1958, so immediately after the General Election in 1959 I went on a special visit to Paris to see if I could promote better relations again. General de Gaulle said, 'I would like you very much to come into the EEC, but you cannot come in from your point of view unless you bring your Commonwealth with you. We cannot have you in, if you bring your Commonwealth with you, so I'm afraid there can be no agreement'. As simple as that. One argued with him and so on, but he was absolutely straight; that was his view then. In fact, in fairness, M. Couve de Murville, who was his Foreign Minister, had put the same point to me in 1958, the year before. I think we hoped very much to persuade them, we wanted to find out their position, it became clear to us that we couldn't do that unless we made a formal application.

SELWYN LLOYD

I believe the decisive moment in Mr Macmillan's own mind about the Community came in the winter of '59–'60 when he went over to Washington. It was made quite clear to us by the Americans that if there was a split in Europe between the six and the seven, America would support the six. Of course, America was never united about this, but I think it was not until '59–'60 that the die was cast in Macmillan's mind for trying to negotiate. Then there was a very decisive moment in the Foreign Office in 1960 when, for the first time, a research section of the Foreign Office was concerned with this subject. Then the Foreign Office seemed to me to swing over quite violently; it's rather like St Augustine: 'Too late, if I know thee, thou ancient beauty'. There was quite a sudden extreme change of view, it seems to me, between the Foreign Office attitude of the fifties and the Foreign Office attitude of the sixties.

LORD BOYLE

supra-national element in the administration of the Free Trade Area – 'a managing board' as Macmillan called it in a later Minute to Thorneycroft. He added: 'this might well be called a 'supra-national' institution. But does it matter?' He went on to say, 'We cannot afford to wait... some initiative... with a political connotation seems to be necessary... we must not be bullied by the activities of the Six. We could, if we were driven to it, fight their movement if it were to take the form of anything that was prejudicial to our interests. Economically with the Commonwealth and other friends, including the Scandinavians, we could stand aside from a narrow Common Market. We also have some politico-military weapons... we must take the lead either in widening their project or, if they will not co-operate with us, in opposing it.'

The Free Trade Area did not appeal to all the signatories of the Treaty of Rome. Free trade meant the lowering of tariff barriers; the French in particular had been persuaded to sign the Treaty of Rome on the basis of tariff protection. This incompatibility was exacerbated by political bitterness towards Britain after Suez.

The French were worried enough by the might of German industry, without an additional threat from Britain. Within a Common Market situation the French felt they could manipulate the situation, but with Britain and additional countries in her train, their security would be undermined. Negotiations dragged on against a background of chronic French political instability, with the British showing a remarkable capacity for making their concessions a stage too late.

Pressure from those who wanted a community-based Europe built up against the British initiative which was seen as an attempt to dilute the provisions of the Treaty of Rome. A major political upheaval in France which resulted in the return of De Gaulle to power with strong army support from generals fighting the Algerian war, sharpened French hostility to any possible economic concessions. While Macmillan welcomed his old wartime comrade to his new office, De Gaulle shut off negotiations with Britain through his minister, Soustelle. The British negotiators, Maudling and Eccles, the President of the Board of Trade, in a quite natural fit of bad temper, which was to be held against Britain later, denounced the French as small-minded and threatened to establish a rival organization that would 'wring that young European capon's neck for good'. The European Free Trade Association (the outer seven) was born a year later. By 1960, French proponents of the E.E.C. were laughing at E.F.T.A.: 'What is the use', they would say in the comfortable hindsight of 1970, 'of a group of countries that could only offer the same goods to each other at fundamentally the same prices?' Although the verdict is too harsh, Britain was by no means the real beneficiary from E.F.T.A.

Any seed that Macmillan wished to sow on European ground in 1960 could not be expected to take root quickly. But on 31 July 1961, formal application to join the Common Market was lodged. Had the bid been successful it would have altered the course of British politics during the sixties and profoundly influenced her political future thereafter.

As with most of Macmillan's major initiatives, the decision to apply for membership was presented slowly, with no trumpeting and as if British policy was to shift slightly in emphasis. It was almost as if the Prime Minister himself had not made up his mind and was sounding out the ground. Many commentators, and indeed some of his own Cabinet, found it increasingly difficult to distinguish between impression and reality, and the series of feints and play on politics led people to doubt his sense of direction.

But beneath the Edwardian *bonhomie* that had concealed so much of Britain's real decline in the late fifties, very positive steps were being taken. Also, as a prime minister with a large and restive majority he could not afford to upset the party. Eden had provided Macmillan with an object lesson: the tiresome Right of the party had to be contained, and had the direction of his African and European policy been too clearly visible he would have had a major revolt on his hands. By evasion and blurring of the real issues, Macmillan was able to abandon Empire and confront Europe.

Macmillan was disdainful of those who could not rise to the level of great events, but there was something a little misleading about his own campaign with its emphasis on the economic benefits for Britain rather than for the political grand design which was his real aim. To some, mainly those against the E.E.C. in any case, it seemed undemocratic and more than a little frustrating. Macmillan was playing to win but his methods left an element of mistrust which, deepened by failure, does something to explain Macmillan's later reputation for cheapening politics.

Macmillan's deep depression after the collapse of the summit in May 1960 was countered rapidly by action. Europe had begun to seem the only way forward. In July, Macmillan reshuffled his cabinet. Committed Europeans, some of whom had been far from happy at the botched juggling over the Free Trade Area, were moved to key positions. Sandys, whose European pedigree was even longer than Macmillan's, took on the delicate responsibility of the Commonwealth, and Soames, then the man closest to accepting the Community model for Europe, was made Minister of Agriculture. He was told that Britain's agricultural policy made it unlikely that there could be a move towards Europe: within six months he was reporting that Britain's agricultural policy would have to be changed anyway. Edward Heath, a Macmillan protégé, was moved after only nine months at the Ministry of Labour to take on responsibility for Europe at the Foreign Office. It was little noticed, but his chief, the new Foreign Secretary, Lord Home, was a firm believer that Britain's future, economic as much as political, lay with Europe. Selwyn Lloyd, probably not so sympathetic towards Europe, moved to the Treasury. Maudling, who had made no secret of his resentment at the treatment he had received from the French during the Free Trade Area negotiations, and who was sceptical about too close a link with the Common Market, was denied his strongest ambition, which was for the Foreign Office. His patron, whose equivocations about the issue barely concealed his hostility towards Europe, was left at the Home Office to win liberal applause.

But the changes were hardly noticed for what they were. The press and the Labour party seized on the new Foreign Secretary, the fourteenth Earl of Home, as a fresh monkey for the Edwardian organ grinder, quite intolerably removed from political pressure in the House of Lords. In the autumn of 1960, Macmillan moved by stealth. Even his Chief Whip, Martin Redmayne, learned what was afoot only indirectly, and rightly anticipated trouble from the party. The key figure was Soames who, in January 1961, assured the Prime Minister that nothing, agriculturally, stood in the way of joining Europe. Already, however, before Christmas 1960, Macmillan had retreated to

In late '60, certainly in '61, Macmillan began to talk about the Common Market. He was of course terribly set back by the failure of the summit in 1960 and therefore was searching around for new initiatives. The first time I was conscious that the Common Market was even quietly in the air was, I think, about November of '60. As a matter of fact, it first came clear to me in a conversation with Christopher Soames, Minister of Agriculture, which of course demonstrates that I wasn't necessarily completely in Macmillan's confidence, or at any rate he hadn't thought it necessary at that moment to tell me what was in his mind. Soames simply saw fit to tell me what had gone on between himself and the Prime Minister in this matter, and that the plan was to launch a campaign to go into the Common Market, with which he thoroughly agreed, of course. I was just glad to be informed. The Chief Whip always had to keep, they say, his ear to the ground, and it's a little bit more than the ground you have to keep your ear to. Macmillan wanted to be sure that he was going to be able to make progress with it, therefore he played it slowly, some say too slowly; but I believe playing it slow was undoubtedly a benefit in the parliamentary sense: whether it was a benefit in the sense of achieving the objective, I don't know.

Macmillan, a great parliamentarian of course, realized the climax of the parliamentary year was always the end of the summer. Either you had a great crisis, indeed most years one had a great crisis, or else it was an opportunity to take great initiatives. I'm quite sure that he would have decided that this was best launched at the end of the summer with a considerable fanfare and then left to mutter along while Parliament wasn't sitting, so that there would be a good deal of skill in the timing. It was always his skill; he was a great politician. There was always the possibility of trouble in the party and trouble persisted the whole time. One has to remember, of course, that it never came to the final vote; we never had to make up our minds, as a parliament or as a party in support of government, that we were finally coming down on the right side.

All through this time the Common Market was always sold on the basis that the party would support it if the terms were right, therefore one never got down to a hard core. I would say that the hard core eventually would have been somewhere around thirty; this is what I was conscious of the whole time. But of course it would depend in the end on whether the terms had been accepted or not. I used to be scolded for suggesting there ought to be a full back position; this was regarded as bad tactics. If we were fighting a battle, this is where we got into the soldiery metaphor, then we must maintain the objective, and therefore in fact there was no fall back position to discuss.

LORD REDMAYNE

Chequers and then his country home in Sussex to write a paper on Britain's future. By all accounts it was an historical essay in the best Balliol tradition.

In the next three months amongst and, perhaps, partly because of the distractions of the Central African Federation and South Africa, the Cabinet was moved towards a bid for Europe. In January Macmillan saw De Gaulle and was told that only an application for full membership would be entertained. By 27 February Heath was telling the Europeans that Britain would accept the Common Tariff (a necessary condition of joining the E.E.C.) against all but Commonwealth countries, but the French put an end to such hopes. It was made clear to Heath that the commitment must be more complete. By the end of March, Heath felt confident enough of the Cabinet decision to let an influential member of the State Department, George Ball, know what was in the wind and to seek American reaction. In April, Macmillan visited President Kennedy and received his blessing for the attempt. Certain members of the Cabinet were still doubtful, particularly Butler and Hailsham. Maudling, indeed, told the Commons at the end of April that no final decision had been taken, but less than three weeks later Heath told the House that the Government found full membership of the Common Market the most attractive proposal, and the one most likely to be adopted, given reasonable terms. But the party had to be handled with care. This could not be presented as a rush into Europe, but more as an approach to see what the Common Market had to offer. It was, too, a question of timing: the announcement was deliberately held up until just before the summer recess. Six days before, a new economic device – the regulator – was used to cut back on domestic consumption.

Whatever the political advantages of going into Europe, the main pressure of advice on Macmillan had been economic. Just as 1960 marked a watershed in foreign affairs, so it also saw the beginning of a fundamental rethink in economic policy. The problem centred on the growth and structure of the economy. There certainly were anomalies: after the investment boom of 1959-60, production did not seem to be rising. World trade was buoyant, and although mild restrictions on domestic consumption should have helped, Britain was not exporting enough. Civil servants became excited by the quest for long-term growth: the achieve-

ments of the French Commissariat du Plan, their economic planning agency, caused a good deal of envious self-examination. The obvious problem in Britain's economic performance was her alarming propensity, at the first sign of a boom, to import not only raw materials, but, increasingly, manufactures and machine tools. This gave balance of payments considerations a much greater importance as the sixties progressed.

A concern for long-term growth was paralleled by increased attention to planning – particularly of productivity, wage rates, and prices. Modernization was the theme. Selwyn Lloyd's period as Chancellor compares only in post-war history with Cripps', and has no other equal as a major innovatory period.

Lloyd's greatest achievement was the establishment of the National Economic Development Council – known, not without affection, as 'Neddy'. 'Neddy' was an independent meeting place for industrialists and trade unions to talk over trends in the economy, and to attempt to draw up plans on what should be done. Although the body had no formal powers it was immensely valuable in deepening the appreciation, on both sides of industry, of the type and condition of Britain's economic problems. The council's overwhelming aim was to encourage faster growth, and it was soon to set a 4 per cent target of annual growth. The members felt that a mutual understanding of each other's plans, together with a government commitment to steady expansion, would enable Britain to break free of the dreary circus of 'Stop-Go'. Most of N.E.D.C.'s members recognized that this would involve some controlled restraint of incomes. But it was only harsher times later that produced the cry of increased productivity.

Additional reforms were cumulatively of great importance. Long-term forward looks at public expenditure were instituted. The introduction of the economic 'regulator' enabled the Chancellor to make limited tax changes between budgets, particularly on purchase tax. A new policy was engineered towards the nationalized industries which made it clear they were not simply an extension of welfare schemes. This policy improved morale in the public sector industries considerably, but excited some popular opposition, most notably when some uneconomic railway routes suffered from Beeching, the new head of British Railways,

Getting stuck

I had certain purposes which I wanted to achieve. I felt that the Chancellor hadn't enough power between budgets and that's why I brought in the idea of a 'regulator', which has survived. I felt it was absolutely essential to have a five-year forward look at the expenditure, and that was accepted after the Plowden Report. I also thought that the nationalized industries ought to operate as a commercial undertaking, to make proper provision for their capital investment programmes that we laid down. I also believed that the government had to get control of the gilt-edged market again; that was achieved. But what I thought was more important than any of these things was that we should produce a formula for confidential discussion between government and the two sides of industry, management and trade union. You can't talk publicly about things like restrictive practices and so on, but I felt it was very necessary to have some kind of private forum – a private meeting place – with an independent secretariat so that the other side would have confidence that it wasn't a government-controlled thing; where one could discuss seriously the obstacles to growth, and the ways in which we could promote economic efficiency and expansion. That was my conception of NEDC. It took quite a long time to get it accepted.

Over the NEDC I certainly consulted the Prime Minister throughout and he backed the project. In fact, if he hadn't done so, I don't think we would have ever got it through the cabinet. He was completely in support and fought very hard for it, and we eventually prevailed. I think he completely agreed with the conception that you had to bring the increase in earnings into some real relationship with the increase in production.
SELWYN LLOYD

Macmillan said to me when he made me Financial Secretary, that he didn't want to have to listen to too much economic argumentation, but the idea of the NEDC sent him right back to his old *Middle Way* enthusiasms. I was very struck how tremendously effectively he took it through the cabinet. When you got Mr Macmillan really interested in a subject he felt strongly about, my goodness, he was not just a persuasive speaker, he was also exceptionally good at getting the business through cabinet.
LORD BOYLE

Clobbering demand

From the moment Selwyn Lloyd took over, he realized that the balance of payments might not right itself. It was, of course, the change of the mark early in '61 which triggered off the crisis that year. The thing that stuck out at the Treasury of course was the very strong element of 'cost-push', the fact that you'd had for the first time about 8 per cent or nearly 9 per cent increase in earnings in a single year. Everybody at the Treasury felt that it wasn't enough just to clobber demand, but you had to do something about wages as well. Selwyn Lloyd saw this point very clearly indeed.

LORD BOYLE

The trouble about 1961 was that the revaluation of the mark created a flurry on the exchanges. Confidence was lost in sterling and in one week we lost over £140 million on the exchanges. We thought we'd check that with the help of the central banks, but as the summer went on we found we hadn't. There was still no confidence in sterling, and I believe the absolute essence of the British economy is to have confidence in sterling. As a great trading nation we had commitments and trading operations over the world. The one thing I had to do in October, cost what it may, was to recreate confidence in sterling, and so I had to take some pretty severe actions. Within twelve months bank rate was down to 4½ per cent and we started to reinflate, and one had to be very certain one was right, and one had to take this very disagreeable action to recreate the confidence in sterling. I think by the summer of 1962 we had got a position in which expansion was really possible, in fact during '63 and '64 we had an expansion of the economy amounting to 8 per cent – an average of 4 per cent – the best rate we've ever achieved.

SELWYN LLOYD

I can remember during the last days of the Finance Bill one Treasury official saying to me 'I feel the Chancellor's days are numbered, though he doesn't yet seem to realize it'. There was a feeling that we had got stuck at that moment, that we'd taken on board a lot of new policies but were rather stuck with them, particularly on the incomes side. I found myself thinking there would be a change soon. At the same time I'm bound to say that I think Selwyn Lloyd had taken more measures to reflate the economy than have always been remembered. I don't think Selwyn Lloyd's departure came as a complete surprise to everybody, but I think in fairness to him it ought to be remembered that he had, in fact, done quite a number of things to reverse engines by the time he did leave office.

LORD BOYLE

and his drastic economy measures – 'Beeching's Axe'. And perhaps most significant, Selwyn Lloyd was persuaded without much difficulty to accept the need for an incomes policy. Macmillan himself was enthusiastic about 'Neddy', and he would hark back to a book he had written in the 1930s. 'Have you read my *Middle Way*?' he would say to startled officials who had forgotten his own advocacy of planning. In Cabinet, he saw Lloyd through, against the rooted opposition of Maudling.

Although it is now possible to see Lloyd's chancellorship as a period of great change, much of it enforced, it began in an orthodox fashion. The 1961 Budget, although Lloyd admitted the overriding importance of cost inflation, contained no remedies. Instead, he made surtax concessions which involved him in a good deal of political controversy. A cabinet revolt, led by Maudling, Macleod, and Heath, forced him to introduce a tax on short-term capital gains, but it was lost in the odium of a rich man's budget. The establishment of the regulator, a device for changing consumer taxes by 10 per cent between budgets, did, at the same time however, give Lloyd some room for manoeuvre.

He was quickly to need it. In July 1961 there was another crisis of confidence, not unlike that of 1957. A revaluation of the German mark put pressure on the pound, which was then artificially strong because 1960 had seen a large inflow of 'hot' money – short-term funds held in sterling, but easily changed into other currencies. Lloyd was under heavy pressure from his advisers to take drastic action. Though he moderated their advice, his political standing did not rise. By using the regulator he upped consumer taxes by the full 10 per cent, imposed limits on government spending and bank advances, and put bank rate up to 7 per cent. The July 1961 measures were a matter of too much, too late. Two years of stagnation followed. But the 'July measure' which really excited interest and opposition was the pay pause, a voluntary wage freeze. At long last people had thrust upon them the implications of a wage-price spiral.

The pay pause ended officially in April 1962, although it had been breached before that. In February a paper was issued declaring that money incomes should not rise by more than an average of 2.5 per cent per person per year. This was the

famous 'guiding light' which had at last seen the light of day. But 'Lloyd's light', as it was scathingly referred to, was clearly not enough on which to base a more effective long-term strategy.

Throughout the first half of 1962, cabinet meetings were plagued by rows over what sort of incomes policy should be launched and the degree to which government should be brought in. Lloyd seemed to have no strong preference himself. Macmillan became impatient and angry and in a remarkable initiative, called together officials to establish the broad lines of what was later to be the National Incomes Commission ('Nicky'), similar in conception and scope to 'Neddy', which had held its first meeting in March 1962. Lloyd's 1962 Budget contained but one innovation, a tax on sweets and ice cream. Buoyed up, first by over-optimistic forecasts, and second, by the expectation that negotiations with the E.E.C. would be complete by July, leading to an investment boom, Lloyd miscalculated: the brakes were left on too hard.

Macmillan's impatience with the slowness of economic progress was exacerbated by his party's record in by-elections. The Conservatives in every

by-election before August lost votes heavily. Orpington, which declared in March, was the most sensational result. A rock-safe suburban Tory seat with a Conservative majority of 14,760 was turned into a Liberal victory of 7,855: the Liberal vote had risen by nearly a third. Orpington was a political freak, but compared with similar election results in Blackpool North and Middlesborough East and West, it did not seem so at the time. The credit squeeze could, in a way, be seen to be working.

Clamour welled up from the parliamentary party, too large for political comfort and self-discipline, about the Government's inability to get a grip. Macleod's own position as Chairman of the Party seemed in danger, and, on 10 July, he and Butler pressed Macmillan to make drastic changes and eradicate the 'fuddy-duddy' atmosphere at the top. Their target, it is all too clear, was Lloyd. Macmillan realized the import of these signals and determined to act. He had planned a reshuffle for that summer, and he would do it now. Nobody foresaw what was to happen next.

On Thursday 12 July a front page story in the *Daily Mail* predicted far-reaching cabinet changes and a promotion for Butler. The story was rumoured at the time to come from the Home Secretary. Whatever the source, could Macmillan afford to wait and announce his changes after an orgy of speculation? There was danger of a concerted resignation if Macmillan dawdled; by the end of Friday 13 July, seven cabinet ministers had been sacked. The principal victim was Selwyn Lloyd. The dismissed Lord Chancellor, Kilmuir, complained that his cook would have got longer notice. He was told that cooks were much harder to replace than Lord Chancellors.

Although the July purge gave the party a new look, it did Macmillan great harm. In a party whose internal relations were essentially based on loyalty, Macmillan, at his own expense, made the concept cheaper. He also made powerful enemies and raised questions of his own dispensability. 'Greater love hath no man than this, that he lay down his friends for his life', Jeremy Thorpe wittily observed. Lord Avon publicly declared, 'I feel that Selwyn Lloyd has been harshly treated.'

Macmillan was certain that he could soldier his way to victory: the core of his strategy was Britain's entry into the Common Market. British membership of the E.E.C. assumed the garb of a panacea for frustration and stagnation, and not only did the

MAC THE KNIFE

Lloyd and six others swept out of Cabinet

By LOUIS KIRBY

SEVEN Cabinet Ministers were swept from office last night in the biggest wave of political executions in peacetime memory. In a day of tense drama at Admiralty House, Mr. Macmillan struck swiftly and ruthlessly.

He handed out sensational sackings and promotions aimed at producing a brand-new image for the Government.

Top of the list in the bloodletting of Friday the Thirteenth came the Chancellor, Mr. Selwyn Lloyd, so long protected from savage criticism by the Macmillan umbrella.

After two years at the Treasury he bows out to the back-benches, and is made a Companion of Honour.

The other six Ministers sacked from the Cabinet are: Viscount Kilmuir, the Lord Chancellor; Mr. John Maclay, Secretary of State for Scotland; Mr. Harold Watkinson, Minister of Defence; Sir David Eccles, Minister of Education; Lord Mills, Minister without Portfolio; Dr. Charles Hill, Minister of Housing and Local Government. All were members of the first Macmillan Cabinet in 1957.

WALTER TERRY

COMMENTARY ON THE CABINET SURGERY

MAUDLING last night . . . Chancellor at 45

The decision, which was conveyed to me on the evening of Thursday the 12th of July and implemented on Friday the 13th, was a complete surprise. I had no conception at all that anything like this was in his mind. I was not offered any other position in the government. I think the action he took on Friday the 13th July 1962 was a mistake, both from his personal point of view and the point of view of the interests of the party. I don't think it would be right for me to comment further.

SELWYN LLOYD

In the end, Macmillan must have become impatient with him; I think this was partly due to Selwyn Lloyd's manner. I think he gave the impression to the Prime Minister that he wasn't achieving enough in the time. I think the real cause of the massacre of Glencoe was a genuine desire by Macmillan to give the Conservative Party a younger look. He wanted to do something before the election to establish new men in office. I think he thought if he didn't act quickly there would be dangerous political repercussions which he thought might bring down his government. Therefore, he acted really within a 48 or 36 hour period, which did, of course, lead to a good deal of heart-searching.

LORD BUTLER

One very prominent minister complained that he'd been treated like an office boy caught with his hand in the till. But I don't think Macmillan at all enjoyed this episode, and I think he was also very much embarrassed by it. There is one story of how a personal friend of his, whom he was going to have to ask to resign, came, not knowing that this request was going to be made to him, and Macmillan started talking about trees; the chap was a bit puzzled about this reference to trees, but Macmillan went on and then said 'Well, you really ought to go and look after your trees'. This chap wasn't very interested in trees, but let the conversation go on. Then it became perfectly apparent that was in fact being banished to his estates. Macmillan, in a very uncomfortable way, was giving him the sack.

ROBERT ALLAN

If the leader of a political party gives the impression or lets it be known that he's not going to win the next election, then his head is on the block. When Harold Macmillan carried out his purge and sacked so many of his ministers he let it be known to at least one, possibly more, that he didn't feel the Conservative Party could win the election in 1964. Now that, to a Prime Minister, is the sentence of death.

REGINALD BEVINS

'*Wonderful job, sir. The public were getting bored with the same old faces.*'

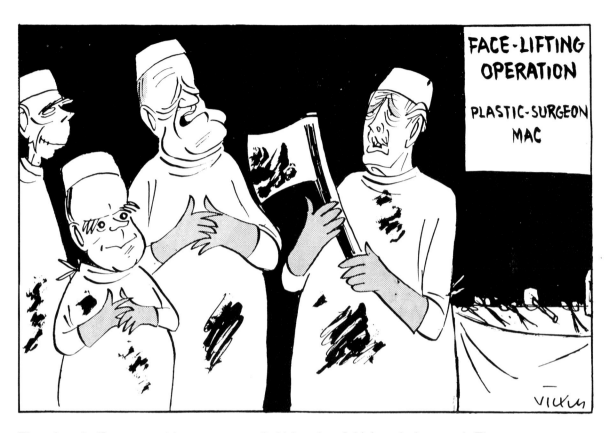

'*Wonderful job, sir. The public were getting bored with the same old faces.*'

The 1962 reshuffle was a positive attempt to refurbish a government which had been in office for a long time and therefore there was a certain amount of discussion of possibilities as to which ministers would happily go. You've got to remember, and this is perfectly fair that I should say this, that all, or nearly all, of the men concerned had signified, either to me or to the Prime Minister, that in due course, admittedly, they would quite happily go. Therefore, however much that operation may be criticized, and it wasn't in fact as brutal as the press comment afterwards made it out to be, or, indeed, some of the comments of the so-called victims made it out to be, you've got to remember that now we have a Conservative government in again, and that a great deal of the strength of that government derives from the fact that these men achieved experience in high ministerial office from 1962 onwards; this was part of the object. The whole timing of that operation was the subject of a great deal of discussion. You will recollect that the Common Market negotiations were going along very well. It was thought during the summer that it might be necessary to recall Parliament in September or October to come to a final vote on it, I can only comment as to the short-term timing of it, but in fact it was intended to be a brisk but fairly leisurely operation over a long weekend. It was for a variety of reasons that it was

then, I think, rushed too much. There was an apparent leak in one of the leading papers; it seemed that someone had blown the gaff. In the light of the speculation that then arose, on the whole it was better done quickly. But there's no doubt at all if that leak hadn't occurred then the chance of getting away with this major surgery would have been very much better than it was.

LORD REDMAYNE

A more special relationship

prospect seem a cure-all for Britain's economic ills, but there was the political promise of new horizons. A mood of self-flagellation seized the nation. Too many people reached for their pens, and the 'Suicide of a Nation' was seriously debated in *Encounter*. Penguin cashed in with a wildly successful 'What's wrong' with everything series. Even the most modest politician felt that a new age was about to dawn. Always sensitive to atmosphere, Macmillan took his chance.

In a speech at the Conservative Party Conference in October 1962 he came across in what was, to the public, a new light. He revealed his long-held convictions about the political importance of Europe with considerable fervour. Before, he had always been careful to place the argument in the more humdrum terms of greater markets and opportunities for British businessmen. His new approach was quite different in tone and degree, as it was intended to be. Helped by Gaitskell's forthright opposition on grounds of historical tradition, Macmillan appealed to a glorious future. He carried the conference with him: the few dissidents were made to look like fools who had interfered with a great historical progress.

Macmillan had been to see De Gaulle at the Chateau de Champs in July. The meeting had been cordial, and De Gaulle had accepted that Britain would be joining and had been pleasurably surprised by the vigour with which Macmillan advocated the European cause. In November, De Gaulle had his mandate confirmed overwhelmingly in the presidential election: he was more secure, with the Algerian problem settled and a Franco-German alliance established, than at any time since his extraordinary drafting to power in 1958.

Macmillan had agreed to see De Gaulle at Rambouillet in December for further talks. But just before they met there were dramatic developments which threw into sharp relief the priorities of British statesmen. December 1962 was a momentous month in British history, but by no means as important as has since been made out.

To illuminate the rapid developments in December 1962, it is necessary to go back to March 1960. Macmillan then talked with Eisenhower at Camp David, the President's country retreat. He explained that the missile Blue Streak, the future basis of Britain's deterrent, was becoming too expensive and too vulnerable. Eisenhower offered

Skybolt, a stand-off bomb carried under a bomber's wing, which could be unleashed 1,000 miles from its target, as part of a tripartite American approach to defence: the other two parts were Minuteman – an intercontinental ballistic missile housed in silos on American soil – and Polaris, a submarine-based I.C.B.M., which had the great advantage of being manoeuvrable and virtually undetectable and indestructible.

Macmillan accepted the American offer with alacrity; he paid the price of allowing Holy Loch to be used as a Polaris staging point. Britain's independent deterrent now had a projected life into the late sixties. But Skybolt ran into trouble, this time under a more cost-conscious American administration. Macmillan, despite his initial uncertainty because of their difference in age,

had quickly established an extraordinarily close relationship with Kennedy; throughout the Cuban missile crisis in October 1962, the two men were in touch by telephone three times a day. With Lord Harlech in Washington as Ambassador, the bond between Kennedy and Macmillan was greatly strengthened.

The Cuba crisis held up reconsideration of Skybolt, but in November, McNamara the American Secretary for Defence told Thorneycroft, now restored to grace as Minister of Defence after a stint at the Ministry of Aviation, that Skybolt could be cancelled. Hints had been dropped before, but this was a definite shift in policy. Thorneycroft quickly sensed the political dangers of Britain losing her independent deterrent, and he reacted very shrewdly by doing nothing and expecting the Americans to come up with a replacement, if, indeed, Skybolt was to be cancelled. Discreet, but strong, representations were made to the U.S.A.F. that it was in their interests too to see that the 'Air Force deterrent' was not lost. Skybolt continued to fail tests as the telephone between Macmillan and Thorneycroft continued to remain silent. It was a sign of changed times that McNamara did not feel the urge to offer a replacement to keep Britain in the nuclear front-runners; such an oversight would have been inconceivable in Eisenhower's latter days.

The British became alarmed: one cabinet minister said he felt he had been left without his trousers. Thorneycroft and Macmillan decided to try for Polaris. They set off for Nassau on a long-standing engagement to meet Kennedy. Kennedy, flying down from Washington with Harlech, had had made clear to him, apparently for the first time, the domestic political implications of Britain's loss of an independent deterrent. Macmillan, although he was studiously filmed watching a calypso, was worried. He was blunt with Kennedy. Give us Polaris, and the British will make over all British nuclear forces to NATO, with only a saving clause about independence.

Although McNamara was heard to mutter that if the British got Polaris they wouldn't know what end to put the missile in, the American delegation were surprised by the British concession over NATO, which fitted in well with their nascent notions of a mixed manned fleet of NATO ships deploying nuclear weapons. The major exception from the American side was George Ball, who

There was a prior doubt on Macmillan's part, I understand, as to whether he could establish the kind of relationship with President Kennedy that he had enjoyed with President Eisenhower. He felt the generation difference, and he was very uncertain about it, but in point of fact they got along extremely well. They were both ironists, they enjoyed each other's conversation; the President was quite entertained by the mask of weary Edwardian langour under which the Prime Minister would pursue his objectives, and rather quickly a fondness developed between them.

There was a good reason why Skybolt did not receive full attention, because this was the autumn of the Cuba missile crisis. When the Americans returned to the consideration of the problem, it was not until November. At that point the decision was communicated to England from Defence Department to Defence Ministry rather than from State Department to Foreign Office, and Secretary McNamara, I think, assumed that Peter Thorneycroft, who was Defence Minister, would immediately undertake contingency plannings of various sorts.

President Kennedy supposed that if this was going to cause a great crisis in England, Macmillan would call him about it. But then there were equivalent misunderstandings on the other side. Macmillan really refused, I think, almost to believe it unless he heard it directly from Kennedy, and you had this curious situation of both Washington and London hanging by the telephone expecting a call from the other. I think you had this situation partly because of false analogies, Britain assuming that Washington saw one thing while Washington was seeing something different, and vice versa, and partly because of simple blockage in the channels of communication.

There was, in the State Department, a group which became known as the Europeans who were led by George Ball who became Under-Secretary of State. They were very much influenced by Jean Monnet and believed very strongly in the necessity of economic and military integration of Europe. They felt it was most important for Britain to enter the Common Market.

The cancellation of Skybolt certainly was seized upon and perceived as an opportunity by the Europeanists in the State Department. It was a providential opportunity to force Britain into Europe; they were therefore very much opposed to any notion of a substitute for Skybolt, like Polaris, for example, which would have the effect of prolonging the British nuclear deterrent well into the 1970s. Their object was to end the independent British deterrent and to end the special relationship to push Britain into Europe.

ARTHUR SCHLESINGER

De Gaulle's get-out

I thought it was very important that Britain played its role in Europe because it seemed to me that this was the only way that a soundly built structure could ever be erected in Europe, a political structure which would avoid all the destructive rivalries of the past. Therefore I felt that one had to look at the British nuclear relationship which was very heavily dependent on the United States, that the renewal and the extension of this relationship was bound to impair Britain's ability to play the role in Europe, which seemed to me to be a very desirable one. So that looking at it in those terms, from the point of view of what American policy should be, it seemed to me that we ought to discourage the extension of the nuclear deterrent into succeeding decades – which of course, is what we didn't do at Nassau. The effect of the decision at Nassau with regard to Polaris was to ensure that Britain would continue to be a nuclear power into the seventies and perhaps even into the eighties and I think that this is obviously one of the elements which resulted in de Gaulle's decision, on 14 January 1963, to deny British entry.

I had tried in Washington before we came to Nassau, and I tried in Nassau, to make the offer so qualified in terms of multilateral arrangements, and so on, that it wouldn't have had the political effect in Paris that I was afraid of. But actually the decision was pretty well made on the President's plane going down to Nassau the morning before the conference opened, in which the President had spoken with David Ormsby-Gore (later Lord Harlech), who was the British Ambassador in Washington at that time, and with whom he was very close. But the President really showed his inclination very clearly. His inclination was to be as helpful as possible to the British government and to be generous with them in view of the fact that there had been the decision to cancel the Skybolt project. He recognized that the cancellation of the Skybolt was primarily an American decision, and if one partner in a venture decides not to go along with it, it necessarily puts the other partner in a very difficult posture. When you add to that the fact of friendship, the fact that there was a good deal of sympathy and *rapport* between the Prime Minister and the President, I think the decision wasn't a very surprising one. We did talk at Nassau about the effect this would have on France and General de Gaulle, but Macmillan didn't seem greatly concerned about this, he thought the General would understand – at least he gave this impression to us.

GEORGE BALL

The offer of Polaris to the French was a perfectly genuine offer. Their immediate reaction to it was quite cool. I just don't know whether it could have been followed up more forcefully, and I'm quite sure that if it had been followed up more forcefully it wouldn't have made any difference. The French tended to regard it entirely as a symbolic offer, as a sop thrown to them.

ARTHUR SCHLESINGER

argued that the Americans had been keeping the British in the independent nuclear business far too long; it made the problem of limiting the proliferation of nuclear arms more difficult, and since Britain was about to join Europe, she should accept nuclear parity with other European powers. This view was regarded by both sides as too 'anti-British'. Macmillan got Polaris at a very reduced cost. When, a month later, McNamara tried to get the British to shoulder more of the costs in what was an outrageously uneconomic deal, Macmillan telephoned Kennedy asking, who was in fact the President? McNamara's attempt to up the stakes was crushed. Polaris gave Britain full nuclear status into the seventies – and, possibly, later.

The end product of Nassau had been predicted a week earlier by Macmillan to De Gaulle. He told De Gaulle at Rambouillet that he was going after Polaris. The General understood and did not pursue the matter further. But the atmosphere of this meeting had changed a good deal from Champs, six months earlier. De Gaulle was less helpful and friendly. It is commonly said that Macmillan and De Gaulle were labouring under linguistic difficulties at Rambouillet but this is not true. Macmillan's French was good, the General's English not so good. Frequently, the General did not allow his interpreter time and brushed him aside. As both the General and Macmillan were inclined to speak in the elliptical terms of broad historical analysis – their similarities have never been done full justice – there was room for misunderstanding. But Macmillan demonstrated clearly to the General that he had a vitally important topic on his mind – Polaris. It gave De Gaulle an opportunity to use this preoccupation with '*les choses nucleaires*' as a pretext.

The agreement at Nassau was essentially traditionalist. Macmillan had negotiated for the prolongation of Britain's independent nuclear deterrent for the third time in his administration. He had secured the release of nuclear information in 1957; persuaded Eisenhower to give him Skybolt in 1960; and in 1962 at Nassau, had persuaded Kennedy to produce Polaris at a ridiculously low cost. The 'special relationship' seemed to be becoming very special indeed.

There was some discussion, both at Rambouillet and Nassau, that there might be an Anglo-French nuclear deal. The Americans were in favour of this

NON!

The Friday before the Monday of General de Gaulle's press conference I had been doing very much the same thing in Paris that Edward Heath had been doing. We had each been canvassing the various ministers of the French government to find out exactly what the progress was in Britain's application for membership of the European Community. I think we had got very much the same answer: a very affirmative response from the French government, the feeling that things really were moving quite well. I myself had a meeting with the French Minister, M. Couve de Murville, in the afternoon. I told him I'd heard some rumours as to what the President's press conference might consist of. I found them rather lurid and I was very much concerned about them and I described them in very much the terms of what actually occurred. M. Couve de Murville didn't seem very upset about this, he simply said there were no ideas of that kind in this house. I reported that to Mr Heath that night, when the two of us dined together, and he rather confirmed all the impressions I had had, that things seemed to be moving rather well.

GEORGE BALL

The breakdown of negotiations over the EEC was a different sort of disappointment to the summit meeting in 1960, because we'd all recognized that the negotiations quite easily might break down. It was just the speed and, perhaps one might say, the brutality of the way in which it was done, which was unexpected. There were a lot of other people who didn't agree with what they'd done and said so. So that although it was disappointing and was a setback it didn't bring one to realize suddenly that something had changed, as the '60 summit did.

SIR PHILIP DE ZULUETA

195

Perhaps this was the moment that he should have declared before history, that his act had ended. At any rate from January 1963 onwards one had this continual sense of slipping, and never being able to regain a hold. Even so, even in those circumstances, he was a very formidable manager of a cabinet. I remember thinking as I sat at that table: I don't know whether it's true that he arranged for me to sit on the same side as himself so that he shouldn't have to look at me, as is reported; but I remember how, looking along, I used sometimes to think that it must have been something like this to have been in Henry VIII's Privy Council, to be sitting two or three places from the man upon whom it depended, with a flick of his hand, whether one's head was off, well, at least one's political head. He had decapitated seven in one weekend a few months earlier. People don't realize, you know, this effect on those immediately around him, his court as it were; the absolute power of political life and death the Prime Minister possesses. I think even in his last few months there was no mistake that Harold Macmillan was a man who was not reluctant to do butcher's work which he said, and rightly said, 'to be a Prime Minister's work'. I don't think it was his grip on his cabinet that was slipping; that's the last grip which ever slips. You lose the public, you lose the press, you lose the party in the House, but the men whose heads you can cut off before breakfast you lose last. The most difficult operation there is is for a cabinet itself to depose a Prime Minister. So it was everything else that slipped around Harold Macmillan before the cabinet itself. This I think is the nature of things.

ENOCH POWELL

I think Churchill had rather a bad influence on Macmillan as Prime Minister. I think that he rather interfered with the integrity of Macmillan's own thinking. I think it was partly because of this susceptibility that he had to the patrician tradition in England; he was that much more susceptible to Churchill, who is such a supreme embodiment or expression of it. I also think he perhaps saw himself as a continuation of Churchill, in being another British Prime Minister with an American mother, and this gave him the same sort of mistakes and assumptions that Churchill had had about the special relationship between this country and the United States. This I think became very significant at the time of our negotiations for entering the Common Market; Macmillan's personal negotiations with the French, I think, were marred by this sub-Churchillian attitude towards the British supposed special relationship with the United States.

JOHN GRIGG

as they hoped it would arrest, and then reverse, De Gaulle's views on NATO. The General, and many Frenchmen shared his view, disliked the American military umbrella and economic penetration in Europe. There were strains of anti-Americanism in the French withdrawal from NATO and the '*force de frappe*' – France's own nuclear deterrent, but one which lacked a convincing delivery system. The General was put in a spot by the Anglo-American proposal for a nuclear deal: on the one hand it would inevitably increase France's dependence on the Anglo-Saxons, but on the other, it would give France access to nuclear information that she was expensively acquiring for herself. This was tempting, but if Britain were to come into the Common Market, which she was now poised to do, the balance of power would shift from France, and Western Europe would no longer be the third force that the General so anxiously desired.

De Gaulle wrestled with this problem for three weeks after Rambouillet. In the end his political conception of a Europe dominated by France, without special ties to the United States, won.

The General's mind was much more divided than has been suggested. Macmillan's warnings, that in the long run France could not withstand the growing strength of Germany, worried the General, though he dismissed suggestions that it might in the long run be Germany, and not France, that was to open doors to the East. De Gaulle used the Polaris agreement as a pretext to veto Britain's application to join the Common Market. It is absolutely untrue that Macmillan deceived De Gaulle over his intentions to get Polaris, even though Macmillan's public denial of deception is not normally taken at its face value.

Nevertheless, once De Gaulle vetoed Britain's application Macmillan was, politically, in a very exposed position. No line of retreat had been prepared; and there was no clear area where a major initiative could be taken. The most ambitious and far-reaching of Macmillan's dreams, and one which inspired him with almost lyrical fervour, lay in ruins by the act of one deeply divided man. Macmillan's position was now weakened as much as De Gaulle's was strengthened. 'Never had it so good' looked very tarnished by the spring of 1963, with the highest unemployment figures since the war. Macmillan's studied calm and unflappability lost the strength and appeal they had had in the post-Suez era. It became too easy to see Macmillan

Macmillan and Soames on the grouse moors.
Sitting targets for satirists. But in both cases the
outward form of the aristocrat disguised the
inward grace of the radical

as an anachronism, a reflection of some Imperial past that he himself had made reality.

In the Conservative Party there was growing restiveness. Macmillan had lost a lot of his usefulness to them after De Gaulle's veto. The satirists moved in to help create, before they themselves were overtaken by it, a mood of nostalgia and absurdity for the elderly gentleman who sat in Downing Street. The satirical television programme 'That was the Week That Was', could bring 12 million people out of the pubs on a Saturday night. There was an air of decline, and this atmosphere was soon to be strengthened by wild rumours and sensational disclosures. People who should have known better talked of Rome in the third century. They were right in one respect: the imperialism of the past was now dead. It remained to be seen how soon Britain could find a new role in the world and how soon people would come to accept it.

NO H-BOMBS
— NOT EVEN NYE'S!

Fight and fight again

Morality returns to politics

There had been various groups in the middle 1950s campaigning against atomic and nuclear weapons. Those groups were effectively brought together by Canon Collins and Kingsley Martin, editor of the *New Statesman*. The articles, I think, that set it off were written by J. B. Priestley and Bertrand Russell in the *New Statesman* in the autumn of 1957. Many of us assembled at Canon Collins's house where we had a discussion about amalgamating the groups that already existed and initiating a campaign on the basis of Priestley's and Russell's articles. That was the origin of it. There was a march which had already been fixed for the subsequent Easter which became associated with the CND and from that moment onwards CND became more the movement that swamped all the others that were in this field.

It became much bigger much more swiftly than anybody had imagined. There were a number of people in the House of Commons who were associated with it; it certainly did reflect the mood of the time and I believe that it did have a very powerful effect on the government. This I think is revealed in Eisenhower's memoirs. Not many people read Eisenhower's memoirs, but if anybody does they will find in it a description of the talks between Macmillan and Eisenhower, with Macmillan using the fact of the great protest movements in this country about nuclear weapons as the lever on Eisenhower to try and get him to move towards a test ban. I think that CND led the way to the test ban. Without CND the veil of secrecy would never have been torn aside about nuclear weapons, and without the veil being torn aside there would never have been the movement towards the test ban, which is the one great victory for sanity in international affairs in the last twenty years.

MICHAEL FOOT

I was particularly interested at the time because in 1956 I had a baby who was born with a very serious blood disease and he lived for only eight months. Those eight months made me realize what the suffering of a mother would be with a child affected by any kind of damage due to nuclear warfare. When they talked about the possible risks to babies yet unborn I felt they knew what they were talking about.

In 1959 we set off from Orpington by coach at eight o'clock in the morning and reached Reading about mid-day, and then we went on towards Aldermaston. It was a thrill being there and seeing coach-loads of people coming in from all over the country, with the names on the backs of the coaches indicating where they had come from. At the head of the march were some of the political figures with the big banners. Following behind were the different groups from all over the country with a banner in front of them. There were young people and students; there were political groups, of course, and there were mothers from this town and that town. As we set out there were very few people there except the people actually on the march. As we moved towards Reading, there were more people watching us. We were just approaching Reading and we were looking across a valley; the road wound across the valley and the procession looked like some mediaeval pageant. It was a gorgeous day, the sun was shining, and all these flags were fluttering in the breeze. We really felt that we were part of something very colourful and exciting. The young people were there playing guitars, there was a West Indian steel band, and there was lots of singing as we went along. It really was something I'd never quite experienced in that way before; everybody with the same idea, young and old, long and tall, coloured people, white people.

The composition of CND was rather wider than we'd had in most such organizations before. It wasn't only what I liked to think of as the stage army of the good, we had more extras in our army this time than we had before. We had rather more headmasters, heads of training colleges; we had the Church a bit stronger, and the Methodists and other parsons helping more than we'd had in the past. There were the young people who were gradually moving into a position of revolt, if you like to call it that. They found in CND some means of attacking the older generation, with whom they had now lost a lot of common ground. We had a few Labour councillors. I tried very hard to get the Conservative councillors to come in, saying this was an enormous threat to our city; perhaps that was trying too much.

ALEC HORSLEY

CND had undoubtedly an essentially political role, because what we wanted to do was to get a change of policy. To do this we obviously had to make some political impact so that what we aimed at was a mass protest movement. We didn't have any great hopes of capturing the Tory Party so we concentrated our hopes in capturing the mind of the Labour Party; to decide that it would stand for our policy if it were returned to Parliament. We weren't trying to take over the Labour Party. What we wanted to do was to give the Labour Party the assurance that if they followed what we believed to be the right policy in this matter that they had the backing of the vast majority of the people of Britain.

In 1959 we changed the direction of the march. We marched from Aldermaston to London quite deliberately, because our policy being a political policy of changing government, and we hoped defence policies, we decided it would be a good thing to come from Aldermaston where the main work was done for nuclear weapons, to London, which is the political centre. So we marched the other way. It was, of course, a most astonishing success.

CANON COLLINS

Certainly CND articulated some very passionate moral feelings: post-Suez, post-Hungary, then about the H-bomb. But very strong moral feelings were, after all, far outside CND. If you take the protest over Suez and Hungary, far, far more people than were in the CND had passionate moral feelings about those issues. So I don't quite see that one can say they re-introduced morality to the Labour Party, although they obviously did articulate the whole thing for perhaps a section of the population that came to politics for the first time, a section of the population that was larger numerically than it had been before the war. To a number of students, and a number of young university lecturers and so on, CND may have had some wider social significance, but in political terms I would say that it did not have any long-term influences or significance. It didn't achieve its immediate aim of converting the party into unilateralism. If I'd asked myself in Grimsby, my own constituency, whether the political argument was different from what it would have been if CND hadn't existed, I think the answer is clearly no.

ANTHONY CROSLAND

We lost the 1959 election because the country wanted some more 'Never had it so good' Toryism. And the people felt they hadn't and so they didn't want a change. But the fault of the Labour Party is losing. You see, it's a strange idea that you can win an election if people didn't want you to. People didn't want a change and nothing we said at the time would have made them want to change. It's true that Gaitskell made one mistake when he promised there wouldn't be an increase in taxation. People said that was the turn of the tide. But it was quite clear, looking back, that the people of the country had decided that they wanted another dose of Macmillan's brand of Toryism, and that's that in England.

RICHARD CROSSMAN

I think Labour lost the '59 election for one basic reason. That from 1951 to 1959, when the Conservatives were in, there was something like a 20 per cent increase in real living standards, as compared with a zero increase from '45 to '51 for

post-war reasons. Before that you had war; there was virtually no increase. And of course the inter-war period showed only the slowest possible increase. I think it's that one, simple, basic fact.

ANTHONY CROSLAND

I believe that the Labour Party never had a chance of winning the 1959 election because of the general malaise in the party, which had been spread by the previous three or four years. I think that the leadership had put itself in a position of great hostility to the bulk of the Labour Party throughout the country. It was that unresolved quarrel between the leadership and the rank and file which led to the demoralized state in which the party went into the election, which we really should have won. There was also the fact that after 1956 the leadership of the party failed to exploit the Suez episode in the way that they could have done. I think that if ever an election was lost by the leadership over the previous few years, that was it.

MICHAEL FOOT

Bitter fruit

Opposite: Gaitskell in defeat: post-election press conference

While Gaitskell's parliamentary troops were slogging their way towards the unexpected and intensely disappointing election defeat in 1959, the Left had turned to the country. They had a highly emotional cause to argue, and one that made a deep appeal to many outside the Labour Party and, indeed, outside politics altogether. J. B. Priestley, in an article in the *New Statesman* in November 1957, caught the developing mood of the Left as he had not done since the war: 'The British of these times, so frequently hiding their decent, kind faces behind masks of sullen apathy or sour, cheap cynicism, often seem to be waiting for something better than party squabbles and appeals to their narrowest self-interest, something great and noble in its intention that would make them feel good again. And this might well be a declaration to the world that after a certain date one power able to engage in nuclear warface will reject the evil thing for ever.' His plea was promptly answered: within three months the Campaign for Nuclear Disarmament was under way.

Although C.N.D. was initially, as one of its members A.J.P. Taylor said, 'a movement of eggheads for eggheads', its influence spread rapidly. Its aims fitted well with the traditional moral fervour and the rejection of 'big-power politics' on the Left. But to translate its politics into action it would have to capture the Labour Party. Not only could it call on practised propagandists, many of them exiles from the Communist Party who had been appalled by the Soviet invasion of Hungary in October 1956, but with the success of the first Aldermaston March against nuclear weapons in Easter 1958 it proved able to capture support from constituency members and shop-floor trade unionists. It was a potential threat to the leadership. 'We are not seeking to disrupt the Labour Party.' A. J. P. Taylor said, 'nor to challenge its leadership. We are seeking to win it over; we offer it the moral leadership of the world.' Gaitskell proved more sceptical of this intoxicating dream than some of the trade union leaders who, like Frank Cousins, were to be found in the crowd at Trafalgar Square at the end of the 1959 Aldermaston March.

C.N.D. did not score its first major success in the Labour movement until June 1959, when Gaitskell's own union, the General and Municipal Workers', hitherto absolutely loyal, voted by 150 votes to 126, with 75 delegates not voting, for the unilateral renunciation of the manufacture and use of nuclear weapons.

To mitigate this pressure the leadership invented the idea of a 'non-nuclear club' – a woolly notion. It was enough to paper over the cracks in the pre-election run-up, but it was shot through with too many inconsistencies to win over the Left, or to outlast the election atmosphere.

The 1959 election result was an enormous personal disappointment for Gaitskell, who expected to win. For the fourth election running the party had lost votes: the Conservatives had an overall majority of 100 in the House of Commons. It was clear that there was something badly wrong with Labour's appeal. In an age of consumer boom, the party's 'image' began to be actively discussed.

Broadly, two views emerged from the 1959 election, and both evolved around how the party should treat the electorate. On the Left, changes in the electorate were not acknowledged as important. The accent should, it was argued, be placed far more on converting the voters to socialism, with a thoroughgoing radical and distinctive policy of unilateral renunciation of nuclear weapons abroad, and further nationalization at home. The Right thought this unrealistic. On some issues Labour's message was getting across all too well. Half Labour's support thought that nationalization was out of date. To the Right, Labour had to be made a party of power at least as much as a party of protest. But this raised a fundamental question. Was the Labour Party nothing more than the humane and reformist manager of a sufficiently transmuted capitalist society? Surely, the Left argued, they were going to build socialism and transform the very natures of men.

In the light of this dispute the power structure of the party became crucial. The parliamentary party, acutely conscious of the electorate, was dominated by reformism, while the Left, although often beaten there, spoke through conference and the N.E.C. They resented the growing elevation of the parliamentary party and its leadership, which to them marked the end of internal party democracy.

If their domestic remedies seemed a little musty, in unilateralism the Left had a cause which made a widespread appeal to moderate members at conference and in the parliamentary party. What was more, Gaitskell was about to present them with an even more fundamental issue which would bring the whole dispute over Labour's purpose into dramatic relief.

Gaitskell, the defeat hardly a month old, launched a frontal attack on Clause 4 at the party conference of November 1959. This was a great deal more than an argument on the extent of nationalization, and it was more dangerous for Gaitskell in that the Left could summon up unilateralism to rock the leadership's boat further.

'The class war,' Macmillan had said after his victory, 'is obsolete'. This stung the revisionists. Symptomatic too, was a sociological survey into popular attitudes about the Labour Party, whose flavour was caught by the title 'Must Labour Lose?' Labour was shown to be closely connected with the 'cloth cap' image and nationalization. Here was the spur for a powerful revolt by the leadership against the fast-dating thirties image.

Gaitskell did not suggest a disavowal of Clause 4, but he did argue that nationalization should take a more subordinate position in the establishment of an egalitarian and classless society. Central to his position was the acceptance of a mixed economy: public ownership in all its forms was a means and *not* the overriding end. To the Left, this was a masterly evasion of the roots of the problem. Gaitskell argued that Clause 4 should not necessarily be regarded as binding, and that further extensions of public ownership 'should be decided from time to time'. Clause 4 was to be qualified by a rider to the party's constitution.

The N.E.C. accepted this in March 1960. It was one of the very few occasions that the Right had instituted a major shift in policy. But the rank and file in the unions were hotly against any tampering with the constitution at all, and pressure built up before the annual conference for individual unions to vote against any alterations. Sensing that conference defeat was inevitable, the N.E.C. in July decided not to proceed with the addition to Clause 4, contenting themselves with recommending it to conference as 'a valuable expression of the aims of the Labour Party in the second half of the twentieth century'. This was carried at conference, but union resentment at revisionist activities spilled over into a different issue – defence.

The leaders of the old Bevanite Left were identifying themselves with C.N.D. by the spring of 1960, and by the early summer a number of large unions had slid into the unilateralist camp. The defection of the distribution workers, the A.E.U,

the railway men, and the T.G.W.U, controlling among them over two million conference votes, left the leadership vulnerable.

The death of Bevan in July 1960 tragically removed a possible architect of compromise. But the worst blow to the leadership was the cancellation of Blue Streak, apparently destroying the British-owned deterrent, which Gaitskell had been determined to support. The N.E.C. changed its line: in July they accepted that the British contribution to NATO would increasingly be in terms of conventional forces, not the obsolescent H Bomb-carrying V-bombers. It was too late to change the big unions' line, nor did Gaitskell want a compromise. The Labour party remained firmly committed to NATO, while the clear implication of the unilateralist line was a move towards neutralism. This was an issue on which Gaitskell was determined to defeat the Left.

Domestic and foreign policy issues had now fused: those supporting Clause 4 were for unilateralism, while those advocating a revisionist statement supported NATO. The Left, however, used foreign policy for their main line of attack, while the Right concentrated on domestic policy. But behind these policy issues lay a bitter fight for the soul and leadership of the Labour party.

The unilateralist motions at the 1960 party conference did not call explicitly for neutralism, but Gaitskell had no difficulty in showing that the rejection of a defence policy based upon the threat of using nuclear weapons must mean Britain's withdrawal from NATO, and that it was pure semantics to think that the Left's policy could be reconciled – as both Wilson and George Brown argued – with the N.E.C's policy. Gaitskell made this abundantly clear in perhaps the most remarkable of all post-war political speeches, in which, knowing that the Left was likely to defeat the platform, he committed himself and his supporters to 'Fight, Fight and Fight Again' to save the soul of the party they loved.

The Left won, but by only a small margin: 3,282,000 votes to 3,239,000, splitting the party down the middle. Gaitskell had won a remarkable share of the consituency vote, and prevented the two-thirds majority which would have committed the party to neutralism. But his leadership was in question. The *New Statesman* in an editorial, 'Wanted – a leader', admitted that the vote 'was largely due to distrust of Mr Gaitskell'. But the

The cloth cap image

I believe myself that the party in 1959 had allowed itself to get a bit out of date in the sense that there was still the cloth-cap image. There was a sort of idea that the ordinary Labour supporter was an unemployed miner, living on unemployment benefit, and everything was rather run on a shoe-string throughout the party. There was a sort of myth that the Labour Party stood for what was then called nationalization, and almost nothing else. I think these two things were harmful. If I had to guess I would say that it was more these two handicaps on the Labour Party which the more up-to-date real policy failed entirely to overlay. There was a sense of phoney prosperity which was somehow associated with Harold Macmillan's moustache.

The fundamental thing was to get away from the cloth-cap image, the cloth-cap talk, and realize that the Labour Party had got to move into being really a left-centre majority party, as the Democratic Party is in the United States, as the Liberals had been in this country in the second half of the 19th century.

DOUGLAS JAY

After the '59 election there were those who said we had not been socialist enough, which meant, conventionally, not put a sufficient emphasis on public ownership, and those who said we should change our name and perhaps amalgamate with the Liberal Party. There was a strong feeling that Labour should become essentially a party complaining, protesting, but waiting for a cataclysm of some kind to change the political climate. A number of us felt we had to make ourselves look like a party whose policies were relevant to the problems of the 1960s. It was no good talking about problems that had been solved; we had to accept that people were very much better off and rejoice in it. In the spring of 1960 Gaitskell sought to change the constitution of the Labour Party by changing Clause 4. I think we might say with hindsight that this was a mistake and that to attack Clause 4 frontally really was provoking. Some people in the Labour Party who shared his view on many issues were reluctant, if you like, to see the Ark of the Covenant broken. It was the nature of the reaction really which was frightening to us. The unwillingness to modernize, to recognize the need for change, and the fact that to be in politics you have to combine principle, a very strong belief in something and, in the case of the Labour Party, in social equality, with recognition that you can't be arrogant enough to be indifferent to the views of the electorate in a democratic country. You've got to try and persuade them and offer them something which is relevant to them: you can't simply say, you must vote for us, because this is what we believe in, you have to recognize you're trying to serve people and not simply to advocate your own particular view.

It was against this background that in 1960 a number of us – broadly speaking, younger members of the party, in our twenties and thirties – started the Campaign for Democratic Socialism.

WILLIAM RODGERS

After the '59 election they were suddenly confronted with an attempt (a) to change the constitution of the party; and (b) – some suggested – to change the name of the party (that had been proposed in the interim after the election) and generally to carry through the whole revisionist programme in the rush of the aftermath of the election. Some people thought that this was a conspiracy on the part of the Right to force their way into a much bigger say than they had succeeded in having in previous years. Bevan took that view and was horrified by the action which Gaitskell took. He himself took steps at that conference to rescue the party from the aggression from the Right, which is what we regarded it as on the Left of the party. The party was thrust into an appalling controversy over the next year because of Gaitskell's attempt to rewrite Clause 4; indeed that was obviously one of the factors which led to Gaitskell's defeat in the subsequent conference over nuclear weapons. Clause 4 was a ridiculous controversy, anyhow – for the leader of the party to say 'We've set out to rewrite the constitution'. In the end, in order to satisfy Gaitskell's pride, a whole new document had to be concocted, even though he'd been defeated at all the conferences. So he had to be rescued from his own follies and undoubtedly the party was weakend by these controversies greatly, and it was weakened because the leader didn't understand for one moment how the minds of most of his followers worked.

MICHAEL FOOT

The precise history of how it came in, was this. He was working on his speech for this post-election conference, and I was giving him a great deal of help on the speech and was writing parts of it. He wrote most of it himself. I was sitting in the library at the House of Commons reading a bit of the speech, and I came to this section on Clause 4, and was slightly taken aback by this. So I went to see him in his room, and asked him 'Do you really want to raise this hoary constitutional issue? It will create an awful upset, and I'm not sure that any great good will emerge.' And he said, 'Well, if as leader of the party I can't even mention the party's constitution, this seems to me to be a very ridiculous state of affairs, and I propose to mention it'. So I said, 'All right, I quite see the point'.

ANTHONY CROSLAND

Clause 4 was a really important thing for Hugh, although I felt that it was a slight strategic mistake at the time. He felt that the Labour Party was not a Marxist party, that we were not going to nationalize everything and that the European Socialist Democratic parties had also given up the idea of wholesale nationalization. So he didn't want the tablets of stone to remain as they were and give the impression that we were going to nationalize everything.

LADY GAITSKELL

CND in a way represented in an extreme form the reaction against the power elements in politics, which the Labour Party as a whole, I think, came under in the years after its defeat in '51. In a way CND was an anti-political movement because it had no policy. It simply was a movement of moral protest against what it saw, rightly in a way, as the obscenity of nuclear weapons. There is no doubt that for a year or two it had a great deal of influence right through the Labour Party. On the other hand, I think it's also true to say, as Frank Cousins made clear when he spoke on the disarmament resolution at the Scarborough conference, that a lot of the people who supported the unilateral abandonment of nuclear weapons as proposed by the CND did so because they were appalled by the proposal to write Clause 4 out of the party constitution. I don't think, in fact, unilateralism would have conquered the Labour Party, if it hadn't been for the shock and disturbance among many sections, at the idea that one of the Ten Commandments should be abolished. Though I'm bound to say, of course, that until Clause 4 was mentioned, nobody knew it existed.

DENIS HEALEY

The high point of CND was, of course, the Labour Party conference in 1960. That looked as though we were really making headway with a major political party. But I think the highlight really, to me, looking back, was the fact that Mr Khrushchev told me in Moscow that it was largely CND, and corresponding European movements that had influenced him in deciding to sign the test ban treaty with America.

CANON COLLINS

My position over nuclear weapons was rather difficult. Everything in my heart agreed with the moral attitude towards the H-bomb; we hated it, and we all thought that it was the most obscene thing which had ever afflicted humanity. I agreed with all the CND people so far as moral attitude was concerned, but I was a parliamentary candidate in a highly marginal constituency. I had the good fortune to discuss this matter privately with Aneurin Bevan for a considerable time and our attitudes, I think, were identical. Our attitude was this: supposing all the preaching of the moralists were successful and Britain became the most moral country in the world as a result, the result would be that the most moral country in the world was the most defenceless. The result was that possession of the atomic and hydrogen bombs by the United States and the Soviet Union would merely intensify the polarization of the world, if there were not a third force. It would make Britain's bargaining power *vis-à-vis* the world powers rather derisory. With the greatest reluctance I tried to sit on the fence and give lip service, I must admit this, to the CND movement, but at the same time I wondered whether, if it came to a crunch, I might not sell out on them.

JACK FOORD

Daily Mirror Thursday, October 6, 1960   No. 17,669

I WILL FIGHT ON

Gaitskell's triumph in defeat on day of tremendous passion

From SYDNEY JACOBSON, Mirror Political Editor, Scarborough, Wednesday

AFTER the most magnificent, most stirring and passionate debate I have ever heard at a Labour Party conference, Hugh Gaitskell was defeated on the H-bomb here today.

But the Labour leader plucked a treble triumph from defeat.

FIRST. He made the greatest speech of his life. A speech crammed with courage, sincerity and brilliant argument rising finally into anger against the men who had attacked him. "How wrong can you be?" he demanded. It caused a storm. But it got results.

It won Gaitskell an unexpected majority of the traditionally Left Wing local Labour Parties' vote.

Some observers here estimate that three-quarters of the million votes from the local parties went to Gaitskell.

SECOND. The majorities against Gaitskell were far smaller than anticipated —so small that they startled the 1,300 delegates.

THIRD. Gaitskell made it crystal clear that he will fight on, and that he is confident of the backing of a big majority of Labour MPs.

Applause...boos...

In the closing seconds of his speech, while the Conference was in uproar with scores of delegates on their feet applauding or booing, he leaned over the platform table and declared that he would fight on to

Continued on Back Page

Hugh Gaitskell making the most courageous and stirring speech of his life yesterday.

The Fight, Fight and Fight Again speech? Oh, I was enormously exhilarated and encouraged by it. It was clear that we were going to be defeated, that the motion in favour of unilateral nuclear disarmament was going to be carried. Gaitskell made such a fine and tremendous speech that people were visibly being won over during the course of the speech, and the majority against us was much less, substantially less, than everybody including us had expected. We were therefore very exhilarated that he'd raised a standard for us. I was in my room in my hotel within half an hour after the end of that conference, there was a spontaneous gathering of 20, 30, 40 people, mostly Members of Parliament, planning how we could fight back.

Meanwhile, simultaneously, a movement of people who were not yet even candidates in many cases and certainly were not yet MPs were meeting to decide how on earth to save the party. These two things of course came together. I was really the chief intermediary between the parliamentary party, the right or centre of the parliamentary party and these people outside Parliament, and I helped to draft the manifesto which launched the Campaign for Democratic Socialism.

PATRICK GORDON WALKER

Right began, as they had done a year earlier, to take the initiative: the so-called Campaign for Democratic Socialism launched a campaign to reverse the Scarborough vote. Their target was to pull the union block vote round and to inform every Labour activist about the direction in which the party was heading. Many Labour supporters found themselves in the uncomfortable position of realizing that moderates were not in control, and that they had to do something about it. In short, the Right had to adopt the tactics of the Left. It was a novel experience for many, but to more hardened Rightists, it enabled them to indulge in 'bashing the Left'; to turn the tables on the fifties, during which, they felt, the whole achievement of the Attlee Government had been besmirched. At first C.D.S. was by no means sure that Gaitskell was the appropriate standard-bearer.

Adding momentum to C.D.S.'s campaign were stirrings among the parliamentary party. There was a feeling that Gaitskell had been tactically too abrupt by forcing the issue on Clause 4 and unilateralism. Among centrist M.P.s, the feeling grew that Gaitskell might be destroying the unity of the party and that he should try to be more accomodating. Certainly, he had given way over the N.E.C.'s statement on Clause 4, and again over defence, but his stance at Scarborough seemed too aggressive to those who did not wish to see the trade union and parliamentary wings divide. It was partly for these reasons that Harold Wilson decided to stand against Gaitskell for the leadership in the autumn of 1960. Gaitskell defeated Wilson by 166 votes to 81.

C.D.S. continued to work on the unions, many of whom, initially surprised and even pleased by Cousins' capacity to challenge the leadership after the all too predictable policies of Deakin, saw some advantage in cutting the T.G.W.U. down to size. The rot, as far as the Left was concerned, set in when U.S.D.A.W. voted for a compromise multi-lateralist motion in May 1961. C.D.S. members of that union played an important part in the decision. This pattern was mirrored later by the A.E.U. decision to reject unilateralism.

C.D.S., in fact, appealed to the traditionalism of the party; great play was made of unity and, more important, questions were asked as to where the decisions of Scarborough would take the party. If most trade unionists had felt able to allow Labour politics to degenerate into a slogan shop,

C.D.S. would have had no effect. But many trade unionists, however much they resisted the airs of the intellectual Right, were not prepared to allow the party to deny itself the fruits of office which they hoped would bring appropriate reward to trade union members. The weakness of the Left's case, although the questions they were asking about Britain's future role have never been satisfactorily answered, was that the revisionists had a clearer idea of where they wanted to go. On domestic issues the revisionists were egalitarian, a difficult position to challenge from the Left; on foreign affairs, they were for multilateral disarmament. The Left did less than justice to their cause. 'Were you better red or dead?' was the question of the hour. But neutralism could not be an answer, without a challenge to the legitmacy of NATO, over which the Left themselves were confused.

During 1961 most of the large unions abandoned the stance of 1960. This in itself has never been fully explained, but there were external factors which did not go unnoticed. The Conservative Government was running into economic trouble of a kind which gave rise to doubts as to whether the British economy was not fundamentally sick. Conservative free enterprise, it seemed, was no longer an answer, but the party of planning had grounds for hope.

Perhaps more significant was the growing realization that Labour's leaders were as much against the British contribution to the deterrent as anyone in the party: neutralism was less attractive as a policy goal. The A.E.U. made the swing against the 1960 decisive, and the official defence policy was given powerful support: 4,526,000 votes to 1,756,000. In many respects, however, the official position was now more radical than the early programme of C.N.D.

The reversal of 1961 had profound consequences. Because Gaitskell had put himself so firmly in the forefront of the defence of Labour's official policy, the vote of confidence in it rebounded in his favour. By the end of 1961 Gaitskell was the master of the party, and his personal prestige as a man who had stood and fought for his principles was far greater than that of any contemporary figure, echoing far beyond the bounds of party. As it became fashionable to deride Macmillan as a somewhat *passé* trickster, so Gaitskell's stock improved, and by the end of 1962, he was being thought of as the country's next leader. His

The Right counter-attacks

From '59 to '60 there were many people who had been alienated from active political work by some of the controversy and the way it had been carried on. There had been things said of a very unpleasant kind, and a very common thing to say, of course, was that you weren't a socialist if you didn't believe in, say, the nationalization of 80 per cent of industry. We found that the great impact that the Campaign for Democratic Socialism had was in making individuals in the constituency parties and in the trade unions discover they were not alone in taking the view they did in supporting Hugh Gaitskell, because the very nature of the campaign against him in '59–'60 almost seemed to imply that, apart from the parliamentary Labour Party, the constituencies had turned against him. We very soon discovered this simply wasn't the case.

This form of democratic socialism had a very wide appeal; people had been frightened out of active politics because they thought they were a tiny, unrepresentative minority. Shortly after we had launched the campaign, I was telephoned one morning by a member of the Hendon Labour Party who said he was very glad we'd launched our manifesto because he took the view that what we were saying was right, that he was in a minority of one and now he felt he could speak out knowing that there were those who were in support. Later the same day somebody else telephoned and said they were a member of the Hendon Labour Party – they were the only one in Hendon who took our view and they were glad that we were there and speaking for them. We were essentially an extra-parliamentary body. We felt that the parliamentary party had blundered, that they'd failed to hold together after 1959. I ought to make it clear we were not supporting Hugh Gaitskell irrespective of what he was saying and doing. This was not a personal campaign, it was a campaign which became personalized.

WILLIAM RODGERS

CDS (Campaign for Democratic Socialism) had been stimulated by annoyance at the fact that Gaitskell had compromised on Clause 4, and this lot wanted to fight it right out to the end, and it was slightly critical of Gaitskell. The manifesto which was being drafted was going to be a little critical of Gaitskell. It was the great Fight, Fight and Fight Again speech at Scarborough which altered all this, because CDS then realized that here was the issue which you simply must fight about – both unilateral disarmament and also the right of the parliamentary party to determine its own policy, and not be ordered about by the conference. I don't think that Gaitskell ever knew to his death that it was slightly anti-Gaitskell when it was first conceived.

It was the sudden success of the manifesto that we sent out amongst constituency parties that really launched CDS properly. What had happened, I think, was that the Campaign for Nuclear Disarmament had managed to penetrate a good many local Labour parties and rather tyrannized them, you know. This often happens, minorities can do this. And there were a lot of people who were a little scared to stand up in the party and be laughed at. What the Campaign for Democratic Socialism did was really to show these people in every party there were lots of other people like them, ready to stand up, and they suddenly began all standing up and found a majority in the local parties. I was also in contact with trade union leaders. I remember a meeting, maybe three or four months after the Scarborough conference, where Gaitskell and a number of leading MPs were there. Gaitskell was speaking in terms of being defeated again at the conference, that he would have to resign and so on. I was the only one who was actively in touch with the trade unions, with these youngsters who were not yet launched but who were about to launch CDS, and I remember at the meeting saying, 'No, I think we're going to win, great gains are coming our way'. At that time Gaitskell was still expecting to lose again, but he was going to fight hard.

PATRICK GORDON WALKER

CDS were perfectly entitled to argue for their views about nuclear weapons and all the rest, but what they were not entitled to say, in my opinion, as Democratic Socialists, was that those who disagreed with them should be drummed out of the party. That was my complaint against the Campaign for Democratic Socialism. Its predecessors in the party were the heads of some of the big unions which organized the campaign for Gaitskell earlier, and those inside the parliamentary party who resorted to these methods is something that the people forget: that the Left of the party never proposed that the right-wingers should be expelled. It was the Right which tried to drive the Left out, and it was that which gave rise to the bitterness in the party, of course. It's hardly credible now that people like Gaitskell should have tried to drive Bevan out of the party, altogether on two or three occasions, which is what they did. But that is what caused the ferocity of politics inside the Labour Party in the fifties, and it must never be overlooked or forgotten by the CDS historians who are, I'm sorry to say, engaged in smudging these facts at the present time.

MICHAEL FOOT

CDS were the people who organized the counter-revolution. They were very efficient and they worked for Gaitskell and they did a highly efficient job. They won partly, of course, because of the fact that most of us did not want to split the party. We didn't want to, we wanted to end the row which had been going on for much too long. In the last resort, if the leadership is there, you accept the leadership and that's that. But I was very, very doubtful whether a Labour Party led and dominated by Gaitskell and the CDS was going to be able to do very much.

RICHARD CROSSMAN

A personal triumph

personal ascendancy was remarkable. Less noticed perhaps was the fact that, at least for some years, he had tipped the balance between conference and parliamentary party decisively in favour of the latter, a point which Harold Wilson was to take to heart.

The emergence of the Common Market issue further helped the Labour Party. Although there remained a plurality in favour of entry, Gaitskell's hesitant, but in the end clear, rejection of entry on any but impossible terms, did much to reconcile the Left. Gaitskell's own closest friends, mostly in favour of entering Europe, were upset, but the party came together behind the conditions he laid down in a way that showed that power and purpose could be reconciled in a Gaitskell Government.

The issue itself was soon finished. De Gaulle's veto removed the last trace of disunity in the Labour Party. But within four days Gaitskell was dead. It seemed a national loss and the nation mourned. It is perhaps a tribute to his all-pervasive influence that there is still a Gaitskellite strand in the Labour Party, and Labour M.P.s are still prepared to invoke his name.

But his heir was not a Gaitskellite. George Brown seemed too erratic to command the Right's full support. Compromise candidates like Patrick Gordon Walker were canvassed, and one, Jim Callaghan ran. With the Right split, Harold Wilson emerged. Left speaking to Left perhaps, but with a clear purpose: to make the Labour Party the national party of government, as the Democrats were in America. Within a short time little was heard of the old divisions. There was more Socialist rhetoric, indeed more rhetoric perhaps, than Gaitskell would ever have used, but no retreat from the revisionist position. With great skill Wilson captured the new issues of managerial efficiency and 'the white heat of the scientific revolution' to mobilize the new and younger middle classes in support of the Labour programme. Left and Right were welded together to damn the feudal and the amateur, and the theme of modernization and the wholesale application of technology contrasted tellingly with the forthcoming accession of a fourteenth Earl to the premiership. What was surprising about the 1964 election was not Wilson's victory, but its tiny margin.

By 1961 when the union conferences were coming along it was a question of 'Can we save the Labour Party?' – Hugh Gaitskell's own words. We played our part early in '61 by helping to make this clear, and again helping to equip those members of trade unions who wanted to speak at their conferences to do so with a certain amount of information behind them . There was, I think a very noticeable change of climate in the trade unions in the space of about a year.

I thought, in the spring of 1961, Scarborough would be reversed. It was clear that a sufficient number of unions had changed their policy to ensure that, but we were still concerned that it should not be, as it were, a block vote which was seen to reverse a decision; we didn't want to bring in the big battalions except in so far as their votes were necessary. We were still anxious that the constituency parties should be convinced on merit of our case and should be prepared to speak for it at the conference in 1961.
WILLIAM RODGERS

I don't think I was surprised at our reversal in 1961, even in those days; certainly not in retrospect. The hard core of the Labour Party, the establishment of the Labour Party, had never really been touched. We'd got into the strong intellectual fringes, the trade unions, their ordinary membership, but we hadn't really got into the hard core of the Labour Party. The hard core of the Labour Party was a little bit – well, it will always vote in the last analysis where its leaders tell it to vote.

One always hopes that mankind will have the sense that he hasn't got; the hope that one will persuade public opinion to arrange that their masters, the politicians and the scientists, will use their energies for constructive rather than destructive purposes. This is how the young people were seeing it at that time. Alas, it hasn't worked out that way.
ALEC HORSLEY

A national loss

Gaitskell was certainly the most formidable personality that I've ever known in politics. A man of immense conviction, of immense strength of will and strength of purpose. Certainly he had these qualities more than I've seen anywhere else in politics myself. He was, in addition, a most attractive man, a very kind man, with a great sense of personal enjoyment. One not only admired him as a very effective political figure but one was deeply attached to him as a personal friend.

The people who want to make a case against him as a political leader say that almost all his major battles were fought over what appeared to be very trivial matters: a few million pounds on teeth and spectacles in 1951, and Clause 4 which was simply words in a party constitution. One could look at it like that: the difference between two conference resolutions on unilateralism, which probably the huge bulk of the public were completely unaware of. This is the case against him, so that the argument is that in doing this, in having these huge battles, often on the point of words, and carrying them through in such an emotional way, that he alienated a section of the party, which is the duty of a party leader not to do.

I think the case on the other side is that throughout those years there was a real battle to be fought in the party. If you like, revisionism, as against traditionalism. Put it over simply like that, that this battle couldn't have been fought and couldn't have been won unless there had been some direct clashes, and direct confrontations; it didn't matter so much precisely what the confrontations were nominally about. What matters is that they had to occur, the party simply had to have an argument and come out at the end of the day on one side or the other, and the triumph of Gaitskell was that at the end of the day he came out firmly as a revisionist in home affairs, and foreign affairs, as the leader of a party with a patriotic defence policy.

Gaitskell could be inflexible on quite small points, I think that's undeniable. But whether you make this a general criticism really consists of saying that none of these battles needed to be fought at all, with a little more flexibility we could have got through without any difficulty in the party and it would have been united. Now whether you agree with that or not, depends entirely on the answer to a prior question, do you think there was a battle to be fought about the kind of party wanted after the '59 election? I think there was a battle to be fought. myself, whether we wanted a broadly unilateralist party or a party committed to the West and committed to NATO, the Western Alliance, and so on. And on home affairs, whether you wanted a party, whatever you think of Clause 4 as a set of words, whether you wanted a party that was fundamentally traditional, or one that was fundamentally contemporary and revisionist. In other words, I think it was a repetition of the arguments of the 1950s, brought about by what was a staggering defeat which nobody expected to be as bad as it was.
ANTHONY CROSLAND

I am extremely prejudiced about Hugh Gaitskell. I am extremely prejudiced about him because I did regard him as the main obstacle to Bevan achieving the power and influence that I thought was his rightful destiny. But his chief virtue was undoubtedly his courage and his capacity to stand up to the battery of politics. His chief defect was his pedantry: he was always dealing with small matters, he would argue for ever about a clause in a document. He was a stickler for matters which could be settled by an intelligent compromise. He wasn't intended in my belief ever to be the leader of a great political party. He was much better qualified to be a high-powered civil servant and he introduced the ways of the civil service into politics. Bevan was an artist in politics, Gaitskell was the civil servant, a pedant in politics. It's not surprising that they quarrelled. Bevan also believed that Gaitskell didn't understand the working-class base of the Labour movement and how essential it was to preserve that base, which was another cause of their quarrels and another reason why I do believe that Gaitskell's leadership did greatly weaken the Labour Party.
MICHAEL FOOT

Hugh never personalized politics and so he never bore grudges. This was shown in his dealings with people generally, despite the fact that I heard recently that both Dick Crossman and Barbara Castle thought that if Hugh became Prime Minister he would not give them a job. This was completely untrue. I heard Hugh ask Clem Attlee why he hadn't given Dick a job, and a couple of months before he died, he saw Frank Cousins and they'd actually discussed jobs. He always regarded the party in opposition not just as a party to attack the government, but always bore in mind that the Labour Party was the alternative government.
LADY GAITSKELL

I was at school with Gaitskell and I had the great disadvantage that I was the head boy and he was not. And we never got the right relationship after that because he thought I would treat him on a basis of equality, and I couldn't help it really. My personal view is, that if he had not died and if he'd stayed leader, we would not have won the '64 election and, if we had, we'd have split. I think he was an awkward man and a very pertinacious, ambitious man, but he didn't have this skill which Harold Wilson has of keeping people together. He was a divider rather than that, and this is why this disaster went on in the conference in 1960 with nuclear weapons. I mean, a competent leader should never let that happen in the Labour Party. The first quality of the leader of a party is to hold the party together. And my great feeling about Hugh Gaitskell – who had great qualities, tremendous integrity, statesmanship – was that he hadn't the elasticity, he hadn't the subtlety necessary for the man in the middle. The leader's the man in the middle in our highly democratic party.
RICHARD CROSSMAN

One key to understanding Gaitskell was that he was an intellectual; he put too high a value on purely intellectual ability. But he also had tremendous depth of moral commitment. Now these, of course, gave him the strength to fight after the defeat at Scarborough over unilateralism. They also, however, made him a little more rigid that a party leader should always be. He tended to feel that people who disagreed with him were both intellectually disreputable and morally dishonest, and this was by no means always the case. I think he also had a weakness which nearly all intellectuals have when they start in politics – he was always concerned to educate people rather than to persuade them. He wanted their agreement rather than simply their consent. Now, of course, in a busy political life it takes a hell of a long time sometimes to get understanding and agreement. You have to settle for acquiescence, but Gaitskell was always determined that people should not only agree with what he did, but understand why he did it. Sometimes I think he allowed an argument to go on longer than it need have for this reason. But I think the overwhelming characteristic of the man was this tremendous moral commitment, which was allied with a total moral fearlessness. It was this which in the end gave him a resonance in Britain far beyond the limits of the Labour Party itself.
DENIS HEALEY

It looked like a straight race between commoners. But it was Home by a short head. Butler (left) played the statesman, but Home (right) sniffs victory

11 W

SERVATIVE BRITAIN IS A POWER FOR PEACE

t about the peers?

A question of confidence

I'm absolutely clear that Macmillan was unhappy about the Vassall case, about the way Galbraith had been treated, and, may I say, no minister has ever been worse treated by the press, senior or junior, than Galbraith. This did affect Mr Macmillan's handling of the Profumo episode. I've no doubt about that at all. He was absolutely determined not to be unfair to Profumo and he hated, as he always said to us in cabinet, dealing with any minister on the basis of rumour, which I think is a good fault in a Prime Minister. But, looking back on it, Profumo's statement was a bit of a muddle. I mean, if it was a personal statement, what were other ministers doing presiding over the drafting of it? If it was in effect a government statement which pledged the credit of the government, I think it ought to have really been put to the cabinet. Certainly, if it had been, one or two members of the cabinet would, I think, have raised some questions.
LORD BOYLE

I know that Macmillan was very upset by the Galbraith–Vassall case. But one can't help feeling that he wasn't all that well advised. It's so absolutely incredible that anyone could have thought that Galbraith could have had homosexual relationships with Vassall, that when the request came for his resignation it was bound to raise criticisms about the advice being given to the Prime Minister. And I dare say it was because of that mistake, and I think it was admitted to be a mistake, that the Profumo case was played in exactly the opposite way and no action was taken; no great effort to persuade him to do anything was apparently made.
ROBERT ALLAN

Macmillan, like everyone else who had been in office for a long time, began to get very used to it. This is the case with all rulers when they've been in office for a long time, they get satisfied with their position. Rather to his surprise, in 1962–3 there were two cases, Vassall and Profumo. In one, Macmillan thought that the Minister at the Admiralty had perhaps been wrongly got rid of, and with the other he never actually saw Profumo and he didn't actually grip the Profumo event early enough to prevent Profumo making that unfortunate statement about his girl-friend, which the House doesn't really expect. What should have happened in the Profumo case should have been an investigation into security. I think the mistake was that Macmillan accepted the advice overnight, which I understand he read at 9 o'clock in the morning and allowed a statement to be made at 11 o'clock in the morning. I think the statement could have been postponed over the weekend and I would have liked Macmillan, with his great shrewdness – after all there is no man more shrewd living in England today – I would have liked him to have seen Profumo himself and formed his own conclusions, which he never had time to do.
LORD BUTLER

In the spring of 1963, Labour's lead in the opinion polls was the highest for seventeen years; 'Don't let Labour ruin it', the slogan of 1959, was now being rejigged in many people's minds as 'only Labour can improve on it.' The catchphrase of technology could, it seemed, secure the future, an impression heightened by the sight of some unexpected skeletons falling out of some ever more impressive cupboards. Not since the Lynskey report on scandal in high places in 1948 had the British people been able to have such a fulsome opportunity to delight in the doings of the mighty, and to allow themselves the delicious hypocrisy of blaming the evils of 'them', while appealing to the good natured 'us'.

The Vassall-Galbraith case, with its alleged overtones of homosexual goings-on in the Admiralty, in September 1962, was incidental to the future of Macmillan. But its combination of sexual innuendo and espionage fore-shadowed the Profumo affair, which followed within months. The resignation of a wholly innocent junior minister, Galbraith, affected Macmillan's handling of Profumo. Also, the enquiry into certain disreputable activities of the Press, set up by Macmillan after Galbraith had been exonerated, ended in the imprisonment of two journalists. The complete alienation of the Press followed.

This proved a major weakness of the Macmillan Government when rumours of sexual scandals revolved around it the following spring. The central figure was a model, Christine Keeler. Her affair with Profumo, Macmillan's Minister for War, nearly two years before, had taken place at the same time as a liaison with the Russian military attaché Ivanov. Denying that there had been any security risk, Profumo told the Commons that there had been no 'impropriety' in his relations with Keeler. Macmillan accepted the denial, but he did not see Profumo himself. It is possible that, had he done so, the whole business might have been scotched by a ministerial resignation. Macmillan felt that Press innuendo had already misled him over Galbraith. In June, after mounting rumour Profumo admitted that he had lied and resigned. The indignation of the press knew no bounds. Later they gave Profumo a reputation for social work in the East End. They were after bigger game. Suspicion that Macmillan must have known the facts about Profumo's activities evaporated after his doleful confession to the Commons, on

17 June, that he had been deceived, but there remained the taint of incompetence at the top. The atmosphere was ripe for further rumour. The competence of the security services was queried. Dramatic stories were made up of Profumo leaving Miss Keeler's back door as Ivanov came in through the front.

The activities of Stephen Ward, a doctor who was the centre of a circle of attractive girls and who had introduced Keeler to Profumo, and his tenuous connection with Rachman, a property racketeer, were given full prominence in the Press. Although many people began to take more than one paper in the summer of 1963 it was the Denning Report in September – a government publication enquiring into the implications of Profumo – that really excited the greed of rumour.

The first printing of the Denning Report, though larger than most, quickly lost its black market price: there were no revelations about cabinet ministers who, as had been privately alleged, preferred to be behind iron masks while indulging their tastes. Nor could it be dredged from Denning, which minister liked doing what, with what and to whom. People quickly lost interest and Macmillan, who earlier in the summer had seemed to be the harbinger of casino capitalism and a *demi-monde* of prostitution and property racketeering, emerged clearly and rightly as the chief political beneficiary from the report.

Ironically, it was against the background of greatest contempt for the Prime Minister that Macmillan scored one of his greatest triumphs – the Test Ban treaty of July 1963. Macmillan had kept up a strong pressure on Kennedy over dis-armament; he also kept his ear very close to the ground to gauge the right moment to approach the Russians. It was Macmillan who made the decisive move to get discussions out of the deadlock of the Geneva disarmament conference on to a ministerial level. The treaty was the biggest single contribution to peace since the invention of the bomb had made that goal so important, and at last Macmillan's traditional brokerage between East and West had been vindicated. It was seen as a remarkable political favour to let Lord Hailsham handle the negotiations in concert with the very experienced Averell Harriman on the American side.

The Test Ban treaty was a great success for Macmillan, but given the atmosphere of the summer of 1963 it was hardly recognized as such. Specula-

Test ban treaty

I'm sure Harold Macmillan encouraged President Kennedy to go forward with the test ban. President Kennedy was very much concerned over nuclear power because of the Cuban missile crisis. I think that some of Mr Macmillan's ideas about how to do it had an influence. I don't know that it was a controlling interest because I'm sure this was very much on President Kennedy's mind. I think Macmillan was the one who suggested it should be taken out of Geneva. There'd been too much wrangling there for months and months. He suggested that there should be a new team, and, I think, putting it on a ministerial level. The President selected me, and Macmillan appointed one of your ministers, Quintin Hogg. We went together with two very good teams to Moscow to negotiate it. We revised our ideas from a comprehensive test ban to a limited test ban and I think that was very much due to the joint understanding that existed between your Prime Minister and the President.

We broke some crockery in the process; we ended the dreams of some people. It was quite clear that we couldn't have a test ban treaty and try to keep reservations for the use of nuclear devices in the atmosphere. We did it all in two weeks. We had a couple of hard moments. I think that Quintin Hogg was a little bit worried that I was playing it a little bit too hard, but I'd had a bit more experience with the Russians. When one wanted something done one had to be very firm, one couldn't be polite about things which were disagreements; these were certain things which were absolutely essential for us, to get it through our Congress, you know. It had to be ratified by the Senate and therefore some of the things didn't seem to be so important to the British interests. I think Hailsham did send once a message to President Kennedy that I was being a little bit overly tough and to tell me to be a little bit conciliatory. I never got any message from the President, who agreed with me as to what I was doing.

AVERELL HARRIMAN

---

tion on his possible resignation was high and possible successors were suggested. Strength of feeling in the parliamentary party seemed to favour Maudling, a younger man, who would project a new image.

Anti-Macmillanites within the parliamentary party fed speculation as often as they could.

But Macmillan himself was undecided whether he should go on. 'My spirit is not broken, but my zest has gone', he is alleged to have said just before the Profumo debate. The Conservatives had twenty-seven abstentions after that debate, including two notorious anti-Macmillanites, Lord Lambton and Nigel Birch, later Lord Rhyl.

In early September Macmillan talked to the Chief Whip about the procedure Macmillan wished him to adopt to sound out the party for a new leader. The Prime Minister was sensitive to criticisms that his own selection had been less than democratic and he wished that a proper and thorough poll be taken of the party. But he insisted that the poll be taken in four tiers: the Cabinet, the Peers, the Commons, and the regional and local associations. The other constant that Macmillan had in mind was his wish to prevent Butler becoming leader.

Butler did not, Macmillan thought, have enough of two very important qualities in the Conservative Party terms: 'robustness' and 'bottom'. Macmillan had made Butler deputy leader in 1962 and had, throughout his premiership, left Butler in charge.

Butler, as had Morrison in the Labour Party earlier, expected the leadership to revert to him. There were many members of the Cabinet who would have been prepared to serve under Butler, perhaps not entirely for selfless reasons. Butler, to this group, represented somebody who took up a forward position on social policy, was probably malleable and, because of his age, unlikely to do more than one term. Butler, it was thought, could then be persuaded to hand over to one of the 'young turks'.

The 'young turks' were Macleod, Heath, and Maudling; Macmillan had given each his chance. None had quite pulled it off, but Maudling was closest. There was no clear successor from the forty-year-olds; no clear challenger to Wilson; no one of President Kennedy's image. The worship of youth was much in the air. By the end of September, Macmillan, making a great decision alone, decided to stay on. He knew he would have to go to the country by October 1964.

On 8 October 1963, the Tory clans began to gather at Blackpool for the annual conference. That morning, Macmillan had not seemed well at the cabinet meeting. He had had to leave the room, and almost immediately some ministers began to speculate over his condition. Both Lord Dilhorne, the Lord Chancellor, and Lord Home, the Foreign Secretary, offered their services in assessing opinion as to a possible successor. It was to be a sure sign of jumpiness but, alas, as has been so often alleged

Heir apparent?

since, there was no immediate poll of ministers in the cabinet room. Macmillan returned and before the meeting broke up he assured his Cabinet that he would be at Blackpool by the end of the week to give the customary leader's speech.

Macmillan, it was confirmed later that day, was suffering from a disease common to men of his age: his prostate gland was playing up. Prostate gland difficulties can induce periods of lassitude before they become apparent. It is also, medically, very difficult to say quite how serious they may become, or quite how long they may put a patient out of action. At any rate by 9 p.m. Macmillan was on his way to King Edward VII's Hospital in London for an operation. A little later, it was announced that Macmillan would not make the leader's speech at Blackpool. After some discussion it was decided that Butler would make it, as head of Government, in his place. Quite properly, Butler, when he arrived the following day in Blackpool (Wednesday 9 October) moved into Macmillan's suite at the Imperial Hotel.

Home, still in London, went later on Wednesday to see Macmillan in hospital. Macmillan told him that he could not contemplate fighting the next election and urged Home to stand as leader. However, Macmillan had made it clear to his lieutenants before that he favoured Hailsham, another peer, for the succession.

Macmillan's motives for initially backing Hailsham are unresolved. Hailsham would not have been approved by the majority of the Cabinet. But Macmillan knew that in the party conference Hailsham was a very popular figure. A display of strong pro-Hailsham feeling at the conference could only upset Butler's chances and might lead the way open for darker horses. Hailsham might also have had the appeal to lead the Tories out of what looked like certain defeat. None of the 'young turks' looked like swinging the party behind them.

Nevertheless, Macmillan, on the evening of Wednesday 9 October, was not confident enough of Hailsham's chances, and made a play for Lord Home's co-operation. Home had told Macmillan a month earlier that, though he would support any leader, Macmillan ought to think over his position. There was no suggestion of any *putsch*. Home, now that he knew Macmillan would not stay on as leader, was non-commital and had doubts that his peerage would permit his standing.

As far as I can make out, Macmillan was always delighted to have me acting for him. I acted for him on every single occasion that he was out of the country. I remember receiving the minutes at No. 10 Downing Street: 'Mr Butler, I should be obliged if you would act for me as Head of the Government. I can leave everything to you. Do not trouble me when I am away, unless it is vital. Yours H.M.' That happened on every occasion he was away. Every time there was trouble I was sent for to discuss it with him.

After the Profumo incident it was extraordinary how a gust of wind swept the Commons and the Conservative Party in favour of a younger leader. It really was quite extraordinary. John Morrison, now Lord Margedale, who was then Chairman of the 1922 Committee, came around one evening to my house and told me what his opinion of the party was. He thought, immediately after the Profumo incident, that the party would opt for Maudling as leader because they thought it was better to have a married leader than an unmarried leader like Mr Heath. He said that the two favourites were Maudling and Heath. Now that was before the Conservative Party conference. I had established in my mind that it was likely the Conservative Party would like, partly because of the Kennedy image, partly because of the Wilson image, to have a younger man as leader. I was told at the time that my claims were obviously in the ring, but that I was too close to Macmillan, and too much regarded as being with the old regime, and they would really prefer it to go to a younger leader. It did lead eventually to the succession of Mr Heath, after a short period with Alec Douglas-Home. It might have been better, really, if they'd decided to go for the younger leader from the start.
LORD BUTLER

A process of selection

The rivals: Maudling, Hailsham, Butler, listen to the missing man, Home

Q. Was it your impression that Macmillan intended to go on as Prime Minister?

A. Yes, quite definitely. I think he would have listened to any of us who told him that we felt he ought to go, but I have little doubt in my mind that it was his intention to see it through. I'd had my suspicions for some months that he wasn't quite well. At that last cabinet meeting he not only looked ill, but said one or two things that hinted that there was something worse than any of us had realized.

LORD BOYLE

Macmillan was down at Chequers. He'd been thinking about it before and had made an announcement that he was going to fight the election. Then he had second thoughts, but he finally made his decision then that he would fight the election and that he would announce it at the Blackpool conference.

SIR KNOX CUNNINGHAM

Mr Macmillan definitely wanted to go on as Prime Minister and it was entirely his illness, and the fact that Alec Douglas-Home visited him in the nursing home and got a written statement from him, that he decided to resign. But I know that when I left London for Blackpool he wanted to go on.

LORD BUTLER

Blackpool was unprecedented in the sense that a Prime Minister resigned in the middle of it. And unprecedented also in the sense that there was no certain front runner, which is rather unusual in our party. Now the front runners were Lord Hailsham and Rab Butler. But the trouble about them was that those who liked Rab didn't like Hailsham, and those who liked Hailsham didn't like Rab. So I thought when the conference opened that perhaps the best bet would be Maudling. Reggie Maudling had a very important speech, and he made rather a flop of it. His weakness is that he cannot lift a big audience and he couldn't lift them then.

Rather disappointed, I went back because Ian Fleming, who was a very old friend of mine, was giving a party for the first night of *From Russia With Love*. When I got back to London I found that the Prime Minister, Mr Macmillan, had swopped peers in mid-stream. He had been backing Hailsham but he'd turned and was now about to back Home and Home was willing to disclaim. Now I didn't get this from Home at all. I hadn't spoken to him for a year before the conference, but I got it by certain means. I was so anxious to get back after Ian Fleming's party because I wanted to put it around that he was a runner. It was very important the conference should realize that. I think they did realize it in the last day and they did anoint him with a drop of democratic oil with the enormous applause he got at the time of Rab's speech at the end of the conference.

LORD RHYL

Q. Was it a surprise to you when Lord Home came forward as a candidate?

A. A great surprise, yes. I thought he was a peer so it was naturally rather a surprise when he came down, or offered to come down, from the upper house to stand for the Prime Ministership. I think what happened was that this idea, which was a complete novelty at Blackpool, appealed to a great many of the independent Conservative members who suddenly thought 'We'd never thought of that idea'. Alec Douglas-Home had always been popular with the Conservative Party and he was a very good Foreign Secretary and he was a very good Commonwealth Secretary. I think they felt they owed him a certain amount because of his very good performance of his duties and also it was a novelty – whereas I wasn't a novelty. I'd been talked about so much.

Q. When did he tell you he was going to be a candidate?

A. He told me that he was seeing his doctor to have a check-up on the Saturday of the Blackpool conference. I remember each hour of that week

Q. That was just before your speech?

A. Yes, just before my speech.

LORD BUTLER

When it came to the issue, it was left to Martin Redmayne, the Chief Whip, to collect the voices of all Conservative MPs. I saw Martin and I said No. 1, Maudling, No. 2, Butler – with a slightly heavy heart on Mr Butler. He said to me, what about the Peers? I knew who he meant, of course, and I thought, good heavens, what could he mean? So I said to him, what about the bloody Peers? What else could I say?

All this was recorded on foolscap – I can see the paper now – lined foolscap, very old-fashioned, no computer or anything like that, and of course at the end of the day these were added up and presumably shown to Harold Macmillan. But of course, nobody believed, nobody in the Conservative Party could possibly have believed, that a majority of Conservative MPs would have wanted to fetch back a peer from the House of Lords when we had 2–300 perfectly able men in the House of Commons. Well, still, it only took them about twelve months to realize, when the penny dropped.

REGINALD BEVINS

There's a well-known tag of Tacitus about a rather undistinguished Roman Emperor, that he'd have made a splendid Emperor if he'd never been one. I think the opposite exactly applies to Rab Butler: he'd have made a splendid Prime Minister if he'd ever been one. The question is, can one separate the qualities of being a Prime Minister and of becoming a Prime Minister? Certainly, for becoming a Prime Minister a man must be ready to shoot it out. He must be ready to see his rivals off, no matter how. He mustn't mind blood on the carpet. You see, Rab Butler had it in his hands. He could have had it for one shot and we, you know who I mean by we, gave him the weapon. We said, 'You see, Rab, look at this, this is a revolver; we've loaded it for you, you don't have to worry about loading it. Now you see this part here, it's the trigger, if you put your finger round that, all you have to do is to squeeze that and he's dead, see?' Rab said, 'Oh, yes, thank you for telling me, but will it hurt him, will he bleed?' We said, 'Well, yes, I'm afraid when you shoot a man he does tend to bleed'. 'Oh', said Rab, 'I don't know whether I like that, but tell me something else, will it go off with a bang?' We said, 'Well, Rab, I'm afraid we must admit you know, a gun does make rather a bang when it goes off'. Then he said 'Well, thank you very much, I don't think I will. Do you mind?'
ENOCH POWELL

I wasn't actually at the meeting but I am aware that at least four or five or probably more cabinet ministers would have been in my favour had I stood out. The reason I didn't stand out was that I thought the Queen had already visited the hospital. I thought that Alec Douglas-Home had been chosen after a concensus taken by the whips. I was trained on the history of Peel as a young man, I remember the terrible effect he had on the Tory Party by disuniting it. Rightly or wrongly I thought I'd put the unity of the party first.

Q. Do you think the sequence of events which took Lord Home to the Palace was constitutionally proper? It was done very quickly.

A. It's not for me to question constitutionalism in any way that connects with authority, but it certainly was a very quick job. But I think that was really decided by Macmillan. I think he was determined to go ahead and he was obviously told of this meeting which was taking place.

Q. Why did he do nothing about it?

A. I think he was determined to go ahead with Sir Alec Douglas-Home.
LORD BUTLER

I think really from the beginning of that day, although he didn't like the idea of yielding, he did not want to split the party. It was, in fact, Reggie Maudling who showed himself the toughest of the dissidents, who was the hardest to convince about it. I think it could have gone the other way, just could have gone the other way.
LORD BOYLE

But this straightforward view was exploitable. Hailsham, almost at the same moment as Home was seeing Macmillan in hospital, was suggesting that he might renounce his peerage at a Conservative meeting at Morecambe. Because of the persistent activities of Lord Stansgate, later Anthony Wedgwood Benn, peers could now renounce their titles, provided they did so by November 1963. In other words, those who had been regarded as out of the race for premier could now join allcomers. Hailsham's case was advanced by Christopher Soames and Julian Amery.

Thursday 10 October was the turning point in the Conservative Party Conference. Unknown to most, from 11 a.m. to noon Macmillan underwent an entirely successful operation for his prostate. But meanwhile, Home, picking up a written message from Macmillan at the Foreign Office, set off for Blackpool. Home was the first major Tory politician to know that Macmillan was going to resign once a successor had been chosen. This was made public by Home just before conference closed that evening; it was quite right that he should do it, as President of the National Union of Conservative and Unionist Associations.

The fat was in the fire. Most party conferences are bean feasts for representatives and journalists alike, but now, for once, something very important was underway. The 1963 Conservative conference took on the atmosphere of an American convention, except that most people were not sure who their candidate was. This did not allow the political temperature to drop.

That evening, Hailsham disclaimed his peerage, among scenes, as one of his opponents said, that that were reminiscent of the Nuremberg Rally. Hailsham, though now it would be Hogg, seemed about to be drafted on the American pattern. But to some, these hysterical scenes were distasteful and seemed to confirm high-level fears of Hailsham's judgement. Macmillan got wind of Hailsham's influential opponents; by 11 October Macmillan had abandoned Hailsham, who nevertheless strode about the conference hall like an uncrowned regent. But authoritative word was getting through that Macmillan had 'switched peers in midstream'. To Macmillan, Hailsham had ruined his case by being over-enthusiastic. He might well carry the constituencies, but his noisy demonstrations could offend the parliamentary party and particularly the Cabinet. Word was allowed to get about that Home should be watched.

On the morning of Friday 11 October, Reginald Maudling made a flat speech and was unable to stir the party, who wanted to hear strong things. The young lost their champion. But Butler was to speak the following day, and surely he could dispose of an incipient challenge from the 14th Earl of Home who was now, whisper had it, in the race. Butler spoke as acting leader, but just before his speech Lord Home told him that he was going to see his doctor the following week for a check-up. It was a warning, of a sort, that Home was now firmly in the race. Butler gave a moderate speech and the party retired from the feverish atmosphere of Blackpool for formal soundings to take place. The position of the rival candidates at the weekend of 12 October was roughly this: Hailsham was losing ground: Home was gaining ground; Butler, on a snap poll there and then, would have got it; Maudling, Macleod, and Heath, in that order, were not seriously in the running.

Macmillan then put his four-tier soundings into action; the process was unanimously approved by the Cabinet on Tuesday 15 October. By the morning of Thursday 17 October, Macmillan, still in hospital, had the results. Some M.P.s claim they were asked 'what about the peers?' Nevertheless, the results showed a strong minority who did not wish to have Butler; the candidate who had done best was Home, but he did not have an overall majority. Some M.P.s, who had had as first-preference choices people who came well down the list, were asked again to choose between Butler and Home. Home's stock went up further. By the evening word was spreading that Home would have it.

This generated a cabinet revolt in Butler's favour. At Enoch Powell's flat, Powell, Maudling, Macleod, Erroll, and Aldington, the party's Deputy Chairman, all agreed to tell Macmillan that Home would not do. Butler did not realize this move until first thing the following day, when he met the plotters, who had been joined by Hailsham. Macmillan moved quickly. Home had telephoned him and expressed doubts; Macmillan replied, 'All the troops are on the starting line. Everything is arranged. It will cause ghastly confusion if we delay.' By lunchtime, the Queen had asked Lord Home to try to form an administration. Home spent the rest of the day seeing his colleagues. The revolt slowly broke down; of the doubters, Hailsham agreed first, and Maudling last, to serve Home. Two refused, Macleod and Powell. The man who had never made a front bench speech in the Commons before became Prime Minister.

It was Macmillan's last triumph, but his most baffling one. Macmillan's career as Prime Minister ended on a final gamble: he gambled that Home's appeal might go beyond the confines of the Conservative Party. But when the election came in 1964, the 'fourteenth Mr Wilson' (as Home aptly described him), beat the fourteenth earl by a whisker. This gamble, like so many other gambles in Macmillan's long career, nearly came off.

Macmillan's legacy in terms of concrete achievement was small; the Test Ban Treaty remains the outstanding exception. Macmillan's real contribution is, like the man himself, much harder to grasp. A visitor to Britain in 1957 who returned in 1963 would have detected great changes in the climate of opinion. Serious-minded Englishmen were much more worried by the future of their country. Some, like Macmillan, thought the answer was in Europe; that as a member of the E.E.C. Britain could re-establish her economic and political future and would no longer be on her own, but within a structure she could fundementally influence. There were, however, many who were less optimistic, and perhaps the essence of Harold Wilson's success in 1964 was his suggestion that there was hope that Britain could remould her future.

To Macmillan, the failure of the E.E.C. negotiations exposed him fully to the bleakness of the future. It was doubtful that the economy could be put right, or that Britain had a framework in which she could bring her political will to bear. By the end of Macmillan's premiership Britain had lost what had been so marked a characteristic before – self-esteem. In a negative way this was a great achievement. The British people were brought face to face with their own smallness; the way forward. however distant, had had its foundation laid.

The Empire was finally laid to rest by Macmillan. He tried to find her a new role in Europe, while maintaining her old one as an independent nuclear power. He did not see, as those with hindsight have pretended, that this circle could not be squared, because it was never a question of either the E.E.C. or Polaris. Perhaps if Macmillan had been more radical in his approach to Britain's old obligations, his grand design might have succeeded. Paradoxically, he would not have survived politically.

On that very last night of his last Parliament, we gave a dinner party for Macmillan. At the end of it I think there were only two members of the House of Commons, and myself and Martin Redmayne, the Chief Whip; we took him upstairs. Redmayne had to do something else, so I took him into the smoking room, which is in many ways the heart, at least for the Conservative members, of the House of Commons. We went in there and nobody paid any attention to him; nobody came round and sat with him to have a drink on what they must have realized was his last night in the place. There were many people there, certainly some who owed their whole political career to him and there were many others who had been old ministerial friends and colleagues. When he went up to leave the place for the last time, there was no cheer, no greeting, he just walked out. There may have been some people there too embarrassed to talk to him, but to me it seemed a nasty indication of the callousness of ingratitude of many Members of Parliament. I suspect he felt it too, but he was too old a hand to show it.

ROBERT ALLAN

Index

Photo acknowledgments

Radio Times Hulton Picture Library: 1, 8/9, 12, 14, 16, 18/19, 22/23, 44/45 (bottom), 98, 146/147
Associated Press: 34/35, 76/77, 187
Barratts: 20/21
Central Press: 86/87, 178/179, 180
Camera Press: 215
Ewan Duff: 5, 173, 198/199
London Express: 134/135, 142
Fox Photos: 27, 58, 212
Imperial War Museum: 13
ITN: 161, 174
Keystone: 30, 32, 36, 38/39, 46, 56, 82/83, 101, 120, 127, 130/131, 144, 148, 150, 152, 155, 157, 158/159, 171, 175, 192, 197, 202, 210/211, 212/213, 219, 224
British Movietone: 122
Pathé: 10/11, 50/51, 71, 77, 80, 88, 95, 115, 118
Popperfoto: 76, 221
Press Association: 93, 106, 110, 165, 189
Sport and General: 96
United Press International: 40/41, 44/45 (top), 68/69, 109, 124, 125, 138, 140
Planet News: 74/75, 111
United Nations: 141
Visnews: 116/117
Labour Party: 17, 62/63, 72/73
Conservative Party: 72/73

Headline acknowledgments

Associated Newspapers Group Limited: 52, 79, 98/99, 167, 190
Daily Mirror: 78, 206
Daily Express: 195

Cartoons

The following appear by permission of the Daily Express:
Low cartoons: 25, 29, 33, 48, 54/55, 60, 66/67
Vicky cartoons: 105, 128/129, 168, 177, 182, 191, 217
Illingworth cartoon: 42/43 appears by permission of the London Daily Mail.
Illingworth cartoon: 65 and Fougasse cartoon: 54 appear by permission of Punch

Extract acknowledgment

Anthony Eden: 133
The Eden Memoirs, Volume III Full Circle Published by Cassell and Company Ltd